OLD SOCIETIES AND NEW STATES

Old Societies

and

New States

The quest for modernity

in Asia and Africa

Edited by Clifford Geertz

Fp THE FREE PRESS, NEW YORK
COLLIER-MACMILLAN LTD., LONDON

For *information, address:*

THE FREE PRESS
A DIVISION OF THE MACMILLAN COMPANY,
60 FIFTH AVENUE, NEW YORK, N.Y. 10011

DESIGNED BY ANDOR BRAUN

LIBRARY OF CONGRESS CATALOG CARD
NUMBER: 63–8416

COLLIER-MACMILLAN CANADA, LTD., TORONTO, ONTARIO

Second Printing 1965

PREFACE

THE COMMITTEE FOR THE COMPARATIVE STUDY OF NEW NATIONS began its work in 1959–1960 under a planning grant from the Carnegie Corporation. Composed of scholars from the various disciplines in the social sciences, its objects are to seek out, through the comparative analysis of new nations, principles that underlie their social and political development and to train students in theories and methods that, emerging from contemporary research, will enable them better to observe the new nations themselves.

Underlying these objects are several assumptions. The new nations are engaged in a form of social change that makes nation building and material development simultaneous political problems. As a result, all aspects of social life have a heavily political element. In this the new nations are different from most older and established nations. They are characterized by a singular urgency to get on with their tasks. The rapidity of such change creates an element of social stress that poses questions relating to more general social phenomena. Discontinuities appear in tradition, culture, social organization, and material standards and are being met by new cultural and political forms. In their efforts to give meaning and personality to their work, the new nations present fresh political mechanisms, political beliefs, and social attitudes that are not only grist for the social scientists' mill, but also deeply affect the future of us all.

Out of such efforts as those undertaken by the Committee and by scholars elsewhere, our knowledge of major events in the "third world" (as it is often called) must be made equal to the problems they pose.

Our research is limited to the new nations, that is, those which have come to independence from colonial status since 1945. India, for example, is considered a new nation while China is not. Our reasons for making this quite arbitrary distinction are based in large measure on our comparative focus. Rather than emphasizing area specialization, such as Asia, Africa, or the Middle East, we prefer to consider certain common experiences that the new nations have entertained, seeking to compare broadly similar historical stages that they share. After examining these stages, we proceed to the more specific differences among them. For example, all such new nations have gone through the experience of colonialism. This is in itself an important historical event. It is one basis for the reaching out, one to the other, of African and Asian nations in the so-called Afro-Asian bloc. There has also been a common response to colonialism, namely, nationalism, which shows certain basic characteristics. Certain countries that experienced British colonialism, for example, are for some purposes more effectively comparable than two countries in Africa that, living side by side, have had different colonial experiences, for example, British and French. Or, Malaya and Tanganyika, two plural societies, make more revealing comparison than Tanganyika and Uganda, in spite of the latter's contiguity and the similarity of their colonial experiences.

In important respects an analysis of the Philippines, India, Indonesia, and Nigeria is more revealing of the problems of multiparty political systems than is a comparison of Nigeria with Guinea or Ghana, even though the latter three are in Africa. Similarly, in the case of Pakistan, Sudan, and Burma, military rule still prevails in the first two and is now dominant again in the third.

Of course, we do not mean to suggest that comparisons within regions are any less sound than between them. Our object is to avoid becoming imprisoned in area parochialism at the expense of more theoretically useful comparisons. Hence, in our second year, 1960–1961, when full-scale activities got under way, our primary task was to delimit the problems of central concern that could be examined by whatever methods and theories seemed most appropriate. These problems were partly dictated by the interests of each of the members, and partly emerged from discussion and evaluation of what it seemed significant to know and study about the new nations themselves.

The danger of superficiality and erroneous comparison in such an enterprise is, of course, very great. We have hoped to meet these difficulties in the following manner. First, most of the staff of the Committee are deeply knowledgeable about particular areas and have spent one or more years in intensive fieldwork. Second, recognizing that not all problems are susceptible to broad treatment, we try to proceed from the more general to the particular. By this means, we expect to give wider meaning to what might otherwise remain exotic events. Third, none of the participants ignores history. Hence, we seek to relate the new to the old both within the new nations and between them and the Western past.

If comparative theory and research describe the general outlook of the Committee, what are our central problems? A quick glance at the table of contents of this book reflects a few of them. Some members are concerned with problems of tradition and innovation. Others deal with social discontinuity and the development of loyalty and authority. Still others are interested in the comparative role of the military, the politics of economic growth, in processes of socialization and corporate identity, and in law and social change. Whatever the particular interest of the members, however, all are ultimately concerned with the problem of democracy in the new states, the forces that erode it, and the factors that might establish or strengthen it.

Nor is our focus purely a matter of theory and research. An integral part of the program concerns comparative law and comparative education. These aspects, in addition to their intrinsic importance, are designed to increase the skill and knowledge of practitioners of law and education. More particularly, we are interested in those who, from time to time, are called upon to act as advisers and technicians in the new nations. Although this part of the program is yet in its infancy, we plan to enlarge our scope in collaboration with the Law School and the Center for Comparative Education so that lawyers and educators can profit from our labors. Two members of the Committee, Professors Max Rheinstein, in the area of law, and C. Arnold Anderson, in the area of education, are responsible for the more functional aspects of the Committee, in addition to their ordinary work as members.

Although drawn from various disciplines, the members of the Committee share, to a remarkable degree, a familiarity and an understanding of the core theories and work of the social sciences, which are particularly manifested in the Committee Seminar on problems of the new nations. Although largely restricted to members of the Committee, fellows, and students in the program, participation also includes visiting scholars from overseas institutions and other universities. One result of the seminar has been the development of subgroups within the Committee composed of individuals whose interests center around some particular problem, such as comparative social stratification.

The program owes much to the vision and imagination of its Chairman, Professor Edward A. Shils. The idea of the Committee took shape during the year 1958–1959 at the Center for Advanced Studies in the Behavioral Sciences, when Professors Shils, Apter, Fallers, and Geertz were fellows of the Center. In a modest way the Committee has tried to retain some of the characteristics of that place, particularly its loose structure, its spontaneity, and its creativity. Indeed, we remain more interested in ideas than in methods and in creativity rather than in precision.

It will be seen that, with such a philosophy, the program of training undertaken by the Committee requires exceptional graduate students. These latter participate in the seminar and enroll in courses given by members of the Committee. Students work closely with their advisers on the Committee. Ordinarily, only advanced graduate students are given fellowships. In addition to students, fellowships are also awarded to advanced scholars who have been engaged in extensive fieldwork for some years. Thus, our ideal is a small group, sharing a common core of interests in the new nations, working closely with advanced graduate students and senior fellows in order to probe more deeply those facets of human experience that, although they occur in nations that are new, relate to the common destiny of us all. This book reflects some of those concerns.

David E. Apter
EXECUTIVE SECRETARY
COMMITTEE FOR THE COMPARATIVE STUDY OF NEW NATIONS

CONTENTS

PREFACE   v

On the Comparative Study of the New States   1
Edward Shils

Cultural Policy in the New States   27
McKim Marriott

Political Religion in the New Nations   57
David E. Apter

The Integrative Revolution
Primordial Sentiments and Civil Politics in the New States   105
Clifford Geertz

Equality, Modernity, and Democracy in the New States   158
Lloyd Fallers

Problems of Law in the New Nations of Africa   220
Max Rheinstein

Concerning the Role of Education in Development   247
Mary Jean Bowman and C. Arnold Anderson

Political Socialization and Culture Change   280
Robert LeVine

INDEX   305

On the comparative study of the new states

EDWARD SHILS

I

SINCE 1945 the world has acknowledged the sovereignty of the following states: Indonesia, Malaya, Singapore, the Philippines, Vietnam, Laos, Cambodia, Burma, India, Ceylon, Pakistan, Syria, Iraq, Lebanon, Israel, United Arab Republic, Libya, Tunisia, Cyprus, Morocco, Algeria, Mauretania, Sudan, Gabon, Ivory Coast, Madagascar, Chad, Niger, Upper Volta, Dahomey, Togoland, Cameroons, Mali, Senegal, Guinea, the Republic of the Congo, Congo, Ghana, Nigeria, Sierra Leone, Tanganyika, Uganda, Rwanda, Burundi, Trinidad, and Jamaica. The novelty of their sovereignty defines them as new states. Until recently, they have all been colonial territories or were otherwise less than wholly self-governing. They have now acquired full sovereignty.

This minimal uniformity of situation and this minimal common experience of being ruled by Western metropolitan powers and of seeking to free themselves of that rule carry with them a number of attendant phenomena. The constellation of common situation and common experience—and, to some extent, the awareness of this community of situation and experience—has generated a common outlook. These together have defined the major tasks of the new states, and these tasks have far-reaching ramifications, which are in many respects similar from state to state.

In varying degrees, all the founders of the new states face or have faced the problem of establishing an effective government and staffing it with indigenous personnel. They all confront or have confronted the necessity of legitimating themselves before their people. They all accept, more or less, the task of organizing and maintaining a modern political apparatus, that is, a rationally conducted administration, a cadre of leaders grouped in the public form of a party system (whether in a one-party system or in a multiparty system), and a machinery of public order. All this must be done in the context of a traditional society, or, more frequently, in the context of a plurality of traditional societies.

These traditional societies have almost always been agricultural societies, impoverished by contemporary standards of material well-being, and employing traditional techniques of cultivation. This adds another facet to the tasks of the elites of the new states. They almost all desire to create a new, modern economic order to replace the inherited one. This entails the development of new economic institutions and techniques, and persuading or coercing the ordinary members of the society into their acceptance.

Among the tasks unanimously regarded by the elites of the new states as high on their agenda is the creation of modern educational institutions, and a widespread participation in them. In nearly all the new states, the governing elite has received a modern education, often to a high level. It is an education approximating the one they have received, metropolitan in its source and modern in its content, that they would like to give to their people. In contrast with the elites, the mass of the population has usually received no formal modern education. The juxtaposition of an elite educated in a tradition of exogenous inspiration and a mass rooted in a variety of indigenous cultures engenders problems that turn up throughout the world of the new states.

The elites are almost always intensely nationalistic—in most of the new states, the reigning elites and their rivals still belong to the generation that conducted the agitation for independence from the foreign colonial power. As contemporary nationalists, they are not merely concerned with self-rule; they are concerned simultaneously to elevate the dignity of their traditional culture and their standing in the world. But they also wish to have, for the sake of economic progress and because it is entailed in being modern, a modern culture diffused through the medium of a modern educational system that runs from the early years to university. The adaptation of traditional literary, artistic, and moral culture to the techniques and content of modern education, and the development of modern studies of traditional culture, form another of the tasks recurrently confronted throughout the new states.

From this confrontation of the exogenous and the indigenous, of the modern and the traditional, arises another problem that frequently agitates many of the new states. In some of them, it centers about the medium of instruction. Nearly all the new states face a situation in which the language of their modern culture is the metropolitan language, the language of the former ruler. Their modern culture is usually also largely derived from their contact with the metropolis, while the language—more frequently, the languages—of the indigenous culture is neither highly developed nor universally spoken or understood throughout the territory. Yet the official and the cultural use of the indigenous language or one of the indigenous languages is felt to be necessary to their national dignity; to go on using a foreign language is regarded as an act of self-derogation. The use of the indigenous language would reduce the gap, so painfully felt by so many of the highly educated in almost all new states, between the "masses" and the "intellectuals."

The separation of the uneducated "masses" immersed in their traditional culture and the "intellectuals" who have had a modern education is representative of some disjunctions observable in the social structure of practically all the new states. Almost everywhere, the societies consist of relatively discrete collectivities— ethnic, communal, caste, religious, or linguistic—that have little sense of identity with one another or with the national whole. The new states of Asia and Africa have not yet reached the point where the people they rule have become nations, more or less coterminous with the state in the territorial boundaries, and possessing a sense of identity in which membership in the state that rules them is an important component. Political parties that are simply modern forms of traditional parochial interests, patronage and corruption arising from parochial attachments, distrust and hostility toward governmental authority because it is thought to embody an alien parochial interest—these are a few of the manifestations of the simple fact that most of the new states do not yet rest upon a "political society." And correspondingly, in nearly every new state, the conduct of the elite and the responses of the populace are conditioned, in one way or another, by this fact.

There follow, from the problems so sketchily enumerated, a host of others. They are all part of the struggle of the impulse toward a modern society in a situation in which their population is neither modern nor a single society.

The new states are not alone in their situation. There are other states, such as Turkey, Iran, Thailand, Ethiopia, and Liberia, that have possessed sovereignty for a long period and that are, nevertheless, largely in the situation of the new states. They too have largely agricultural economies; they too have a low standard of living. Their educational systems are relatively undeveloped; their modern culture is confined to narrow circles; the mass of the population is traditional and parochial in its outlook; and their civil unity is fragile. They too have young elites (or, more frequently, counterelites) insistent on the modernization of their countries. The states of Latin America are in much the same situation. Their economies are largely agricultural, their masses uneducated, and their elites live under the dominance of the metropolitan cultures. The earlier acquisition of sovereignty does, however, make a difference that distinguishes them from the new states of Asia and Africa.

The older undeveloped states of Asia and Africa and of Latin America have in common the fact of established national elites, indigenous in origin, with their own traditions of political practice and stable relationships with the traditional local elites of their countries. The established national elites are older and more integrated with the economic interests of established agriculture and commerce than are the elites of the new states. The older undeveloped states do have an administration of sorts, staffed by indigenous personnel. Their political elites are usually satisfied with a slovenly pluralism, since on the whole they demand little in the way of enthusiastic affirmation from their people. Their boundaries and their territorial aspirations are more frequently accepted as given than is the case in the newer states. Their politics tend to be somewhat less ideological, and where they are ideological tend to be less populistic and less collectivistic than are the politics of the elites of the new states.

In these societies, "modernity," "dynamism"—that is, the idiom of progress, rational technology, collectivistic organization, social equality and populistic demagogy—are largely the possession of the counterelites. The counterelites in these states have more in common with the elites of the new states. Where the counterelites have succeeded in attaining power, as they have done here and there in Latin America, they must contend with an inherited quasi-modern social structure, such as does not confront the elites in states that have just recently acquired sovereignty from foreign rulers.

The new states of Asia and Africa are not, of course, unique phenomena. They do have marked affinities with all states, and above all with the undeveloped states of their own continents and Latin America. But they have enough that is unique to them and common to them to justify our decision to put them at the center of our attention.

II

WE have undertaken our studies of the new states of Asia and Africa for a variety of reasons. They would at any time be worthy of attention, since they comprise human beings meriting sympathy and understanding; but they are especially worthy of our intellectual effort at present because they now count on a world scale. What happens in them sends repercussions through the rest of the world system and affects the future of all mankind, of ourselves as well as of themselves. We are interested in the new states because they are an important part of the contemporary world, and we wish to fill out the map in our minds and in the minds of our fellow social scientists and fellow citizens.

We wish in this respect to fulfil a publicistic obligation. We wish, no less, to cultivate them as legitimate matters of academic concern, which is something different from even the best of contemporary journalistic reportage and analysis. Like the best of contemporary journalism, we wish to be concrete and vivid, to examine events "on the spot," and to grasp and convey the sense of what they mean to those who participate in them. We wish to do justice to personalities. We cannot, however, be content with these aspirations, however admirable.

We must go beyond the meaning the events have to those who share in them—though we must never forget them. We must do this because we must see the shape events take, their formation into patterns or structures, even where these are not perceived or appreciated by those who participate in them. Our central concern will be with the vicissitudes of the aspiration toward the establishment of a political society. This means that we are to be concerned with the interdependence of the different parts of the respective societies the governing elites of the new states attempt to rule, and it will mean taking into account factors and consequences that are sometimes overlooked or differently interpreted by persons active in the situation. This does not mean that everything is to be explained solely by transpersonal "forces," by "deeply rooted traditions," by "structures" in which the knowledge, reason, pride, and anger of individuals have no part. It does mean, however, that in the study of new states, as we intend to practice it, we must give prominence to the power of the traditional inheritance of beliefs and standards that form and constitute individual minds, and to those inherited norms of institutional life that have the insistence and approbation of significantly placed persons. We shall be interested in the intertwinement of practices vital to continuing life with loyalties to collectivities other than the new states themselves; we shall be equally interested in the dispositions and attachments of the elites and the way in which these influence the ways in which they conceive of their tasks. We shall try to understand the ways in which the traditional patterns of belief and action penetrate into the modern sector of the society, the ways in which the traditional and the modern interact and fuse. The modernization of the traditional and the traditionalization of the modern and outcomes that no one plans, desires, or expects will be among our major themes. In any inquiry into the working of society, as much attention must be given to the quality of performance of the elites and the factors within their own inherited culture, training and experience as to those that are "givens" in their situation. It is especially urgent that the elites of the new states be singled out for study because they, more than the elites of most states past and present, have taken such great responsibilities on themselves to guide and transform their societies. In the action of elites, the given and the chosen encounter each other with momentous consequences. The consequence with which we are most concerned is the extent to which a modern order, in its various aspects, emerges. These interests are dictated not only by the requirements of social scientific analysis but also by our simultaneous preoccupation with opinion and policy.

Through our studies we aspire to illuminate opinion both in the new states themselves and in the English-speaking countries. The opinion in the new states to which we refer is the opinion of the rulers of those societies, of those who aspire to rule, and of those who are sufficiently interested to pass judgment and to seek to influence the way rule is exercised in those societies. Given the present paucity of scholarly study of the problems of the new states, whatever is produced under creditable auspices about their problems has a reasonable chance of entering gradually into the opinion of the educated class, and therewith in some measure into the political class, of the new states. Without harboring many illusions about the efficacy of our studies, we do think that this hope is not entirely a vain one. The elites of the new states are, on the whole, rather well educated. The temptations of demagogy are certainly great among them, but these temptations do not have the field to themselves. Thus, while wishing to avoid presumption and arrogance, we think it possible for our inquiries to be of value to the elites of the new states, helping them to see themselves, their people, and their problems in a perspective that is more comprehensive and more deep-going than actors in a situation, especially busy and harried actors, can ordinarily discover for themselves. Politicians, civil servants, and journalists, pressed and distracted by the demands of daily routine, and immersed in events in a way in which scholars can never be, can benefit from dispassionate and detached observation and analysis. Readers in the new states are not the only audience from the new states for such studies as we are cultivating. The new states send many of their best young men and women, some of whom are destined to enter into the highest positions of authority in their countries, to study in our universities. The tradition of human sympathy, disciplined detachment, and substantive analysis that governs the study of the new states will, we hope, be shared by our students from the new states, as well as by our readers there, so that they may in their turn contribute not only to the indigenous growth of such studies at home but to the enlightenment of opinion and policy there as well.

We are no less interested in widening and deepening the sympathetic understanding of the real situation of the new states among the influential sections of the public in our own countries. Realistic, sympathetic studies of the new states can help to make our policies toward them more understanding, more discriminating, and more helpful. There are benevolent errors to dispel as well as malevolent errors to overcome. We wish to secure the benevolence while dispelling the mythology with which so many well-intentioned persons confront the new states. The differentiated portrayal of the situation of the new states and the subjective and environmental determinants of action might make us, and those who must make policy, more imaginative about the possible lines of development as well as about the obstacles to such development. By a greater realism, coupled with a vivid disclosure of the range of possibilities permitted by the "givens" of life in the new states, and of the capacities of their rulers, we hope also—at least, to some extent—to disarm ill will.

The kind of social research we are practicing is a disciplined extension of experience. The categories we employ are the same as the ones we employ in our studies of our own societies, and they postulate the fundamental affinities of all human beings. Their persistent application in research and the diffusion of the results of research into the circles of influential opinion will, it is hoped, further the process through which that sense of affinity, necessary for constructive policy, is nurtured.

Our undertaking does not, however, intend to attain these moral effects through preaching, exhortation, or manipulation. We seek to do it through enlightenment. Our chosen instrument of enlightenment is systematic research, conducted under the auspices of the best traditions of contemporary social science.

III

THE accumulating body of research and theory, the present level of research techniques, and the generous provision of financial resources enable contemporary social science to achieve that intimacy of understanding of the new states that is required both for the purposes of the enlightenment of opinion and the advancement of social sciences as intellectual disciplines. The existence of the new states offers an unprecedented opportunity for the exploitation of these advantages.

There are now more than thirty instances of societies with very similar situations and problems, each one differing somewhat from the other in tradition, resources, and achievements. They form, moreover, a substantial part of the earth's surface and population. The data are therefore not some minor fragments thrown up in a corner of the world. They are, rather, a massive part of the whole universe with which social scientists must deal. They provide an enormously important, immensely rich field of observation. The emergence of a social order, the formation of the state, the transformation of tradition, the legitimation of new authority—these are only a few of the most fundamental problems of social science that can be studied in the experience of the new states. The approximate identity of their situation and structure affords the possibility of returning again and again to these basic problems. By studying them in slightly differing contexts, with enough in common among them to enable us to estimate the significance of the various factors that operate differently among them, social scientists may regard the existence of the new states, considered simply from the standpoint of their subject, as an exceptional boon.

It is not, moreover, the only one. The intimacy of our understanding of the societies that have now passed into history will never be able to equal the intimacy we can now attain in our intellectual relationships with these still living societies. The study of the new states permits degrees of intimacy and comprehensiveness that are not easily attainable with respect to any other society, either living or dead, larger than a small tribe. This gives it a great advantage over every comprehensive social inquiry, based on fieldwork, except the anthropological study of the village community.

The possibility of the direct contact with living human beings, obviously, does not exist any longer for the societies of the past. We have nothing but documents, and artifacts—only the fragmentary remains surviving, by the accidents of the official intention to survive or of the durability of physical composition, from the full round of life. From these we must try to reconstruct what we think was most significant. These remains only obliquely answer our questions if they answer them at all. In dealing with living societies, we can address our questions directly to participants in those societies. We can obtain from them the data we need to fill in our picture. It permits us to study categories of action that leave no written records or that leave them with a disproportionate emphasis on the literate and official classes. The inwardness with which we can comprehend any section of the population is impossible to attain in dealing with societies and individuals of the past except for a few of the most articulate who have left behind them great deposits of written records.

Of course, not all problems can be elucidated directly from information gained by interviewing of contemporaries and participant observation over short stretches of time. These techniques must be joined to historical research, which provides depth in time and which enables us to correct the errors arising from distortions in temporal perspective. Temporal depth is necessary in all social science studies; but the need is more obvious in the study of the new states, which themselves have such a short history and which are implanted in such a medium of tradition.

The exhilaration of intensive interviewing and the richness of returns from extensive reconnaissance should not be allowed to obscure from our minds the limits of firsthand observation of contemporary events. Human action and its collective forms have a temporal dimension. It is, therefore, necessary to supplement our firsthand observations of the present moment or of a span of a few years in the life of the new states by historical knowledge. We need to know the historical background of the states we study because that discloses to us evidence to which the data elicited by interviews refer but that cannot be understood without an extension of our awareness of the significant past of the society. Furthermore, since human actions and institutions have a temporal dimension, a cyclical or development pattern, interview data on contemporary events alone that are not supplemented by historical research will hide from us important potentialities. Here, it must be admitted, the study of the new states encounters difficulties. In Asia and Africa, historical studies prosecuted by modern techniques are in their infancy. Sources have not yet been assembled and calendared, bibliographies are deficient, and the basic monographic research has not yet been done. The social scientist who tries to penetrate to the indispensable historical depth finds himself compelled to do historical research of a sort with which his colleagues working on Western societies think they can dispense. It is likely that the entry of social scientists into what has conventionally been regarded as the sphere of the historian will give a valuable impetus to historical research on the background of the new states; it might also make social scientists studying contemporary Western societies more aware of the temporal dimensions of their own problems. None the less, social science research on the new states, driven as it is to confront the facts of history to complement the richness of its observations of contemporary events, finds itself in the somewhat perplexing situation of the amateur and handicraftsman in an age of professional specialization.

Indeed, even the field procedures appropriate to the study of the new states correspond to the stage of craftsmanship in the development of research techniques in the social sciences. The techniques of the craftsman were not so precise or rigorous as they have since become. They were not equal to the specificity of contemporary microsociological analysis.

In the sociological study of the advanced societies of the West, sociological research has tended to become technically differentiated and to be concentrated on specific problems. The intimate contact with the whole human being and the whole society under study has been sacrificed to greater rigor and more impersonal reliability. For better and for worse, this stage of scientific advance has scarcely begun to be reached in the study of the new states. Fieldwork in the new states, while it tries to adhere to high standards of rigor in observation, interview, and documentation, cannot at present inhibit itself by the standards of the laboratory or the opinion survey.

The primary need in the study of the new states today is a comprehensive view, a view of the whole society. Owing, perhaps, to the strength of the tradition of intensive one-man inquiry that has been fostered by social anthropology, from which so many of the students of the new states have come and the literature of which is so essential to the understanding of the social setting of the new states, their comprehensive study by techniques that are appropriate has begun in the right direction. Furthermore, owing to the perhaps transient situation in which so little sociological research has been done on the societies of the new states, each investigator in the field of the new states is almost compelled to take a broad view to compensate for the deficient supply of more specialized monographic literature. Whatever the causes, the breadth of outlook in the study of the new states may be counted on to give a powerful impetus to the development of macrosociological analysis in this field and in the course of time, we hope, to its development in the study of other societies as well.

IV

WE intend, through our studies of the new states, to contribute to the comparative analysis. This means more than studying one new state with an eye on the parallel and divergent developments in other new states. Of course, this is necessary and it is already being done. To be genuinely comparative, however, we need also another kind of historical knowledge. That is, we need the knowledge of the great societies of the European and non-European past. Social scientists may no longer neglect this history, even if their primary interest is the understanding of the newly sovereign states of Asia and Africa.

Social scientists must now begin to bring into their horizon what has in the past been left to historians. The original research done by the historians of ancient, medieval, and early modern Europe and the Islamic, Indian, Chinese, and Japanese states is comparable, in its relation to primary sources, to the fieldwork done by social scientists on contemporary societies. The historians' research on these great societies and epochs cannot be redone by social scientists except in rare cases. Their respective schemes of training are too different, as are the linguistic and technical requirements. Unlike the situation that arises when a social scientist tries to reconstruct the historical background from which one of the new states has arisen, there is, moreover, no need for him to try to do the historians' job. The historians have already done it. It is now a task of the social scientist to try to master the results of research on the great historical societies and to adapt them to the purposes of social science.

The great historical societies—the aristocratic city-states, the patrimonial principalities, the bureaucratic empires, the feudal kingdoms, and so on—represent a tremendously significant part of human experience. Any attempt to further our causal understanding of why the new states are developing as they are will be affected by our awareness of the experience of the human race in historical times and not just in contemporary primitive and advanced Western societies.

One of the greatest dangers in the study of new states is that we shall interpret their experience and possibilities within too narrow a schema. At present, our schema is inevitably limited by our own experience of the modern large-scale state. It is not inevitable that the new states will develop in this direction, even though their elites so aspire. Of course, historical awareness will not provide the answer to our questions, since there is no reason to assume that human possibilities have been exhausted by experience of the human race up to the present. None the less, the study of the variety of forms of social and political organization, as these are presented by historians, will do much to diminish our territorial and epoch parochiality. We shall be particularly helped by historical studies of institutions that are associated with authority, such as kingship, dynasties, patronage, and administration. These are the subjects most studied by historians, and they are the ones most relevant to our central problem in the study of the new states. We see in these historical inquiries forms of authority that often bear a close resemblance to the traditional systems of rule with which the elites of the new states must contend and which they would, in some cases, assimilate. But more important than any specific propositions that can be formulated is the enrichment of an imagination about the range of possibilities of which societies and polities are capable.

The orderly understanding of the new states requires that they be seen *sub specie aeternitatis*, or at least within the categories of known human experience. There is an important reason, deriving from our theoretical interests, for this requirement. To escape from *ad hoc* explanations, in which the canons of explanation are historically accidental, we must promulgate categories that are equally applicable to all states and societies, to all territories and epochs—variations must be subsumable within these categories. To attain this end, all societies must be included within our scrutiny. That is why we speak of our mode of analysis as "comparative."

V

THE comparative study of the new states has already made notable progress. The works of Almond and Coleman,[1] of Coleman[2] himself, of Wriggins,[3] Weiner,[4] Morris-Jones,[5] Pye,[6] Harrison,[7] Ashford,[8] Kahin,[9] and others, to say nothing of the writings of some of the contributors to the present volume, show that the subject is under way. The path they traverse has been laid out on a map that comprehends more than the country studied. The mere fact that all these authors are of American or British origin and education has meant that they have begun with a perspective that does not attribute to the situation of the new states a uniqueness so extreme as to refuse any possibility of comparison. They all begin with an awareness of the state systems in which they have lived. They go further, however. Their awareness of variety is tempered by a sophisticated appreciation of the considerable identity of the problems that exist in all polities. They are the beneficiaries of a movement in social science, inspired mainly by Max Weber, which attempts to operate with categories that are of universal applicability or are derivable from such categories.

Comparative study, therefore, treats the new states as instances of the species of states. The same sociological approach pertinent to the understanding of politics in the older existing states or in the great states of the past is regarded as pertinent to the politics of the new states.

"Historicism" asserts the uniqueness of every society, of every

1. Gabriel Almond and James S. Coleman (eds.), *The Politics of Developing Areas*, Princeton, N.J., Princeton University Press, 1960.
2. James S. Coleman, *Nigeria: Background to Nationalism*, Berkeley, University of California Press, 1959.
3. Howard Wriggins, *Ceylon: Dilemmas of a New Nation*, Princeton, N.J., Princeton University Press, 1961.
4. Myron Weiner, *Party Politics in India*, Princeton, N.J., Princeton University Press, 1957.
5. W. H. Morris-Jones, *Parliament in India*, Philadelphia, University of Pennsylvania Press, 1956.
6. Lucian Pye, *Politics, Personality and Nation-Building: Burma's Search for Identity*, New Haven, Yale University Press, 1962.
7. Selig Harrison, *India: The Most Dangerous Decades*, Oxford, Oxford University Press, 1960.
8. Douglas Ashford, *Political Change in Morocco*, Princeton, N.J., Princeton University Press, 1961.
9. George McT. Kahin, *Nationalism and Revolution in Indonesia*, Ithaca, N.Y., Cornell University Press, 1959.

culture, and every epoch. It denies the fundamental identity of
human beings in different societies, cultures, and epochs. It asserts
that these unique features are incomparable with one another, and
so different from one another that no general categories can illuminate any significant aspect of the events that occur in these diverse
societies, cultures, and epochs. Historicism often goes beyond these
methodological contentions, and proclaims a relativity of moral
standards; it often associates itself with a philosophy of history
that is a temporal arrangement of these unique constellations into
a meaningful pattern of growth (or of growth and decay.) We
need not concern ourselves with these latter adhesions to the
methodology of historicism. We are, on the other hand, greatly
concerned about the insistence on the uniqueness that denies the
possibility of any general theory that can help us to comprehend or
account for uniqueness.

We are not historicists. We aim at generalized categories and
analytical propositions, both because we regard them as among the
highest intellectual achievements and because we think they are
indispensable for the better understanding of concrete and particular events. It is obviously necessary to ascertain the unique features
of societies and polities. These are already so apparent that their
detection as such will not cause us any great difficulty. Indeed, the
likelihood that their particularity will overwhelm us is, rather, the
greater danger. Our task in this regard is to find the categories
within which the unique may be described, and in which its differences with respect to other situations may be presented in a way
that raises scientifically significant problems. Orderly comparison
is one necessary step in the process of systematic explanation. The
alternative to comparative description and explanation is *ad hoc*
description that uses categories usually drawn from more or less
contemporary experience. This might satisfy the mind momen-
tarily, but when an effort is made to go more deeply and to be
more consistent, this procedure reveals that it is a superficial make-
shift. Cumulative knowledge, the transfer of insights gained in
one inquiry into another context, is greatly hampered.

Yet the task of description and explanation is nerve-rackingly
difficult when we try to do more than make *ad hoc* explanations.
Explanations of unique events that explain why one society differs
in a unique respect from another society must be made by ref-

erence to some other difference between those two societies. This
kind of explanation is often feasible in an *ad hoc* way. To go beyond *ad hoc* explanations—however truthful and revealing these
might be—demands the stabilization of concepts or categories;
but to stabilize often imposes only a deadening rigidity, an application of concepts improvised in some other intellectual context.
Stable concepts are helpful only if they are applicable. They will
be applicable only if they are of sufficient scope and if they contain
sufficient potentiality for logical extension. More specifically, this
will entail the delineation of the variables and their values at a
level of generality that will render them applicable not only to the
societies ruled by new states but to other societies as well. The
essential constituents of a factor adduced for explanatory purposes
are more perceptible when a given value in a category of events is
scrutinized against a background of as diverse as possible a set of
precipitating conditions. Otherwise, the historically adventitious
features of the precipitating situation can be as prominent in our
minds as the more essential ones.

Let us take a simple example. If we wish to explain why the
military intervened in the political life of Iraq, Sudan, or Pakistan,
it will be helpful to refer, for instance, to Islamic (and Ottoman
and Mogul) traditions, which do not allow for the legitimacy of a
civil order, and to contrast this situation with that of India, where
Islamic traditions are not central and the military has not intervened. This is a plausible effort at explanation, and it is not wrong.
It is only insufficient. After all, the military has intervened in
Burmese politics and in Laos, and in neither of these can Islamic or
cognate influences be found. And this proposition about the intervention of the military would throw no light at all on why it has
intervened on several occasions in France in the past century or
why it was so influential in Roman imperial politics. It could, of
course, be said that there is no good reason why there should be
a unitary explanation. Isn't it enough to explain Pakistan by comparison with India, France by comparison with England, Rome
by comparison with Athens? Our answer is that it is not enough.
The Islamic tradition, for example, is not an irreducible entity; it
is a variant of a general human possibility, and the deeper, more
universally valid explanation will pay explicit attention to that
possibility. If we reject the possibility that the Moslem and the
Buddhist or Hindu cannot be compared so that their differences

may be described in a common language more general in its reference than the language of either of these religious orientations, then we cannot accept an explanation that remains content with their irreducibility.

The variables adduced in explaining a difference among several new states must thus be phrased in the same analytical idiom, and must be part of the same system of analysis, as a proposition that asserts similarities or differences between an old state and a new state, or between two old states. The comparative study of new states is not, therefore, a self-contained discipline. It is part of the systematic analysis of human society, in which all societies are seen as members of a single species. For this reason, the comparative study of the new states must give at least a significant modicum of attention to the great historical states as well as to the primitive and the modern.

None the less, to proceed comparatively does not mean that every piece of research must give equally intensive attention to two states, nor that it must review the situation relevant to its interests in every new state, nor that it must bring in explicit references to the establishment and maintenance of new political orders in medieval Europe or China. Inquiries that do this are certainly desirable, indeed, even urgent; but it will not be imperative that every comparative study assume this form.

Studies that do assume this form will, in any case, be rarer than those that concentrate on the situation of one or another of the new states, and this rarity will not be damaging. Most comparative inquiries need not be designed in a way that systematically and with equal intensity compares two or more new states or compares one new with one or more other states of longer establishment. Each investigator of a situation in one of the new states will, however, have to know something substantial about the corresponding situations in new states other than the one he is investigating. Similarly, in illustrating his analytical contentions, he might well refer to a variety of states. These features will, however, be more a part of the rhetoric of exposition than of the logical structure of the analysis or of the substance and procedure of the investigation.

An inquiry may be considered comparative if it proceeds by the use of an analytical scheme through which different societies *may be systematically compared* so that, by the use of a single set of categories, their identities and uniqueness may be disclosed and explained. The analysis is comparative if the explanation draws on variables and the values of variables that are applicable to the description and analysis of societies widely different in time and place from that under immediate consideration. An inquiry into a particular society will be considered comparative if its descriptions and explanations assert, imply, or permit the systematic juxtaposition of that society or of some section of it with other societies or their corresponding sectors.

How explicit, particular, and concrete must that juxtaposition or comparison be? Cannot the comparison be contained in the general proposition that has made the observations of particular societies "anonymous" by incorporating them into generalized propositions? In principle, it has no larger need for the concrete juxtaposition of particular historical societies, any more than the general theory of society will need such a particularity of reference except for purposes of illustration. When the comparative pattern of analysis becomes more mature, it will be very little different, if different at all, from a systematic theory of society. As these two intellectual undertakings develop, they draw on each other and approximate each other in a way that permits the future pattern to be perceived.

But whatever the pattern of the remote future, there is at present no complete identity of comparative analysis and general theory. There is at present no systematic, dynamic general theory of society of universal comprehensiveness; nor is there, as yet, any analytical or empirical comparative theory of society.

This does not mean, however, that all comparative analysis must at present enumerate painstakingly, for every situation it considers in one country, corresponding situations in a number of other countries. It does mean that concrete comparisons of particular societies are, and will continue for some time to be, necessary. We exist at present in a middle ground, in which the general theory has begun to reveal its main lines and in which empirical comparative analysis, influenced by this theory—and influencing it—has begun to show how it is going to develop. One of the main lines of development of the latter is the macrosociological analysis of a single society, conducted under the guidance of the tentative general theory. This general theory is itself deeply influenced by the comprehensive historical-sociological studies of Max Weber. The enrichment of the general theory so that it becomes more relevant to empirical comparative analysis depends, in part, on the increasing readiness of social scientists to extend their knowledge beyond contemporary America, Germany, France, Russia, Great Britain, and the still-living "primitive societies." Particular comparisons will then be made in more fundamental terms, and the theory that will permeate these comparisons will have become more differentiated.

At present, therefore, we are in the middle phase of the development of the comparative method—from the enumeration and correlation of isolated items, in the style of Hobhouse, Wheeler, and Ginsberg, or of the Human Relations Area Files, to the universal propositions, which are formed from the orderly scrutiny of the full range of societies, historical and contemporary, and utilized in the analysis and explanation of particular instances. Comparative analysis in its present state functions primarily as a standpoint for the case study of particular societies. It is the standpoint that prompts comparison and contains the results of comparison. The standpoint stands in need of elaboration and articulation.

Here is where the study of the new states becomes especially pertinent. The study of the new states cries out for comparative analysis. It needs comparative analysis, and it offers great opportunities for its further development. The mere fact that so many states are in somewhat similar situations, face somewhat similar problems, and have certain similarities of social structure, while also differing from one another, would recommend comparative treatment even if it were not a desideratum for the more systematic development of social science. The inherent necessities of the study of the new states, so numerous, so similar to one another in so many respects, and also so different, would have created the idea of a comparative outlook even if it had not already existed.

But the idea of the comparative point of view does exist. It has outlived its adventitious associations with the theory of social evolution. We now see that it need not be accompanied by any particular philosophy of history, with any theory of stages, of any inevitable sequence throughout the course of human history. The study of the new states provides it with the greatest opportunity it has ever had for a renewed life. Freed from its evolutionary encrustation, and brought into connection with a dynamic conception of social systems, such as it lacked earlier, the comparative standpoint can serve both the broadened human sympathies of this age and the requirements of the more coherent social theory appropriate to this extension of the imagination.

VI

THE central concern of the study of the new states is with the formation of coherent societies and polities. Its concern with particular institutions, beliefs, and practices concentrates on their significance for this process. In other words, the study of new states is a macrosociological study: it is a study of *societies*, and when it studies parts of these societies, it studies their contribution to the functioning of the society as a "whole."

The comparative method as it has came down to us, in a least one of its forms, has often been characterized by an interest in whole societies. The theory of states of social development was one mode of expression of the comparative outlook in social science; it aimed, as a means to the end of formulating a sequence, at a classification of types of whole societies, characterized by one predominant feature. The historicism that in Germany was directed by the desire to construct a philosophy of history had many affinities with the positivistic, empirical effort to construct a theory of stages; it too was dominated by the characteristically German, romantic emphasis on "totality." It emphasized the uniqueness and incomparability of a whole society with any other whole society. Historicism, with its vague and often hidden historical metaphysics, might have muddied the waters of social thought; but its preoccupation with coherent wholes left, besides much else, an invaluable inheritance. In contrast with the ethnographic positivism that took single items out of context, even when trying to establish types or classes of societies, it sustained a tradition from which the macrosociological sensitivity has grown. Max Weber was its greatest heir.

Contemporary work in the comparative study of the new states draws much of its inspiration from Max Weber. He refined and corrected the historicist tradition. He went beyond historical particularity in his grandiose set of categories for the analysis of types of authority. This enabled him to set forth the affinities, the identities, and the differences of the great historical societies in a way that no other social scientist has ever done before or since. Whatever might be the empirical limitations of his work on the sociology of religion, his pursuit of a common problem in societies and cultures as different as China, India, ancient Israel, and post-Reformation Europe sets a standard for comparative macrosociological analysis that it is difficult to equal and that it is necessary to transcend. The great sources of historicism—Hegel, Marx, and Romanticism—came to fulfillment in Max Weber's work in an idiom and imagery necessary for the progress of empirical research.

The study of the new states is the beneficiary of Max Weber's achievement. Its macrosociological intention does not derive from him alone. It also comes from social anthropology, from which it has acquired the tendency of that discipline to study the whole round of life of a society.

Quite apart from the tradition of social science, the reality of the new states and the ways in which their elites define their tasks would compel the study of the new states to take a macrosociological direction. The new states are, as we have said, not based on a society that is coterminous with the boundaries of the state. The elites of the new states are as aware of this as are foreign social scientists. Their efforts to modernize their countries, or at least their aspirations to do so, always include, as the very central element of the conception of modernity, the formation of a nation and of the institutions appropriate to a national society. These institutions include a national economy, a national educational system, a national legal order, a national party system of one or more national parties, and a national army.

A modern society is not just a complex of modern institutions. It is a mode of integration of the whole society. It is a mode of relationship between the center and the periphery of the society. Modern society entails the inclusion of the mass of the population into the society in the sense that both elite and mass regard themselves as members of the society and, as such, as of approximately equal dignity. It involves a greater participation by the masses in the values of the society, a more active role in the making of society-wide decisions, and a greater prominence in the consideration of the elite. This process of integration into a single society is the problem of macrosociology. From this central problem follows a great variety of derivative problems—for example, concerning the role of mass communication in forming an integral society, of the role of military service in enhancing national identification.

Like all states, the new states rest on a prepolitical matrix of institutions, beliefs, and solidarities. In the case of the new states, the prepolitical matrix is in a most rudimentary condition. The constituent societies on which the new states rest are, taken separately, not civil societies, and, taken together, they certainly do not form a single civil society. They are scarcely able thus far to produce a polity that can supply the personnel necessary to run a modern society. They lack the affirmative attitude toward rules, persons, and actions that is necessary for consensus. They are constellations of kinship groups, castes, tribes, feudalities—even smaller territorial societies—but they are not civil societies. The sense of identity is rudimentary, even where it exists. The sense of membership in a nation-wide society, and the disposition to accept the legitimacy of the government, its personnel, and its laws are not great. Society-wide institutions, other than the state, are scant in the societies we are discussing. The interaction among the different sectors is tenuous. Parties are very often communal, sectional, and tribal. Civic associations tend to be tribal; trade unions tend to be creations and instruments of the political parties. Publications are local in circulation; there is no system of mass communications effectively covering the country. The whole infrastructure is meager and fragile.

In so far as there is internal migration, the migrants of each region retain their original identities and, to the extent that they can, retain their previous social structure and loyalties. With the enhancement of the authority of the state, with some measure of political democracy—or at least some responsiveness on the part of the elites to what they conceive to be the popular will—there is a sharpening of conflict over the benefits an interventionist state can confer. The power of the government and unity of the country are placed under strain. This is a fundamental and practical problem in every new state. The maintenance of order, the intensification of exertion on behalf of public ends, the involvement in participation are acknowledged as pressing problems in the new states both by their own elites and by foreign observers, sympathetic as well as hostile. A widespread moral consensus, reaching into the outermost areas of the society, maintained, renewed, and revised by strong personalities and effective institutions, is a real need of the new states.

To estimate the approximations toward, the factors leading toward, and the obstacles in the path of the formation of society and polity, and of a coherent cultural order, requires a macrosociological perspective. The study of the new states that omitted this problem would be of little value either to practical life or to scientific understanding. The study of the new states is thus the par excellence of macrosociological analysis. It could not readily be otherwise, and it could not be more fortunate for the development of our subject.

Macrosociology has been left painfully uncultivated by sociology in recent decades. As sociology and its cognate disciplines have become more refined and rigorous, they have also narrowed the scope of their observations—although these two tendencies are not logically connected with each other. Where social anthropology, which is more or less macrosociological in its study of its traditional subject matter, that is, the small society, has transferred its attention to advanced societies, it has confined itself to the village or small town. Its macrosociological potential has not been sufficiently realized in the study of advanced societies. Indeed, practically no social scientist—none, except for a few quasi-Marxists—has attempted to deal macrosociologically with modern societies; and these because of their inclination to regard power, and above all, coercive power, as the sole means of producing coordinated action, have contributed very little to the formulation or clarification of the macrosociological problem.

Consensus is the key phenomenon of macrosociology. The phenomenological description of consensus is relevant to our theoretical interests. The extent to which the population residing within a given territory is a society, and not just a complex of societies ruled more or less effectively by a single system of authority, is of both theoretical and practical interest. Every constituent institution and stratum of the society or societies of a new state can be studied from the standpoint of the macrosociological problem. Interconnections among the various sectors of the elite, local and national, and their relationships with the rest of the society, the situation of the "professionals" of traditional culture, the growth of the monetized sector of the economy, the adaptation of immigrants in towns, the formation of trades unions—to cite only a few illustrative instances—are all fit subjects of macrosociological analysis. In every instance, the problem is as follows: How does this institution or practice or belief function in the articulation of the society, in attaching or detaching or fixing each sector in its relationship to the central institutional and value systems of the society?

There are all sorts of prospective gains in studying the coherence of a society. It would offer, for example, the possibility of a greatly needed improvement in our understanding of the nature of nationality and nationalism and of their differences. It could disclose the potentialities and limitations of nationalism as a precipitator of persistent and intense effort throughout a society. By permitting the contemplation of the consensual/dissensual pattern of a society, the processes through which it moves, and the determinants of its formation, maintenance, and rupture in a society *in statu nascendi,* the study of the new states offers opportunities for empirical research similar to those which Thomas Hobbes's fiction of the state of nature offered for the purposes of political-philosophical analysis. Macrosociology will "empiricize" and differentiate the discussion of consensus. It will show how much and what patterns of consensus correspond to different states of order. It will show the respective roles of prepolitical and political factors on their growth and vicissitudes.

We may confidently expect that, if this program makes genuine progress in the study of the new states where its urgency is so much more patent, the study of the more advanced societies will inevitably benefit. A central problem will thus be restored to social science, and the process of fragmentation of our comprehension of our own societies will be corrected. Once more we shall be able to see the basic identity of the interests of self-interpretation, the general theory of society, the comparative study of the new states, and the practical management of the deeper problems of the society under study.

VII

IT has sometimes been charged against the present students of the new states that, under the guise of sociological analysis, they are simply using the measuring rod of Western democracy to describe the working of regimes that by tradition and necessity cannot be measured in this way. This charge raises, although in a muddled and confusing way, a fundamental question: How are we to assess and judge the new states? More particularly for those of us who espouse a certain method of understanding, it is proper to ask what our method, comparative and macrosociological, can contribute to a more equitable judgment of the development of the new states.

Is it morally and scientifically permissible for us to be concerned with the fortunes of political democracy, of public liberties and representative institutions, in these states? Certainly we are, and should be, concerned with the political outcome of the interplay of the traditional order and the modern resources, institutional and personal, of the new states. We are interested in the success or failure of the elites in seeking to create a coherent and stable polity. We would, however, certainly be doing less than our intellectual responsibilities require if we were to regard stability or cohesion, as such, as undifferentiated conditions. There are different kinds of cohesion, and different kinds of stability; some are better than others, as well as different in their consequences for the direction of growth in their societies.

Certainly the various forms of society and polity that emerge in the new states must be a fundamental preoccupation. We must, however, avoid an excessively simple classification, which places on the one side the democratic polity such as we know it in the West, and which places all other sorts of regimes on the other side. The danger of such a procedure is that it might regard all the other regimes that are not more or less identical with our present-day Western forms of democracy as falling into the residual category of the simply "nondemocratic." This is a danger a genuinely comparative mode of analysis can help to avoid, just by virtue of its construction of a more diversified classification of types of regimes, and by its transcendence of historical particularism.

It is not a manifestation of Western liberal parochialism for us to be concerned with the growth of individuality and creativity, the institutionalization or the reasonable criticism of authority, and the incorporation into the political order of dissent, or with the range of participation in consultation and decision, or with the institutional forms of respect for ordinary human beings, or with loyalty, amity, and affection among human beings. These are all values of universal validity, and regimes that do not find a place for them and similar values are less good than those that do. None the less, we must not be doctrinaire in our belief about the institutional forms in which these values can be expressed. It would be wrongheaded to think that the institutional arrangements in which these values have attained some measure of realization in Western societies exhaust the human possibilities of creation and contrivance. It would be just as wrongheaded ethically and scientifically as the all too common and quite groundless proposition that the indispensable conditions of economic progress in a new state are the suppression of public dissent and the amalgamation of all organizational activity into one dominant political organization.

The comparative study of the new states need be no more relativistic, ethically, than it need or can be historicist in a methodological sense. The avoidance of relativism must not, however, be accompanied by a freezing of our imagination about the diversity of institutional forms through which our ethical values can be realized. A genuinely comparative study of the new states, within the context of a general theoretical and comparative analysis of all states and societies, will do more to reveal the possibilities of the organization of public life than all the arguments about the inherent genius of the "African personality," the "Islamic state," the "Hindu heritage," or the "Western tradition." It can contribute to the schooling of judgment and the refinement and enrichment of analysis in political philosophy. Thus, it might, by proceeding along the lines of Max Weber, bring to fruition what was begun by Aristotle and Cicero. It will therewith illuminate our spirits while it disciplines our minds.

Cultural policy in the new states

MC KIM MARRIOTT

No STATE, NOT EVEN AN INFANT ONE, is willing to appear before
the world as a bare political frame. Each would be clothed in a
cultural garb symbolic of its aims and ideal being. Can one predict
the cultural fashions of the new states? Can one say what the
nature of a nation's cultural raiment will be—what elements of
culture will be worn by all citizens as the common core of decency
in the new national way of life, what elements will be used to distinguish the new national identity, what elements will be officially
put forward as that state's special claim to respect in the eyes of
mankind?

When, following the Second World War, the nations of South
Asia first crossed the threshold of independence and began to
experiment with cultural policy, the probable outcome seemed
obvious to many observers: there would be a movement toward
the dominant Western culture such as the world had never seen
before. Accelerating programs of technical assistance presumed,
and were thought to be in fact bringing to pass, just such a cultural
overturn.

To other observers, such as the philosopher F. S. C. Northrop,[1] an alternative prediction seemed far more promising: one was about to witness a "resurgence of submerged civilizations," an inevitable outward legislation of what the legal sociologist Eugen Ehrlich had called the "inner order" or "living law" of each national society.[2] The rising tide of the world of 1947, or 1952, seemed to be an Asian and Muslim "culturalism" resembling the romantic nationalism of Europe a century earlier, rather than the secular nationalism familiar in the contemporary West.

Observers of the diversities and of the sometimes sudden alterations of national cultural policy in the new states during the later 1950's and afterward may doubt the possibility of generalizing, much less choosing between these two contrasting predictions about the trend of cultural development. Consider the example of India since her independence: with a population 85 per cent Hindu, India framed an explicitly secular constitution of Anglo-American type, yet followed a policy of indigenous cultural pluralism. She chose as the symbols of national identity and eminence old elements that are largely of the Buddhist and Mogul high cultures. On the other hand, Ceylon and Burma, having preponderances of Buddhism among their peoples, insisted on secular policies for ten and fourteen years, respectively, and then inaugurated strongly religious national and international programs. Muslim Pakistan took a seemingly opposite course, declaring herself Islamic at the outset, framing an Islamic constitution through nine years of debate and religious agitation, then two years later suspending that constitution in favor of a regime of secular character. Equal diversities are evident among the newer West African states: Nigeria stresses the continuity of indigenous cultural pluralism, and Ghana a unitary supertribal myth, while the Ivory Coast affects French culture and a disdain for all cultural history. Neither the fact of world dominance by European cultures nor a knowledge of underlying cultural values in each of the above new states would seem to have much power for explaining or anticipating cultural policies characterized by such variety and instability.

1. F. S. C. Northrop, *The Taming of the Nations*, New York, Macmillan, 1952, pp. 3, 68–69, 303–309.

2. Eugen Ehrlich, *Fundamental Principles of the Sociology of Law*, translated by Walter L. Moll, Harvard Studies of Jurisprudence, Vol. 5, Cambridge, Mass., Harvard University Press, 1936.

The variety and instability of cultural developments in the new states point to one condition shared in some measure by all nations of the mid-twentieth century, and not shared by those of the nineteenth: the presence of modern devices of mass communication. Modern means of communication have been gradually transforming the cultures of many nations for a century, generally without having been made the instruments of intentional policy. But the availability of such means of communication also opens up new potentialities for the manipulation of culture. The possibility of educating their citizens to a newly chosen way of life, of mobilizing them in support of deliberately cultivated values, of representing them to the world according to a consciously created image—all these are open to the elites of the new states, either in actuality or in prospect. Whoever in the new states commands mass communications cannot avoid taking decisions and choosing among alternatives that shape cultural development. Neither the "resurgence" of an "inner order" nor the diffusion of Western ways is likely to take place today without the mediation of conscious processes of "cultural management."[3]

If culture may indeed be managed, then the analysis of cultural policy may be placed alongside the analysis of the other "arts of the possible"—economic policy, military strategy, and politics. In such an analysis, we shall have to attend to varied and changing cogitations as to more and less effective means toward chosen ends.

The intention of this essay is to explore the considerations lying behind the various cultural policies actually chosen by newly independent states in Asia and Africa. The case of India is first explored in some detail as one of the more mature, complex, and explicit in its evolution. The Indian example suggests some general reasons for a new state's choosing indigenous rather than foreign cultural materials, for selecting the highest effective level of culture, for referring to distant phases of history, for recognizing a degree of cultural variety, and for preferring some kinds of external cultural alliance to others. The same issues of choice are reexamined as they recur variously in Ceylon, Pakistan, and Indonesia, and in the new states of sub-Saharan Africa, with the aim of establishing common principles in their handling.

3. Lloyd A. Fallers, "Ideology and Culture in Uganda Nationalism," *American Anthropologist*, 63: 677–678, 1961.

India

THE evolution of cultural policies in independent India is distinguished from all the other national developments here examined for its age and maturity. The long duration of the movement for independence, foreshadowed in the early 1800's and pursued in many forms for more than a century, gave ample opportunity for leaders to experiment with varied uses of Western and indigenous materials.[4] While the early and continuing leadership of nationalism tended to rest with men of strongly Western cultural tastes, the political potentialities of Indian cultural materials were proved again and again by new aspirants to leadership. For a hundred years, religious reformers, poets, and revolutionaries appealed to aspects of indigenous tradition as offering national strength, unity, and dignity. But the structure of Indian civilization was by no means ideally suited for the purposes to which its contents were to be put.

For makers of cultural policy, salient facts about the indigenous civilization of India are that it was large, stratified, and varied.[5] Indian civilization was large in content partly because it had accumulated through the centuries many layers and regional varieties of tradition. The most authoritative or top layers of the civilization tended often to be the most widespread; these "greater traditions" were often also the most specialized, being embodied in archaic languages or complex ritual forms that required professionals to preserve and apply them and to translate their contents into forms intelligible to the layman. Conversely, the lower levels of the civilization—the vernacular cultures, or "little traditions"—tended to be the most diversified from place to place. While many resemblances were shared among the many unlettered little tradi-

4. W. Norman Brown (drafter), "Traditional Culture and Modern Developments in India," *Report of the XIth International Congress of the Historical Sciences*, Stockholm, 1960, pp. 129–162; and the many examples in William Theodore de Bary, et al. (eds.), *Sources of Indian Tradition*, New York, Columbia University Press, 1958, pp. 551 ff.

5. M. N. Srinivas, *Religion and Society among the Coorgs of South India*, Oxford, Clarendon Press, 1952, pp. 213–218; Robert Redfield, *Peasant Society and Culture*, Chicago, University of Chicago Press, 1956, pp. 67–104; Bernard S. Cohn, and McKim Marriott, "Networks and Centres in the Integration of Indian Civilisation," *Journal of Social Research* (Ranchi), 1:1–9, 1958; Milton Singer (ed.), *Traditional India: Structure and Change*, Philadelphia, American Folklore Society, 1959.

tions, their participants generally communicated from one region to another not directly, but only through triangular translations up to the higher levels and down again. In Andhra a peasant would worship Vyankateshvar; in Bengal, Krishna; in Orissa, Jagannatha; in Maharashtra, Vithoba; and so on. Only if all these names of deities were translated into the name of the embracing Sanskrit god Vishnu would the civilization-wide community of worship become apparent; only an expert would so translate. Similarly, Rajputs, Patidars, Reddis, Okkaligas, and Marhathas—all dominant farming and fighting castes, but belonging to separate regions—could become aware of their common claims to aristocratic status in India's mythical past only by reference to the overarching relevant Sanskrit class category of the "Ksatriya." Conceptions of deities and of the traditional class orientations of Brahman, Ksatriya, and Vaisya were essentially plural and divergent even at the highest levels of thought. A consciousness of common culture then could exist only by reference to the top of the civilization, and then only to a limited extent.

Powerful devotional movements during the preceding eight centuries had begun to cut wider channels across the stratification and regional variants of Indian culture with certain simplified religious messages. Now the coming of such means of communication as the printing press and the railroad greatly hastened circulation among the cultural strata. Where all but a tiny class of literati had previously been dependent for civilizational contact upon chains of oral specialists, printing was now employed to publish the great books in translation for a growing middle class. Classical models of the spiritual or aristocratic good life were made more directly available for imitation by rural as well as by urban gentry. Religious fundamentalism appeared in many movements and sects. During the nineteenth and early twentieth centuries, pilgrimage to the civilization's most sacred places accelerated steadily.[6]

The later phases of the movement for independence and the advent of political democracy put heavy new demands on India's cultural policy makers. Leadership shifted more toward figures like

6. McKim Marriott, "Changing Channels of Cultural Transmission in Indian Civilization," in Verne F. Ray (ed.), *Intermediate Societies, Social Mobility, and Communication, Proceedings of the 1959 Annual Spring Meeting of the American Ethnological Society*, Seattle, University of Washington Press, 1959, pp. 66–74.

Tilak and Gandhi, who insisted on Indians' rights to cultural independence from the West. The intricate civilization of India, its higher contents already undergoing widened dissemination to an enlarged elite, had now to be reshaped into a standard cultural package suitable for rapid distribution to each member of a massive electorate. Not just landlords and Brahmans were to be supplied, but also the sons and daughters of shepherds, swine-herds, and sweepers, who would soon be filling the country's schools. A high degree of selectivity had thus to be applied to the vast corpus of Indian culture. The most prominent, universal, and accessible, but not necessarily the most sacred or authoritative, items were often chosen for emphasis by political leaders, pub-lishers, and later by educators and officials. With established gov-ernment and political competition focused at a single all-Indian center and at the capitals of internally heterogeneous British In-dian provinces, regional and local variants in all spheres of culture tended to be neglected in the search for the widest possible com-monalities. Also neglected were the most sacred but esoteric Vedas, the speculative Upanishads, and the limitless variety of puranas. Certain parts of the popular epic literature, and particularly one ethical text from the Mahabharata—the Bhagavad-Gita—were exalted beyond the hundreds of contending holy books. The Gita gained something like the status of a unified Hindu "Bible" where none had existed before. Some of the resulting adaptations of ancient materials, freshly fabricated as the common core of na-tional culture, were as unfamiliar to many of the older literati as they were to the newly arriving peasant citizens.

In modern cultural policy,[7] compromises have constantly to be made between the aim of reaching a broad audience (necessarily by means of choosing a higher—and therefore more prestigious and remote—level of culture) and the aim of moving the audience deeply to loyalty or action (necessarily by means of a more local, intelligible, and lower level of appeal). Linguistically, a sufficiently heavy borrowing from Sanskrit can sometimes carry a speaker of one Indic or Dravidian language across the boundary of another language of the same family in which he has no more than rudi-

7. The following observations, where no other source is cited, are largely based on field research by the author in Uttar Pradesh, 1950–1952 (with sup-port through an Area Research Training Fellowship from the Social Science Research Council), and in Maharashtra, 1955–1957.

mentary grammatical knowledge; but that much borrowing from Sanskrit will at the same time generally lift his words above the understanding of all but the most educated listeners.[8] The happiest general medium to find for rebuilding a stratified culture such as India's would seem to be the highest level compatible with effective comprehension—a level generally somewhere between the middle and the top.

The search for the "right" level of culture for mobilizing the Indian peasantry goes on in every sphere. Consider a typical debate between one rural development officer and a conservative Brahman farmer, a key man in his village.[9] The officer's aim was to persuade the farmer to adopt the practice of sowing, then plowing under a green crop in order to enrich the soil for subsequent planting of grain. The development officer's initial secular appeals to economic advantage had gone unheeded, and had in fact been exposed as not only self-seeking but also sinful, since plowing a crop under involved taking the life of the destroyed plants. The officer next appealed to the doctrine of duty as set forth in the sacred Gita. Here his words went over the heads of most villagers, while failing to equal the much greater traditional textual learning of his Brahman antagonist. Success came to the officer only when he put himself into the nonliterate peasants' own dilemma and spoke of the need for reconciling the inevitable sins of farming with the possibility of earning greater spiritual merit by applying the farmer's wealth to the performance of social and religious duty.

Even if he is acquainted with the more local variant of culture, hesitancy about descending to too low a level is always present on the part of any public figure. The lower levels of culture are liable not only to command a more limited range of communication but also to imply the lower social standing of the user. Even regional and communal minority parties have felt constrained to keep toward the upper end of the civilizational hierarchy: thus anti-Brahman agitation has rarely gone so far as to exalt elements of peasant religion, but has rather asserted the right of non-Brahmans

8. John J. Gumperz, "Language Problems in the Rural Development of North India," *Journal of Asian Studies*, 16:251–259, 1957.

9. Albert Mayer and associates in collaboration with McKim Marriott and Richard L. Park, *Pilot Project, India: The Story of Rural Development at Etawah, Uttar Pradesh*, Berkeley, University of California Press, 1958, pp. 207–210.

to practice Brahmanic rituals. Similarly in Madras, Tamil partisans of a Dravidian state, while attacking the northern bias in the Ramayana epic, sought to rewrite the epic story, not to ignore or abolish it.[10] The formula best suiting any determined mobilizer of action in his search for an effective intermediate level of common culture may generally be restated as the lowest level compatible with the dignity of his purpose and office.

The problem of choosing a suitable past is like that of choosing an appropriate cultural level, but here operating on a dimension of time. Symbols capable of exciting loyalty to the state would seem readily available in India's rich history. But even for a single village, there are many pasts to choose among.[11] Critical moments of history remembered as triumphant by one sector of society are all too often remembered as humiliating by other sectors. So it is with Mogul symbolism in India's government: some identification with the Mogul past is hardly avoidable, since the capital city, the achievement of a continental domain, and much of the apparatus of government appear as Mogul heritages in the present. Such symbolic connections with the preceding regime had, of course, been nurtured by India's British rulers. Prime Minister Nehru's own ancestral fortunes had risen in Mogul times: his familial tradition of dress and dialect are on the Muslim side, while his personal admiration goes strongly to the seventeenth century Hindu-Muslim political and religious synthesis attempted by the Mogul emperor Akbar.[12] But for India to go far in adopting a Mogul identity would alienate both India's orthodox Muslims, who regard Akbar as a heretic, and many Hindus and Sikhs, who recall Moguls generally as alien conquerors or rapacious despots. The use of Mogul symbolism by independent India has thus scarcely gone beyond the adoption of Mogul fashions in the "national dress," the uniform of palace guards, and the exploitation of Mogul fortresses for the modern ceremonies and utilitarian purposes of the state.

If Mogul elements cannot without conflict take a very prominent part in India's national culture, neither can reminiscences of

10. Selig S. Harrison, *India: The Most Dangerous Decades*, Princeton, N.J., Princeton University Press, 1960, pp. 127–129.

11. Bernard S. Cohn, "The Pasts of an Indian Village," *Comparative Studies in History and Society*, 3:241–249, 1961.

12. Jawaharlal Nehru, *The Discovery of India*, New York, John Day, 1946, pp. 256–57; *Toward Freedom*, New York, John Day, 1941, p. 16.

any other well-known historic dynasty. The legendary dynasties of the Mahabharata epic relate mainly to northern India, while the great events reported in the Ramayana, which link North and South, are seen by Dravidian separatists in Madras as depicting a hated conquest.[13] India's long, painful search for inspiring glories in the past has therefore had to reach back beyond both documentary history and legend to seize upon an archaic figure once hardly known to exist outside the work of British epigraphers—the Buddhist emperor Asoka. Asoka, who reigned in about 269–232 B.C., has about as much conscious continuity with modern India as the pyramids have with Abdel Nasser's Egypt. Asoka does, however, enjoy the advantage of having been a major indigenous ruler of spiritual pretensions who belonged to no known caste, no embattled region, and no threatened or threatening religion—at least as of 1947. Thus, the lion-ornamented capital of one of Asoka's edict pillars, although it is a work of strongly Persian style and although it had been totally unknown to most Indians, nevertheless became the national emblem of India. Gandhian pacifists could reconcile themselves to the installation of these violent beasts by observing that the lions have drawn in their claws and are smiling.

Witnessing the difficulties of India's search for inspirational symbols in her tangled pasts, one may question whether a future-oriented and quite secular national culture would not serve as well and with less tension. But modernism with its Western biases stands for things like the licensing of new abattoirs to slaughter beef for the Bombay market (anathema to cow-revering Hindus), or legislation for the abolition of dowry and for the institution of inheritance by females (disrupting to the patrilineal kinship systems of most Indian peasants). What little support is to be raised in upcountry India for new governmental measures is more likely to be raised by authoritative reference to their parallels in the forgotten Vedic past rather than by invoking the thinly held values of the modern, utilitarian international pattern. India's national anthem, "Janaganamana" by Rabindranath Tagore, has as its text a poem of such international type, a recitation of the names of provinces and rivers; the text is there, not because it moves citizens through tradition to loyalty, but because secular leaders felt

13. Harrison, *op. cit.*, pp. 217–218.

the necessity of displacing the emotive but obviously Hindu anthem of the independence movement, "Vande Mataram."

The same restraints do not govern opposition parties, but the same cultural hierarchy of relative effectiveness operates. Thus Communist political songs of the 1957 elections dwelt, like "Janaganamana," upon land, and also upon workers, toil, sweat, blood, and other high symbols of international Socialism with little response. Communist orators heard in rural areas of Maharashtra interested and moved their audiences best not by high ideological exegesis (scarcely attempted in any area) but by recitations of stories from the generally secular, originally Hindu epic Mahabharata. In the epic, of course, the speakers identified themselves with the heroes, and the Congress Party with the villains and demons. Deculturated modern appeals simply will not do the same sort of rousing job.

That India should be a secular state—that is, that there should be no state religion—is a fundamental principle of her constitution, yet a truly sterilized secularism has proved far from possible. In fact, the first fifteen years of independence saw the flourishing development of a multireligious cultural policy. For political as well as intellectual reasons, governmental support has been given generously to a major center of Islamic studies at the Aligarh University, to the restoration of the Hindu temple of Siva at Somnath, and to dozens of other religiously oriented projects. Government officials, sometimes men of the "wrong" religion, or of no religion, have become the managers of thousands of temples taken over under new statutes designed to prevent the wasteful or corrupt management of the temples' economic resources by private authorities. National and state calendars of holidays include not only such secular occasions as Independence Day, Republic Day, and Gandhi's Birthday, but also the birthdays of Krsna, Siva, Buddha, Mohammed, Jesus, and Guru Nanak. Some thirty holidays, largely religious, are already officially recognized in most states; and since a large number of additional holidays are constantly requested by adherents of the nine major religions, legal ceilings have had to be fixed. In the name of "cultural education," school texts try to incorporate materials on the beliefs and leading figures of all the religions of India, just as "cultural activities" programs at schools attempt to teach children of all faiths the techniques of worship appropriate for the many religious festivals. The contents of many religions are incorporated into the new national civilization not because of their inherent spiritual authority, but because they are high parts of an existent national "cultural" mosaic. Thus, orthodoxy withers, while a kind of religious revival blossoms.[14] In the eyes of the world, this Indian device of cultural pluralism, conceived internally as an agnostic policy and probably secularizing in its long-term effects, nevertheless preserves for India a distinctly spiritual aura.

In foreign as well as in domestic cultural policy, India tends toward pluralism. But among the many guises in which she might present herself, India's emphasis goes constantly to those that are most broadly regarded as admirable.

The broadest cultural phenomenon of which India can claim a part is the modern world culture of industry and science. As a peripheral recipient of some of the latest technological developments of the West—the newest plants for manufacturing steel, refining oil, or generating electricity, the newest laboratories for scientific research or the latest medical techniques—India can sometimes claim to be more up-to-date on a limited scale than even the donor countries. By comparison with other developing nations, India can generally show further technological progress. But if she emphasizes only this claim to world respect, India cannot in the foreseeable future aspire to the highest position, for she is still largely an importer rather than an exporter of such cultural goods, and thus second best to the West. Many elements of modern international culture link her with a wide world, but that world and its culture are in some senses not her own.

The second most widely spread segment of world culture in which India participates is the Islamic. In her centuries of Muslim rule, India was a leader of world Islamic civilization, and even today, after partition, she remains the third nation of the world in numbers of Muslim citizens. But India's claim to Islamic fame is inherently subject to qualifications like those affecting her claim to modernity, and to other qualifications as well. Indian Islam is an import, even if it is an old one, and has often been suspected of dilution or corruption by its pagan milieu. Furthermore, the 1947 partition had seemed to signify a rejection of allegiance to India on the part of most of her Muslim citizens: a

14. Taya Zinkin, *India Changes!* New York, Oxford University Press, 1958, p. 120.

strongly Islamic identification would therefore have been regarded as invalid by many.[15] Top leadership of Islam in South Asia seemed destined to fall to Pakistan, while leadership of world Islam seemed likely to remain in the smaller but more vociferous and historically central Islamic states of the Middle East. India's presentation of herself to the world as possessing some secondary eminence in Islamic culture usefully serves to sustain her sympathetic communication with other Muslim nations and to preserve her competitive position vis-à-vis Pakistan, but Islam cannot provide a credible total identity for the state.

For signaling her unique identity among the nations, there is no doubt that India could best choose to emphasize Hinduism. Hinduism is no import, but developed on Indian soil. The disqualification of Hinduism on the international scene is simply that it is so closely associated with Indians. It seems never to have succeeded as a world religion apart from Indian people: when it has traveled (anciently to Ceylon, Southeast Asia, and Indonesia, and recently to Africa, Fiji, and Trinidad), it has traveled always in the persons of Indians. Hinduism therefore retains the rather embarrassing character of a tribal, although national, religion. India would gain even less of world favor from adopting Hinduism as her official religion than Israel would by making herself into a Judaic state. Hinduism offers a basis of understanding with no other nation.

Generalizing on the difficulties of cultural policy that India has experienced in dealing with modern industrial culture, with Islam, and with Hinduism, one may say that the ideal segment of a nation's culture for international presentation is that which is neither too narrow, nor an import, but rather a widespread export. For India, Buddhism is just such a commodity. From its beginning as an Indian sect, Buddhism spread to most of central, eastern, and southeastern Asia and to the Indonesian archipelago as well as throughout South Asia. That it had nearly disappeared in India by 1947 was, if anything, an asset to India's taking it up as part of her international image, for no important internal group seemed likely to gain or lose by the illusion. As a somewhat vague and abstract doctrine, Buddhism has had relatively high marketability, or at least intelligibility far beyond its area of religious acclimatization

15. Wilfred Cantwell Smith, *Islam in Modern History*, Princeton, N.J., Princeton University Press, 1957, pp. 256–291.

in Asia. As suggesting either extreme spirituality or some sort of radical reform of less desirable pagan cults, Buddhism has seemed a respectable religion to many even in the Christian West.

The Government of India's symbolic adoption of the Buddhist robe had been presaged in her internally convenient selection of the Buddhist emperor Asoka as premier national hero. The international development was to be seen silently but forcefully stated in the Buddhist ornamentation of new architecture in the capital city (in the gateways of expositions and in such permanent structures as the Vigyan Bhavan and Asoka Hotel), in India's interested participation in the many conferences and exchanges of relics among Buddhist countries about the time of the twenty-five hundredth anniversary of Buddha's birth (1956–1957), in her archaeological efforts (for example, at Nagarjunakonda), and in her production and subsidy of numerous documentary films on Buddhist themes, and so on. The robe proved a serviceable garment in publicizing India's efforts to dissuade China from action in Tibet in 1954; the "Five Principles" (Panch Sheela) of coexistence propounded by Nehru at the time were cast in Buddhist cultural style and resounded widely in Asian public opinion. The Five Principles again proved useful in the Asian-African Conference at Bandung in 1955.[16] Efforts toward retaining the loyalty or friendship of the Indo-Tibetan frontier areas—Ladakh, Bhutan, and NEFA—also stood to gain from a Buddhist cultural policy. If there was one regret on the part of some Indian policy makers, it may have been at the possibility that they had oversold their goods on the internal market, for in 1956–1957 three million untouchables searching for equality in separation left the Hindu fold to become Buddhists.

External and internal cultural policies are, of course, not wholly separable: in order to attain a harmonious over-all policy, a nation needs to find a suitable core of internal culture that can also be satisfactorily used for broad external self-representation. In India's cultural foreign policy, the minor emphasis upon Islam and the major emphasis upon Buddhism cannot be entirely hidden from the Hindu citizens of the country. "Our Panditji is a Muslim!"

16. W. Howard Wriggins, *Ceylon: Dilemmas of a New Nation*, Princeton, N.J., Princeton University Press, 1960, p. 443; George McT. Kahin, *The Asian-African Conference, Bandung, Indonesia, April, 1955*, Ithaca, N.Y., Cornell University Press, 1956, pp. 8, 12, 14–15.

said North Indian peasants in the early years of independence on hearing Mr. Nehru's dialect, seeing his costume, and learning of his solicitous concern for Muslim Kashmir and for the welfare of Muslims generally. In the later 1950's, one could hear the prime minister called a "Buddhist" by conservative southern Brahmans, who regard Buddha as an evil form assumed by Vishnu to tempt untrue Hindus from their faith.

Pressed by demands and criticisms from many sides, the Indian Government has naturally preferred to have its external cultural policies all ways at once. In place of its saffron-colored, Buddha-decorated *About India* pamphlet of 1957, the Information Service of India in 1960 issued *India Today* on the new cover, a shadowy background of Hindu, Jain, Sikh, Buddhist, and Muslim shrines is overprinted with silhouettes of steel mills, oil refineries, and hydroelectric works. Selections from the Indian constitution intended for the Western external audience emphasize that document's provisions for the uplift of women and the abolition of untouchability;[17] selections from the same document preferred by government spokesmen for the internal peasant audience may rather emphasize provisions for cow protection, and include little about revisions of caste and family.

Granting the contrasting contexts in which external and internal policies must operate, India's cultural management shows a notable consistency of aims. When modern communications and political democracy required a transformation of the country's stratified civilization, India's cultural policy makers compromised upon selections from the higher and intermediate levels of the indigenous cultures, revived a forgotten (and therefore less conflictful) phase out of the country's many pasts, and sponsored a secular flowering of religious multiplicity. Contrary to predictions, they neither seized the West's symbolic secular apron strings nor paraded India's most dominant Hindu insignia. Externally, they chose at first to give primary display not to India's achievement along the international technological continuum, nor to her own major historic civilization; instead, they celebrated her importance within world-wide Islam, and especially her old origination of Buddhism. Given the great range of cultural alternatives presented by the highly cumulative and still living Indian civiliza-

17. *About India*, Washington, D.C., Information Service of India, 1957; *India Today*, Washington, D.C., Information Service of India, 1960.

tion, such choices had to be highly selective. The choices were not unconscious, nor were they the results of a blind "culturalism," nor were they entirely consistent with one another in content. They did appear to respond rationally to piecemeal calculations of the most suitable cultural emphases for promoting the state's prestige and for facilitating broad and unconflicted communication in the contemporary world.

To what extent can it be said that the cultural policies of others among the new Asian nations follow similar lines of calculation? A survey of the contrasting cases of Ceylon, Pakistan, and Indonesia suggests that they have much in common with India's problems, if not always with her success in solving them.

Ceylon

CEYLON's experience demonstrates what seem to be opposite cultural policies pursued within a civilization similar to India's. Scrutiny indicates, however, that the management of that civilization before independence had been markedly different from India's. Until 1947, power and pride of place in Ceylon had been given to secular English education and its products. Nine-tenths of the Sinhalese majority population—the rural Buddhists—had been left to shift for themselves in vernacular schools, while preferment in governmental appointments had gone to deracinated urbanites, Eurasians, and mission-educated Tamils.[18] The lack of a strong and early independence movement in Ceylon also meant that Ceylon's leaders had accumulated little experience in manipulating cultural symbols to arouse support. Ceylon's great Buddhist tradition had therefore undergone much less of that selective transformation that modern means of mass communication had begun to work before independence in India. That Ceylon's first free government was a wholly secular one in taste and policy stood for the larger fact that a great gap of non-communication existed between the political elite and most of the rural people.

In Ceylon, problems of choosing appropriate variants and levels of indigenous culture for national communication seem scarcely to have been recognized as problems before independence. Hindu Tamils had taken pride in Tamil history and ancient culture;

18. Bryce Ryan, "Status, Achievement, and Education in Ceylon," *Journal of Asian Studies*, 20:463–476, 1961.

Buddhist Sinhalese had dwelt upon the glories (and Tamil-inflicted tragedies) of their own past as depicted in the communal Mahavamsa history, or in the restored ruins of Anuradhapura.[19] Regional groupings among the Sinhalese likewise diverged in their views of the civilization, present and past. No group or leader seems to have conceived the possibility of dredging up some hero or heroic epoch suitable for the whole nation's emulation. The accepted formula for coexistence between the two largest ethnic groups of the island had been an official disregard for all indigenous cultures.

Since independent Ceylon was in fact a secular state, it is not surprising that her cultural policy makers at first saw few opportunities to exploit cultural commonalities internationally. Her own slight technological progress and her recent status as a restive colonial dependency in any case discouraged emphasis on any Christian or Western orientation. Distaste at the dominating international position of neighboring India, and anxiety over India's Tamil separatist agitators, barred emphasis upon Ceylon's very great cultural sharings with the Hindu world.[20] The small size of the minority of Moors left little profit in an Islamic identification.

Competition for mass support in the three elections following independence soon gave a series of jolts to this acultural state of affairs in Ceylon. The ruling and opposition parties both aimed especially to mobilize the rural Sinhalese voter for the first time. They did so by appealing to the interests of the Sinhalese Buddhist clergy and of rural homeopaths. The clergy, along with Buddhist laymen, replied with new unified forms of organization and with a novel resort to the public platform, press, and radio. Fundamentalist agitation was begun, seeking Buddhist control of the educational system, moral reforms of many kinds, and governmental assistance in the administration and financing of the Buddhist religious organization—all new political measures justified as a "return" to the legendarily virtuous days of the Buddhist monarchy. As conceptions of a third, neutral force in world politics developed through Asian and Afro-Asian negotiations, the Government of Ceylon began to recall the country's important ancient religious role. International Buddhist ties were then cultivated in

19. Wriggins, op. cit., pp. 231–240.
20. Ibid., pp. 399–400.

earnest, especially at the Buddha's anniversary celebrations of 1956–1957, and later.[21]

Ceylon's late and sudden Buddhist revival, like India's more comprehensive cultural programs, selected and propagated a neglected high level of indigenous culture, connected present efforts with the dignity of a remote past, and linked the new state with one broad and relevant range of culturally similar states. But the cultural policies of Ceylon fell far short of comprehending the whole nation. When the newly aroused Sinhalese claimed a privileged position for theirs as the only state language, and moved toward establishing Buddhism as the state religion, they began a phase of communal politics characterized by violence in relations with the country's Tamils and Hindus, and fraught with the potentiality of future conflict with neighboring India.

In Ceylon's first fifteen years of experimentation with cultural policy, a limited unity and an extreme intensity of action were thus achieved, but at the expense of maximal breadth and ease of communication.[22]

Pakistan

THE initial simplicity of her cultural policies sets Pakistan off to some extent from all others among the new states here examined. With an 86 per cent majority religion, she could afford better than Ceylon to reject pluralist policies at the outset. That Pakistan—if there was to be a Pakistan—would be an "Islamic state" had actually been determined long before creation of the state in 1947. The determination for Islam had been made according to the political necessity of the Indian Muslims, notwithstanding the paradox in setting any national boundary upon that universalist faith. Most proponents of Pakistan, excepting only some of the top secular leadership, seemed agreed at least that in the desired nation there should be a much closer relationship between the higher ideals of Islam and the actual practices of men. This relationship should be closer than any that had obtained in British India, and closer by far than any that might obtain in the either Hindu or secular India whose development after independence was projected.

21. *Ibid.*, pp. 171–174, 184–210.
22. *Ibid.*, pp. 251–270, 337–348, 255–358, 366–369.

But the difficulty of defining a satisfactory "Islamic state," and the reluctance of anyone to choose in advance of independence among the differing definitions held by literati, politicians, and the ordinary man, served to maintain a maximum of unity among those who were mobilizing to attain the state. Development of a standardized, popular version of the culture of the new nation was thus postponed until after the attainment of independence.[23]

Three points of view evident in the constituent process indicate the range of civilizational levels as well as the range of Islamic pasts among which Pakistanis had to choose. Traditionalists would rely upon centuries of historic experience and on legal doctrine as handed down and interpreted in the present day by those learned in the law—the ulama. Modernists emphasized the doctrine that holds that the right ways for today are shown by the legislative consensus of the present community of Muslims. Fundamentalists, the most radical, would return directly to the words of the Prophet and the ways of early Islam variously interpreted without benefit of subsequent history or the accumulations of expert knowledge.[24]

Compromises conceding something to each of these points of view were painstakingly worked into a draft constitution through nine years of discussion, 1947–1956. Political strains brought first a dismissal of the drafting body, then enactment of a partly similar, substitute document in 1958, then suspension of the substitute in 1959. The total effect was not a rejection of the widely held ideal of an Islamic state, but rather a realization of some of the measures necessary to achieve it—a mass program of Islamic education, direct entry into electoral politics by the ulama, and greater efforts to mobilize the citizenry in support of Islamic policies. Fundamentalism, with its innovating tendencies, seemed destined to gain[25] as higher levels of Islamic tradition were being brought closer to the average man by such easier communication. Meanwhile, groping for an immediate, if vague, unity and stability, the Government of Pakistan supported publicization of the country's monuments both from the Mogul past and from the Indus Valley

23. Myron Weiner, *Party Politics in India*, Princeton, N.J., Princeton University Press, 1957, pp. 193–196.
24. Leonard Binder, *Religion and Politics in Pakistan*, Berkeley, University of California Press, 1961, pp. 7–9.
25. *Ibid.*, pp. 374–375, 378–379.

civilization of the third millennium B.C. If India could sense her continuity with Asoka and if Ceylon could find inspiration in early Buddhist kingdoms, then the new Muslim state might find retrospective comfort in contemplating the previous "five thousand years of Pakistan."[26]

To find her broadest area of prestigeful communication internationally, Pakistan needed to look no further than to her own basic political identification with Islam. Given a technology lagging behind even her neighbors', she could hardly have supported a claim to fame of Western or internationalist type; later, under military rule and Western alliance, a secondary image of this sort was projected. The advantages and disadvantages of an Islamic foreign cultural policy for Pakistan are much like those already noted for India. (India's alternatives of Hindu or Buddhist policies were, of course, not readily open to Pakistan.) Pakistan is, moreover, the world's second Muslim nation in population, and could well claim a position of future leadership on that score. But it is noteworthy that Pakistan's calculations as to the cultural emphasis most useful to her for breadth and prestige did not confound her calculations of immediate political advantage. Pakistan did not link herself politically with the Islamic Arab League or with the largely Islamic African-Asian group in the United Nations; her experiences with those groupings were, in fact, disappointing if not disillusioning. On the contrary, Pakistan joined the Southeast Asia Treaty Organization and the Baghdad Pact when those partly extra-Islamic alliances promised best to serve her need for support against Muslim Afghanistan and part-Muslim India.[27] Pakistan appealed to Islamic solidarity to mobilize friends and to neutralize opponents, but not to exclude possible allies who are Christian or pagan.

Indonesia

OF Indonesia, a nation 98 per cent Muslim and containing more Muslims than any other in the world, one might have expected a "resurgence" of Islamic cultural policies paralleling their

26. Sir R. E. Mortimer Wheeler, *Five Thousand Years of Pakistan*, London, C. Johnson, 1950.

27. Keith Callard, *Pakistan: A Political Study*, New York, Macmillan, 1957, pp. 314–318, 321–322.

rather straightforward adoption in Pakistan. But while some recent developments of Islamic communications in Indonesia are much like developments in Pakistan, the unifying potential of Islam is far less in Indonesia than it had been in the Indian Muslim League before partition. Consideration of Indonesia's more acute difficulties in settling on an initial cultural palicy in fact moves us closer to the problems of the new African states.

The distress of Indonesian cultural policy appears to result from the country's lack of a comprehensive, deeply entrenched domestic great tradition. For a millennium and a half, varied mixtures of imported Hinduism and Buddhism had overlain the popular animistic cults of the region without displacing them. The very late spread of Islam had been for the most part nominal and superficial, intense only in certain restricted areas or movements of the past three generations. At the time of independence, self-conscious Islam was the property of less than half of Indonesians (the santris), while the Javanese prijaji elite that dominated the civil services of the nation remained aloof, essentially Hindu in its aristocratic culture.[28] Purely pagan pockets also remained, some having respectable bodies of ethnic custom codified under the Dutch regime, but lacking connection with any overarching layer of pan-Indonesian civilization.[29] Dutch colonial policies had been explicitly pluralistic, favoring the retention of Western culture in pure form as the preserve of a small native elite, while encouraging the separate and unaltered continuance of all regional and local cultures.[30]

The problem of cultural selection for Indonesians is then in part a problem of choosing among essentially differing traditions, more nearly as in Buddhist versus non-Buddhist sectors of Ceylon or Burma, rather than only a problem of choosing among a graduated series of connected cultural layers, as in India. Cultural pluralism could not well serve, since the Islamic overlay was weak and since Islam would by doctrine admit of no competitors. Pluralism was additionally in bad repute politically as a Dutch

28. Clifford Geertz, *The Religion of Java*, New York, The Free Press of Glencoe, 1960, pp. 123–126, 228–231.
29. Edward M. Bruner, "Urbanization and Ethnic Identity in North Sumatra," *American Anthropologist*, 63: 508–521, 1961.
30. Lucian W. Pye, "The Politics of Southeast Asia," in Gabriel W. Almond and James S. Coleman (eds.), *The Politics of the Developing Areas*, Princeton, N.J., Princeton University Press, 1960, pp. 91–94.

device for keeping the country disunited. A genuinely common level of communication was hard for Indonesia to come by. Before independence, the Indonesian nation observed but a single widespread holiday, had no national language, no embracing myth.

The cultural task of Indonesian nationalism has thus been to determine and propagate any serviceable existing features that could be found, or else to create such features. A search into the remote past would lead only to mythological links with preciviliz-ation, to the times of early historic colonization by Hindu and Buddhist foreigners, or to epochs in which one island dominated the others, as in the indigenous but Java-centered empire of Madjapahit. Excavated memories of Madjapahit may have proved inspiring to some Javanese, but have been able to contribute to the all-Indonesian sense of nationality little more than the enigmatic national emblem, the Garuda, mythical bird-vehicle of the ancient Indian gods. Malay, a previously undeveloped tongue but a widespread lingua franca, was pressed into more serious service as the new state language. Even the minority of enthusiastic Indonesian Muslims recognized that a significant common allegiance to Islam could not be assumed, but needed the establishment of a Ministry of Religion and special curricula for its ultimate development. Until the country had been more fully Islamicized, the problem of choosing among competing traditionalist, modernist, and fundamentalist versions of the "Islamic state" ideal could hardly arise sharply as it had in Pakistan.[31]

Meanwhile the existing paucity of identifiable common cultural content leaves a gap that Indonesian policy makers have attempted to fill with numerous secular and nationalist holidays, the activities of new nationalist associations, patriotic anthems and speeches. While these efforts appear to have meaning for a small but rising sector of the new national elite, they remain empty formalities for the majority of Indonesians. A genuine pan-Indonesian nationalistic culture above and beyond the orientations of peasantry, old elite, Muslim, and regional minorities seems likely to develop only slowly by the necessities of political compromise and the training of a new generation of culturally uprooted youth.[32]

Indonesian choices in external cultural affairs may be related to the same issues as those governing the policies of India, Pakistan,

31. Geertz, *op. cit.*, pp. 185–214.
32. Pye, *op. cit.* p. 122; Geertz, *op. cit.*, pp. 370–374.

and Ceylon. The ideal pose of an originator of a great ancient culture exported to the world is hardly available for Indonesia to assume, for Indonesian civilization is itself an amalgam of well-known imports, many of them relatively recent. The Indonesian versions of Hinduism, Buddhism, and Islam have not generally been recognized as authoritative at any time in the past. But given her notable lack of any basis for claims to a more modern cultural eminence and the improbability of excavating a more flattering image from the remote past, Indonesia has had to content herself with portraying herself as she is—a well-known importer, perhaps even a connoisseur of Asian civilizations. Indonesia's status as cultural dealer served her well when she hosted the Asian-African Conference at Bandung in 1955, and the same modest, non-threatening role may serve her interests at least moderately well in the future. Her historic international cultural role has at least something to recommend it as compared with the roles necessarily taken by the culture-poor states of the new Africa.

Sub-Saharan Africa

WHILE the new Asian states generally struggle with problems of managing the many levels and variants of their inherited civilizations, most of the new states of sub-Saharan Africa struggle to compensate culturally for their lack of full participation in any recognized civilization. The remoteness of the new African states from Asian or European great traditions does not remove the problems of choice among cultural levels, however. Instead, it makes those problems more acute. Just as in Asia, in Africa expanding literacy and education create a void, while considerations of political dignity and national purpose require that the void be appropriately filled. If the Africans do not suffer from the civilizational *embarras de richesse* that now typically confronts the Asians, they suffer instead from the dilemma of having either to relate themselves to some foreign great tradition or somehow to convert elements of their many indigenous tribal cultures into a new entity worthy of civilized respect.

Identification with a European high culture may supply a great traditional background, but may also bring special pain, for such identification generally implies a deprecatory view of an African state's domestic cultures.[33] Solutions to this painful dilemma have sometimes been extreme. One extreme solution for an African state is to ignore the background of its own indigenous tribal cultures, while emphasizing perfect adherence to the foreign model: such has been a common tendency among the elites of French West African territories, such as Guinea and the Ivory Coast; the same has been true to various extents in Belgian and in other French territories, as in Dutch Indonesia, where the European cultural assimilation of a select few of the subject peoples was stressed.[34] The total disrespect for the national heritage that is implied in that ignoring has naturally enough produced a strong reaction with independence, precisely, it seems, among some of those who had gone furthest toward cosmopolitanism. Their reaction—the movement to discover a vague though highly respectable quality called "negritude," or "African personality"—moves on an international plane far above any lesser tribal or local traditions.[35] Senghor of Senegal and Sartre of Paris may join hands in such a movement. Their program is to create the missing African great tradition from above through refined, synthetic restatement of indigenous cultural materials, hopefully extant and widespread, but still waiting to be identified.

Lying somewhere between these extremes of either surrendering to European civilization or fabricating an African counterpart are several alternative policies evident especially in the states of former British administration. Instead of the full French dress of Sekou Touré and Félix Houphouet-Boigny, one finds in the wardrobes of Kwame Nkrumah and Sir Abubakar Balewa a mixture of tribal robes and business suits. Nigeria exemplifies a splitting of orientations between the strongly European inclinations of the civil-service elite and the continuation of indigenous aristocratic traditions by the former agents of indirect rule—the native chiefs. At the same time, most of the Nigerian intelligentsia remains

33. St. Clair Drake, "An Approach to the Evaluation of African Societies," in *Africa from the Point of View of American Negro Scholars*, Paris, Présence Africaine, 1958, pp. 16–24; Fallers, *op. cit.*, p. 685.

34. James S. Coleman, "The Politics of Sub-Saharan Africa," in Almond and Coleman, *op. cit.*, pp. 269, 281–282.

35. See, for example, *Africa from the Point of View of American Negro Scholars*, Paris, Présence Africaine, 1958; Coleman, *op. cit.*, p. 353; and Léopold Senghor, "What is Negritude?" *West Africa* (London), November 4, 1961, reproduced in *Atlas*, Vol. 3, No. 1 (January 1962), pp. 54–55.

marginal to both these higher cultures, and pursues mixed eclectic
cultural policies.[36] Ghana exhibits the policies of a nationalist
intelligentsia taking power suddenly in opposition to traditional
leadership and legitimizing its position by rapid new borrowings
from foreign sources: a new state culture is created by translation
from Russian Socialism ("Black Star Square"), Judeo-Christian
messianism (Nkrumah the "Redeemer"), and the symbols of
former colonial power (a renovated Christianborg castle, and so
on).[37] A third and uniquely explicit alternative cultural policy is
evident in Uganda, where much of European culture has been
embraced without conflict under the fiction that it and its agents
are mere instruments of the continuing Baganda tribal state.[38]
The rapidity with which these formerly British territories have set
about filling their cultural gaps may be related to the more urgent
demands resulting from the greater extent of education within
them.[39]

The varied African efforts to obtain the equivalent of an Asian
or European great tradition demonstrate that awareness of the
problem of cultural levels is by no means absent. A high and
comprehensive culture of some kind must be had, and if any
African elements are to become a part of it, those elements will
probably be elements of exalted local status—for example, the
robes, rituals, and insignia of the highest chiefs and priests. Fragments of tribal culture of high significance may be usefully incorporated into modern state ceremonies of only a limited range,
however: the golden stool of the Ashanti tribe has political
potency in only a small quarter of modern Ghana. Nigeria, with a
federal constitution, is more likely to continue policies of cultural
pluralism.[40] But political competition in the unitary political
systems of other states has discouraged central resort to the identifiable tribal symbolisms of subordinate groups.

36. James S. Coleman, *Nigeria: Background to Nationalism*, Berkeley, Uni-
versity of California Press, 1958, pp. 50–54, 157–158, 162, 411; Coleman,
"The Politics of Sub-Saharan Africa," *op. cit.*, pp. 267, 283–285; Hugh H.
Smythe and Mabel M. Smythe, *The New Nigerian Elite*, Stanford, Calif.,
Stanford University Press, 1960, pp. 111–114,145–159.

37. David E. Apter, *The Gold Coast in Transition*, Princeton, N.J., Princeton University Press, 1955, pp. 226–230, 241–251, 304–305; *Time*, "Dirt
under the Welcome Mat," November 10, 1961, pp. 37–38.

38. Fallers, *op. cit.*

39. Coleman, "The Politics of Sub-Saharan Africa," *op. cit.*, p. 352.

40. David E. Apter, *The Political Kingdom in Uganda*, Princeton, N.J.,
Princeton University Press, 1961, pp. 22–27.

Translating from tribal beer into London gin may modernize and give wider utility to a traditional tribal libation, while orchestral arrangement may embellish the "mammy dances" of the Accra market place. Such African elements are not likely, however, to contribute much at the middle or lower levels of the cultures of the new states. Except where Christianity has been officially domesticated, as in Uganda, the African states seem not to have felt able to employ explicitly European religious means for political legitimation at the top. The contents of the higher levels of the new state cultures must therefore be largely provided from the secular, future-oriented culture of the Europeanized elite, regardless of the disjunctive consequences that may ensue. The resulting composite cultures thus seem generally to bring together foreign secular elements at the top with some elements of generalized indigenous sacred significance below. Outside the Baganda kingdom,[41] the effectiveness of such composites for conveying a sense of identity and purpose has yet to be measured.

If the choice of appropriate levels for national communication sets up difficult dilemmas for African cultural policy, the choice of suitable pasts likewise raises extreme problems. To say that many new African states lack evident connection with indigenous great civilizations of the past is not to say that evidence of such connections has not been sought, and where necessary created. Unfortunately for the desires of some Africans to associate themselves with the respectability of the Islamic civilization that has for centuries been influential in Africa, exploration has too often shown the superficiality (in Guinea and Senegal as in Indonesia), or the sectional limitation and divisiveness (in Ghana and Nigeria as in India) of the possible emphasis upon a Muslim identity. Ancestries closer to home have therefore been preferred. The preference for links to illustrious if obscure empires of African history is manifest in the states of Mali and Ghana, which take their names, however inaccurately, from putative ancestral African empires of the western Sudan in medieval times.[42] The search for roots had led naturally to exploration of the histories of units smaller than the present states, as well as of previous empires. Numerous cultural and political histories of tribes and regions were

41. Fallers, *op. cit.*
42. Apter, *Gold Coast*, op. cit., p. 22.

produced in Nigeria and elsewhere just before and just after independence, each history promoting some cultural unit of smaller scope as a candidate for higher recognition.[43] Of course, a state's history during recent centuries is not the only, or necessarily the best, source of cultural materials for its use. Just as in Israel of the present day and in all the competing nationalities of Europe through the past century and more,[44] so in the new African states official expenditures on prehistoric archaeology have soared. As in so many new states elsewhere, the vagueness and remoteness of the archaeological pasts have proved to be distinct virtues when dealing with fluid aspirations for new unities. Since archaeologists of the new African states have until now found no local Harappa or Anuradhapura, however, their mood seems more akin to desperation than to satisfaction with their contribution to filling the urgent needs for an appropriate continuity of cultural content. The African states' strong orientation to future time may thus be seen to represent not a disinterest in finding cultural reassurances in the past, but a failure to find them.

African positions in external cultural affairs remain as problematic as do African orientations in past time, and for many similar reasons. The most satisfying external posture—that of an old exporter of civilization to the world—is not easily assumed by any of the sub-Saharan states. A recognized indigenous civilization existed on the African continent only in ancient Egypt, and the new African states have yet fully to exploit the plausible contention, so difficult of documentation, that ancient Egyptian civilization grew out of an identifiably African cultural base, and in turn carried the light of Africa to the world. One may at least expect that older, opposite interpretations of West African cultures as "degenerate" derivatives from high Egyptian, "Hamitic," or Semitic prototypes[45] will be restated in terms less offensive to the cultural dignity of the new states. Egypt, and to a lesser extent Israel, have already found the interested ear of some African states for scholarly assertions to the effect that Africans were

43. Coleman, *Nigeria, op. cit.*, pp. 327–328.
44. Gutorm Gjessing, "The Teaching of Archaeological Anthropology: Archeology, Nationalism, and Society," in David G. Mandelbaum, Gabriel W. Lasker, and Ethel D. Albert (eds.), *The Teaching of Anthropology*, Berkeley, University of California Press, 1963.
45. For example, see J. Olumide Lucas, *The Religion of the Yorubas*, Lagos, C. M. S. Bookshop, 1948, pp. 14–15, 341–359.

ancient importers of, if not emigrants from, the main centers of civilization to the northeast. These are second-best statuses, but more creditable than those of the aping savage or the isolated barbarian.

Efforts by some Africans to stress the Islamic component of African civilization have evidently been tempered, as noted above with respect to Nigeria, Ghana, and the Ivory Coast, by the potentialities of supporting faction, since such nations are Muslim only in minor part. Islamic claims even in the Sudanic and new East African states have been moderated by knowledge that no African state below the Mediterranean could claim much past or present eminence in the wider world of Islam. The ancestors of the new states were consumers, never producers of works dear to the Mohammedan faith.

Cultural exports by the eighteenth and nineteenth century ancestors of the new sub-Saharan states have impressed the Western world, but largely at low levels. Those exports include elements of folk and popular music and dance, and features of illiterate American dialects, as well as sculpture to feed the fads of Parisian primitivism. The origins of the borrowed forms of music and dance are known to certain scholars and artists,[46] but not to the non-Africans who make the most use of them. The export of these popular items seems unlikely to become a matter of prideful recall to anyone, least of all to leading Africans. Such exports have accordingly been little stressed in the self-representations of the new African states.

The modern ideological movement in western Africa to discover a quality called "negritude," or "African personality," shared by both native and expatriate Africans, may be understood as an effort to raise the level at which African gifts to man's higher cultivation are to be examined. It is also in essence an effort to give positive cultural meaning to membership in the "African" or Negro race. Just what that membership may be made to mean for Africans, and whether these conceptions may be successfully extended to include the peoples of eastern, northern, and southern Africa, remains to be determined. For the western Africans themselves,

46. Melville J. Herskovits, *The Myth of the Negro Past*, Boston, Beacon Press, 1958; James A. Porter, "The Trans-Cultural Affinities of African Art," pp. 119–130, and Lorenzo D. Turner, "African Survivals in the New World with Special Emphasis on the Arts," pp. 101–116, both in *Africa from the Point of View of American Negro Scholars*, Paris, Présence Africaine, 1958.

"African personality" is neither an export nor an import, but a feature shared by citizens of many states; it may serve to promote concerted action beyond the single state, such as the act of union among Ghana, Guinea, and Mali. That the concept has been taken up and applied very unevenly needs no racial or other internal explanation, but may be understood as responding—like pan-Arabism or pan-Slavism—to the divergent political interests of the various African states.

Given their inheritance of unpromising cultural traditions, one should feel no surprise that the new African states, while striving imaginatively for indigenous materials with which to cover their nakedness, have generally chosen to retain an emphasis that would seem a bad fourth choice for most new nations of Asia—an approximation to the cultures of the Western or Eastern European blocs. Although their present achievements in European cultural spheres are not inspiring, their aspirations may nevertheless be safely projected for the time being toward a bright role in a world only now beginning to unfold.

Conclusion

EACH new nation without exception strives to clothe itself in the dignity not only of culture but also of civilization, for each enters an intercommunicating world of civilized states, and each is equipped with an apparatus of communications by which it can achieve its desires. Particular choices to use foreign or indigenous cultural materials appear to rest upon calculations of relative advantage, given certain preexisting features of each state's cultural context.

A classification of preexisting cultural situations relevant to the choices before the new states might first distinguish those states characterized by overarching civilizations from those states lacking them. Where indigenous or anciently borrowed "great traditions" are present, as in India and Pakistan, cultural policy is necessarily concerned with simplification of those traditions for mass use. Where such greater traditions are present, but no one tradition is effectively predominant, as with Buddhism in Ceylon or Islamic civilization in Indonesia, a larger task of propagation must be taken up along with the tasks of selection and adaptation. Where no overarching civilization is deeply established, as in the new states of Africa, more strenuous cultural policies must be formulated as to the borrowing of civilization or the building up of a new civilization from indigenous cultural materials.

Several issues of cultural policy recur in the states of each category—issues of choosing an appropriate level of culture, of dealing with cultural variety within the state, of finding a suitable orientation in time, and of relating internal to external culture.

The choice of levels in states of old civilization raises problems of compromise between higher and lower traditions of the civilization. The tendency in all our examples is toward a leveling down, toward a democratization of convenient features from the higher levels. In African states where higher and lower levels of culture are disjunctive owing to recent importations at the higher level, compromises are less readily achieved: except where arbitrary intermediate choices are firmly made, attempts to deal with both indigenous and foreign materials generally run to unsettled extremes of acceptance and rejection, unstable mixture, and innovation.

Monistic rather than pluralistic tendencies are the rule in the new states here examined: if indigenous culture is not ignored, one variant or combination of elements is commonly propagated at the expense of others. The process of civilization is itself, after all, a process of synthesizing some diverse cultural materials while rejecting others. Variety is readily incorporated within a new state's chosen culture only under special conditions, and these conditions cut across the civilizational classification outlined above. The long previous interlacing of several high traditions, as in India, or the previous recognition of several regional cultures, as in Nigeria, under federal systems with secure central government—these are some factors whose rare combined occurrence seems essential for a policy of cultural pluralism in a newly independent state. Detailed consideration of issues in the handling of ethnic diversity is found in the paper by Clifford Geertz in this volume.

New states of elder and younger civilization alike seek continuity with respectable pasts promising future unity and success. As the recent historic pasts of nearly all new states are troubled, the cloudier glories apparent through ancient history, archaeology, or mythology are everywhere preferred. Where these vistas are not open, as more commonly in the states of younger civilization, then attachment to the future itself regularly becomes the main orientation in time.

Advantage in external cultural policy is sought along two dimensions that are not parallel: respect and breadth. Choices seeking to maximize respect may be ordered in a series in which an emphasis on anciently exported culture is preferred to an emphasis on more recent exports; old imports are preferred to new imports, and all exports are favored over all imports. The new states of elder civilization are generally better provided with the substance for commanding greater respect. But the dimension of breadth is separable: what is older (for example, Hinduism) may be narrower in distribution than what is newer (for example, Buddhism), and hence the newer may be preferred. Reckoning by either dimension, the new states lacking deeply established civilizations of their own may rationally choose to ally themselves culturally with civilizations of foreign origin, while the states of indigenous civilization may rationally choose to do the opposite. In effect, their choices are the same, for they show regard for the same conceptions of relative advantage.

Striking in all these examples of cultural policy is the tendency for the new states to converge toward a middle ground of similar choices, or to suffer by deviating from it. The Asian states, in sifting out many levels and pasts and variants on their civilizational themes, respond to pressures in the modern distribution of power and information that are the same pressures as those to which the African states must also respond. If the African states lack some of the Asian subtleties, they dramatize for us all the more starkly the fact that the "national culture" of every new state is a product of modern manufacture.

Political religion in the new nations

DAVID E. APTER

I

TODAY IT IS VIRTUALLY IMPOSSIBLE to read a scholarly journal in
the social sciences without somewhere encountering the terms
"development," "modernization," "industrialization," or "Westernization." The meanings of these words ordinarily overlap, but
they do share two main emphases. One is that the poorer nations
are interested in increasing their wealth by enlarging their own
productive capacities. A second, related to the first, involves increasing differentiation and complexity in available roles in developing societies.

An increase in productive capacities can proceed along several
lines, of which industrialization is the most striking. Recognized
models for successful industrialization are Japan, which became a

I would like to record my indebtedness to the Institute of Industrial Relations
and the Comparative Development Group of the University of California,
Berkeley, for their assistance and support while writing this paper. I would
also like to thank Professor Neil J. Smelser for reading and commenting on
the manuscript. The original stimulus in developing these ideas came from
my colleagues on the Committee for the Comparative Study of New Nations at the University of Chicago, particularly Professors Edward Shils,
Lloyd Fallers, and Clifford Geertz.

traditionalistic society adapted to an economy based on industrial enterprise, the Soviet Union, which achieved the same goal swiftly by drastically altering the pre-existing social framework, and the Western complex of nations, where the process occurred more or less piecemeal and over a long period of time. Much scholarly enterprise has gone into efforts to determine the relevance of these experiences for the new nations.

In this enterprise some scholars have attempted to ascertain the character of those roles necessary for industrial societies. Notwithstanding these efforts at understanding, many unsolved and pressing problems remain—the relations between new élites, administrators, and professional men and traditional roles, the social tensions arising from the increase of wealth and the reorganization of roles, and the political problems emanating from these tensions.[1] Taken together, the problems of increased productivity and material welfare, as well as role alteration and integration, identify crucial areas of social tension and political sensitivity around which a large number of other, more secondary political problems arrange themselves.

Efforts to understand these matters have naturally led to the examination of countries where successful modernization has occurred. The political needs and urgencies of new nations has led us to look for historic parallels elsewhere. Examples most commonly referred to are the Soviet Union and the Western democracies. Among the new nations of greatest concern, precisely because they use the language of militant socialism and an almost Leninist reliance on control of the state by a single political party, are those countries that have set out to modernize at a very rapid rate, with particular emphasis on industrialization.

Among these are nations disinclined to handle development problems in terms of democracy, pluralism, and individualism, even though, in practice, to draw a clear line between these and other new nations is more difficult than it sounds. States with autocracy, monolithic structure, and community imperatives are not wholly different from the others. All face the complexities resulting from increased productive capacities. All are troubled by the same need to create, fit, adjust, and integrate new role systems.

States with monolithic structure, autocratic government, and a

1. See Kingsley Davis and Wilbert E. Moore, "Some Principles of Stratification," *American Sociological Review*, 10 (April, 1945).

wide range of community imperatives face a particular political problem. This problem stems from the fact that productivity and role integration become primary concerns of government, with the result that all social life becomes politicized in some degree. When social life is heavily politicized, government requires exceptional authority. Such authority tends to be monopolistic. Monopolistic authority needs to replace older belief about other forms of allegiance. New political forms are developed that have the effect of providing for the continuity, meaning, and purpose of an individual's actions. The result is a political doctrine that is in effect a political religion.

The effects of political religion are such that they strengthen authority in the state and weaken the flexibility of the society. Hence it becomes difficult to change from autocratic to more democratic and secular patterns of political organization and social belief.

My conclusion is that the combination of autocratic-structural arrangements and reliance on political-religious authority in several of the new nations creates latent instabilities in the development process that, once they become apparent, cannot be resolved either by democracy or totalitarianism but by something different from either. Political "solutions" will take the form of new theocracies partly because of the failure to achieve massive industrialization as a means of raising productivity, and partly so that new and modernized roles can be regulated and integrated by central values expressed as political religion. This will blend older roles and newer ones in the context of a modernizing autocracy.

The states with which I am immediately concerned include Guinea, Ghana, Mali, China, and Indonesia. Other examples could be cited, but these are most relevant to our discussion. I should like to show that in the beginning of the modernization process these seem closer to the Soviet or even to the Japanese examples. The important point is, however, that no matter which model they resemble, none will evolve in the Western pattern.

Hence we can distinguish between those new nations that accept autocratic solutions to the problem of rapid change from those preferring democratic ones, even if the lines of demarcation are blurred in practice. The new nations indicated above are more autocratic in political structure and authority than Nigeria, India, Senegal, and the Federation of Malaya.

However, even the most autocratic of the new nations differs from the Japanese and Soviet patterns in one very important respect. Few of them can modernize through massive industrialization because only one or two have the potentialities for large-scale industrial enterprise. *Modernization* and *industrialization* are not the same. Failure to recognize their differences is a common weakness among many contemporary political leaders, who see the need to restructure roles primarily as these are functional to the industrialization of society. By viewing productive capacity in industrial terms, they discipline the population to achieve the unachievable. The resulting internal problems are met by stringent political methods increasingly backed up by a new moral code expressed in religious terms.

Thus, while both the Soviet Union and Japan dealt vigorously with the problems of social discontinuities produced through the unevenness by which institutions and values were adapted to the development of industry, they were at least engaged in the actual process of industrializing. Managerial and fiscal changes no doubt worked hardships on prevailing habits of savings and investments and on patterns of organization and control of commercial and social life and, as well, on belief systems, but these were rendered compatible with industrial techniques.

The Soviet Union, beginning in revolution, developed a particularly stringent system of political control that was bolstered in great measure by political beliefs devoted to the worship of science and technology. In Japan, incompatibilities resulting from industrialization resulted in a more gradual harmonizing of discontinuities accomplished by increasing the veneration for the emperor and meanwhile militarizing crucial sections of the community.[2]

These forced-draft methods of modernization are attractive to political leaders in several of the new nations. That is why in some of them virtually all aspects of social life are political. However, under such conditions, the tasks of government become extremely burdensome. Certainly government is more complicated than during the colonial period. Discontinuities appear in the sphere of values and beliefs during a period of modernization, and also appear to threaten government. This is because most of the govern-

2. Indeed, the "military" solution is one of the characteristic ways in which traditionalism and innovation can be conveniently blended to restructure social life.

ments of the new nations are weakly legitimized in the first place. Government is not fitted into that range of cherished objects included in the central values of a changing community. As a result, political leaders tend to use force in order to retain authority and instill in the citizens attitudes of respect and devotion to the regime. Such a tendency to use force drives a wedge between government and the people.

What bridges the gap between ruler and ruled, individual and society? Not the actualities of industrialization and a restructuring of social life on an industrial basis. Rather an ideological position is put forward by government that identifies the individual with the state. Modern political leaders come to recognize quickly, however, that no ordinary ideology can prevail for long in the face of obvious discrepancies between theory and practice. A more powerful symbolic force, less rational, although it may include rational ends, seems necessary to them. This force is what I shall call political religion. It feeds its own categorical imperatives into authoritarian political structure on the one hand. On the other, as we shall indicate, it affects the most fundamental needs of individuals by specifying through the state religion the permissible definitions of individual continuity, meaning, and identity.

In this sense the Soviet and Japanese patterns are different from new nations in so far as they successfully industrialized, and similar mainly in so far as they used political religion, in the first instance, and religion politically in the second, to support authority. The Soviet experience is more relevant on the organizational side since most of the more autocratic new nations use a Leninist party and governmental structure as well as the language of socialism. However, they will become more similar to the Japanese as they develop in a theocratic direction.

Although most of the new nations will not industrialize, they will continue to modernize. Internal markets and resources are too poor and limited in size for rapid industrialization. The new nations are short of capital and skills. Although their infrastructures can be improved to handle commercial and extractive enterprise, it will be a very long time before they can anticipate deriving the major part of their gross national product from industry. Hence, the industrialization process cannot be used by them ultimately to resolve role discontinuity or increase material welfare, the two key political objectives.

Modernization is possible. At a minimum, modernization means that two conditions are present, neither of which is limited to industrial societies: a social system that can constantly innovate without falling apart, including in innovation beliefs about the acceptability of change and, as well, social structures so differentiated as not to be inflexible; and second, a social framework that can provide the skills and knowledge necessary for living in a technologically advanced world, including the ability to communicate in terms of the technology. These are what I shall regard as the minimal attributes of modernity.

A lack of understanding about modernity, reflected in the belief widely held by leaders of new nations that only industrialization can bring modernity, means that the discontinuities in the modernization process cannot be appraised realistically by many political leaders. This is why I have said that solutions to the problems of weak legitimacy, excessive politicization, and lack of industrial opportunities are sought in the state as a moral and regenerative force, a force that has independent validity and that, requiring discipline and obligation on the part of the citizens, will in turn give them both new dignity and new religion. In this way political religion becames a form of modernization with or without other forms. It is indeed this aspect of modernization that makes the Soviet Union significant to the developing areas, rather than its successes in industrialization. Moreover, a political religion that can universalize values linked to the widespread desire for better material conditions stimulates modernization by raising material and mundane ends to the level of the sacred.

Having sketched in the nature of the problem, I shall illustrate my remarks first by showing the nature of theocratic rule, and second by indicating how this differs from more secular pluralistic systems, although the latter evolved from theocracy. Finally, I shall indicate the role of political religion in some of the more autocratic countries, particularly as this relates on the one hand to the structure of authority and to the structure of personality needs of individuals on the other.

My point of departure is J. L. Talmon's interesting book *The Origins of Totalitarian Democracy*. More clearly than any other contemporary theorist, Talmon has pointed to certain contrasts and tendencies in Western political practice that I believe have been given a fresh relevance in some of the new nations. Specifically, I have in mind Talmon's notion of totalitarian-democratic practices, practices that have a strong appeal in the new nations.

The term "totalitarian democracy" is an invidious one. It stresses a particular theory of popular autocracy implicit in the notion of extreme popular sovereignty. As such, I do not think it entirely appropriate for an analysis of the new nations, and I shall employ a somewhat different set of terms. However, many of the qualities that are found in the notion of totalitarian democracy are also to be found in systems that I shall call "mobilization systems," that is, those that are profoundly concerned with transforming the social and spiritual life of a people by rapid and organized methods.[3] Talmon describes the totalitarian democratic school as one based upon the assumption of a sole and exclusive truth in politics. It may be called political Messianism in the sense that it postulates a pre-ordained, harmonious and perfect scheme of things, to which men are irresistibly drawn, and at which they are bound to arrive. It recognizes ultimately only one plane of existence, the political. It widens the scope of politics to embrace the whole of human existence.[4]

This "school," Talmon claims, began in the French Revolution, although it was implicit at an earlier time among the French *philosophes*. It forms a continuous tradition of Jacobinism, emerging in modern times around the twin problems of political freedom and social revolution. Modern Jacobins in Africa and Asia have been stimulated by these two problems to create new communities whose political philosophies can be blended with militant organization for a moral purpose. The result is a mystique that has a compassionate concern for men, while acting in a ruthless manner against the enemies of the "cause."

The contemporary Jacobins of the mobilization systems follow a classical pattern of leadership. They unite practice and philoso-

3. The typology used here was developed in collaboration with my colleague Carl Rosberg, and first published in our joint article "Nationalism and Models of Political Change in Africa," *The Political Economy of Contemporary Africa*, D. P. Ray, ed. (Washington, D.C.: The National Institute of Social and Behavioral Science, 1959). Subsequently, I altered the terminology somewhat by replacing the concept of "consociational" with "reconciliation," the term used here.

4. J. L. Talmon, *The Origins of Totalitarian Democracy* (London: Secker and Warburg, 1955), p. 2.

phy in a conscious synthesis. They are doers who are writers, and shapers who are thinkers. They wish to make their mark not only upon their countries but also in the realm of political ideas. They are practical prophets rather than idealistic reformers.

In contrast to these, Talmon offers the liberal democratic pattern. The latter, he says, assumes "politics to be a matter of trial and error, and regards political systems as pragmatic contrivances of human ingenuity and spontaneity."[5] Here Talmon's point is similar to one made by Popper.[6] It offers a more piecemeal solution to problems of social change.

Talmon's formulation of liberal democracy requires a further structural element, that is, that such systems are organized pluralistically and have diverse centers of power that must be reconciled when basic decisions are made. I prefer to call this a "reconciliation" system, to denote its organizational structure. Ideologically it conforms to Talmon's description.

These two systems challenge each other even when they have certain ultimate ends in common. In the reconciliation system the Jacobin tradition is checked by a plurality of ideas that are entertained by diverse effective power groups. Alternatively, it is not possible for the mobilization system to adhere to basically liberal attitudes. To do so would limit the power of the state and undermine its effective freedom of action vis-à-vis the citizens. However, the mobilization system makes certain of the liberal values into a religious support for the state. By doing so, it introduces a new element into the state, the definition of individuality in purely social and corporate terms.

II

ONE difference between religion and other forms of thought is that religion has more power. So fundamental is its power that one cannot examine individual conduct or desires without reference to it. In that sense religion cuts into human personality in a way in which ordinary ideological thought rarely does.

One can see this in two systems already discussed. In the reconciliation system, society is conceived of as a summation of indi-

5. *Ibid.*, p. 1.
6. K. R. Popper, *The Open Society and Its Enemies* (London: Routledge and Kegan Paul, Ltd., 1945), *passim*.

vidual values held together by a framework of law that is itself highly valued. The mobilization system is represented by valued goals laid down by higher authority and regarded as sacrosanct. There is a difference between the two systems in the way they approach change and consider history.[7]

Talmon points out that despite their differences both have their common origins in modern Western political thought. He turns to the French Revolution and its immediate antecedents in search of the origins of those ideas that are steppingstones to the totalitarian-democratic pattern. This is a familiar technique in political theory, and is certainly valid and useful. My approach, however, is to look at the development of new societies. As their own internal dynamics become more clear, we can see what aspects of political belief are more in harmony with their own internal needs. Indeed, it is the fate of many of the political ideas of the past, including those that provide a common fund of political values, to become altered and twisted in application.

The point is that when political religion becomes a key feature of the polity of a new nation, its likely outlet is a mobilization system of some kind. Mainly these fall into the radical and populist tradition of political religion, but it is not inevitable that they should do so. Consider, for example, South Africa, which has elevated the doctrine of the Dutch Reformed Church into political virtue, and by so doing has changed what was a reconciliation system (at least for the European community) into what is increasingly a mobilization system. It has done so despite the fact that this entails great risk. South Africa steadfastly is cutting its ties with the West, the Commonwealth, and even the United Nations in preference to losing its political religion. It has refused to follow along those lines of more pragmatic change that a reconciliation system would require.

To include South Africa in our analysis confuses the issue somewhat and certainly extends Talmon's notion beyond his intent. Nevertheless it is important to do so because it raises the question of relationships between concrete structure and belief, between political form and religion. It becomes necessary to examine the

7. The one is flexible in its ends but in many ways conservative, and concerned especially with individual rights. The other is more doctrinaire in its commitment to certain ultimate values, while remaining tactically more supple. The classic Leninist formulation of theory and practice, strategy and tactics, is the clearest expression of the latter's code.

relationship of religion to politics, at least in summary fashion, before going on to the specific subject of political religion in the new states.

Political religion begins in man's religious views of the human community. Most ancient societies, and most primitive societies as well, were theocratic. It was the unique achievement of the West to alter hitherto theocratic forms of polity. A number of factors account for this—Christianity for one, the growth of rationalism for another—resulting in the secular polis with its emphasis on the separation between church and state. In turn this nourished the ideal of a common collectivity that raised the political ends of society to a new prominence and, indeed, elevated them to a sacred level. Jumping to modern times, we can view colonialism as merely the overseas extension of conflict between traditional theocracy and secularism as it was embodied in alien political rule. Anti-colonialism and movements concerned with independence and development are the contemporary aspects of the conflict between the secular colonial system and the new political religions.[8]

Secularization involved a genuine liberation from the stuffy closets of theocratic traditionalism. In this sense, nationalist movements evolved in a very Western pattern. On racial, political, and economic grounds they embodied the Jacobin demands for equality and opportunity. As well, they argued for participation by Asians and Africans in government. This at least was the first stage —a stage in which individualism was advanced as a prerequisite to political independence. Examples of this initial process of secularization in the political field were to be found in both the Indian National Congress and the Moslem League in British India, in the West African National Congress, in the Aborigines Rights Protection Society in Ghana and Sarekat Islam in Indonesia. All these sought greater political advance and, with this, education and opportunity as the basis for political progress. After independence the situation changes radically. Not individualism but mass participa-

8. Not that this implies a pattern of inevitable historical evolution. There are theocracies today, such as Pakistan, among the new states. There are successful newly independent nations without political religion, such as Nigeria. There are others where the separation of church and state exists within a context of national solidarity and highly valued political ends. Egypt today is an example of a consciously Moslem country with a strong penchant for sacred political ends.

tion through community action becomes the condition of national success. The ends of the state become elevated to virtually a sacred level. "Human investment," originally a Communist Chinese doctrine, finds its counterpart in Guinea and Ghana. Indeed, the older political programs become identified with conservatism and neo-colonialism, while in many of the new states "guided democracy" and the single-party system emphasize an imposed unity that, by raising the political ends of the society to a sacred level, also serve to define and justify authority.

This pattern is in sharp contrast to much of Western practice, but it is no less modern. Nor is modernization brought about only through mobilization of the community. Arguments over which form of system will more quickly bring about modernization tend to be rather sterile, but one point is clear. Different programs of modernization exact different penalties. In the reconciliation type there may be more personal disillusion, petty politicking, frustration at the inability to solve problems, and the waning of idealism to such an extent that the springs of effective action and responsibility are dried up and society becomes an object of plunder by political élites. In the mobilization type, burdened by self-imposed obstacles and excessive politicization, failures in planning and organization, and a measure of ruthlessness and coercion, create almost pathological conditions of fear, mistrust, and duplicity, coupled with reprisals and oppression if public sentiment gives these voice. It is a sad commentary on Ghana's government today that, amid bomb throwing and large-scale detentions, the President lives surrounded by security measures that no British governor before him ever considered necessary. It is one thing to define the ends of the state as sacred. It is another to translate that into an acceptable pattern of belief.

This pattern is quite unlike the reconciliation system, where secular ends can never really become sacred. In the Western pattern, with the early separation of church and state, the role of the state was to devise better ways through which individual fulfillment could occur. Eventually what emerged was a compromise between religious tolerance and political freedom, a mutually congenial arrangement that resulted in a sharing of responsibility for the running of social life between church and state, and between private and public authorities. Pluralism was thus built into the conception of political democracy.

But, it may be asked, how did this pattern emerge in the first instance? By what fortuitous circumstances did the separation of church and state occur? The answers to this are shrouded in a still earlier Western tradition, a theocratic one. It was a Christian innovation to make the distinction between the sacred and the secular spheres by challenging the state religion of Rome. To that extent the church as a political movement, which would have preferred its own theocracy to any form of secular government, nevertheless created the ideal of temporal rule when it could not substitute its own power for state power. Religion and politics became two separate ideologies that were in competition but continued to coexist, each representing powerful institutional forces.

It can readily be seen that there is a good deal of relevance to these historical situations when we begin to examine modernization in the new states. Theocratic elements, secularization, and political forms all jostle one another and compete for prominence. Each has a significant part to play. If purely traditional theocratic elements have their way, the problem posed is one of resistance to innovation. Most traditionalists tend to see changes as undermining their power. They cannot support the secular outlook because the religious basis of the state would be swept away, and with it the theocracy. Secular systems that welcome innovation provide little in the way of organization and belief. The problem of alienation to society becomes profound, and the unevenness of modernization causes conflict resulting in political instability and chronic dissatisfaction. Where political religion is established, alienation disappears, at least overtly, but oppression obliterates freedom, fear replaces spontaneity, and everything is politicized, from family and kinship to voluntary associations. One has only to encounter the Brigades de Vigilance in Mali, whose task it is to root out "subversion" in the home, the clan, and the state, to recognize what this means.

It becomes clear that these three historical types of political experience still exist in the new states. The theocratic type exists in the traditional systems of most of the new nations—traditions that are by no means ended. The reconciliation pattern has been experienced by most new nations, and indeed its values were at one time regarded as the essence of modernity and democracy. The mobilization pattern is a more recent development that for a variety of reasons has come to prominence. Not only are these patterns to be found in the array of new states; their proponents are present in each country.

So far we have merely presented an overview of some of the key problems with which we shall be concerned. These are secularization, innovation, and authority with respect to the modernization process. Modernization not only involves all three but also arranges them differently in three types of political arrangements: the theocratic, the reconciliation, and the mobilization systems. These three respond differently to the modernization process, particularly with respect to public reactions. In theocracies change must be filtered through traditionalizing instruments; in reconciliation systems it produces alienation and often corruption. The mobilization system has emerged prominently as an alternative to both. A key feature of the mobilization system is political religion. Proponents of the mobilization system argue that such a system is a transitional phenomenon to more democratic practices once modernization has occurred. Political religion may express this millennial view of the political kingdom.

That in sum is the argument. I have deliberately used terms rather loosely to convey a kind of historical sweep in my argument. The processes of modernization now under way have their counterparts in earlier movements. In our discovery of relevant problems in the new nations we ought not to forget that. Indeed, Tocqueville's words about parliament in prerevolutionary France would sound familiar in Sudan, Pakistan, Guinea, Ghana, Indonesia, and several other new nations after the defeat of colonialism:

> But when absolute power had been definitely defeated and the nation felt assured that she could defend her rights alone, the parliaments at once became again what they were before: a decrepit, deformed, and discredited institution, a legacy of the Middle Ages, again exposed to the full tide of public aversion. To destroy it all the King had to do was to let it triumph for a day.[9]

It is now essential to examine these ideas more carefully and to show the relationships between religion and politics in the differing systems outlined above.

9. See Alexis de Tocqueville, *The European Revolution* (New York: Doubleday Anchor Books, 1959), p. 68.

THE THEOCRATIC SYSTEM

I cite the case of classic Greece as a theocracy. Barker comments that in the Greek polis "the state exists for the moral development and perfection of its individual members." It is "the fulfillment and perfection of the individual which means—and is the only thing which means—the perfection of the state."

He points out that "a state which is meant for the moral perfection of its members will be an educational institution. 'Its laws will serve to make men good.'" Thus its offices ideally will belong to "the men of virtue who have moral discernment. Its chief activity will be that of training and sustaining the mature in the way of righteousness. That is why we may speak of such a state as really a church: like Calvin's church it exercises a "holy discipline." Political philosophy thus becomes a sort of "moral theology."[10]

There is much in common between Barker's view of the Greek state and the aspirations of several of the new nations of the world, as well as some of the militantly Marxist ones such as China and the U.S.S.R. True, the specifically religious content that was so much a part of the antique world has been downgraded and regarded as prescientific. Nevertheless, the state provides images of virtue and purpose. The individual's will is bent to serve what the state decides is important. Nor is this done in a spirit of autocracy. Rather, there is an ideal of moral and material uplift that, having as its apotheosis some visible form of political order, presumably will secure human happiness.

In theocracies, political and religious associations are one and the same. Some specialization of political roles is possible, but these have their significance in a religious system of ideas. A king is a spiritual counselor as well as a warrior. He is the classic defender of the faith in addition to being a lawgiver. Justice is tempered with divine guidance. The great difficulty that theocracies faced centered mainly upon the control of despotic and corrupt kings and priests, whose transgressions of law offended human society and natural society.

Theocracies had a system of authority in government that shared power with the wider authority of the gods. Revolutions, changes

10. See E. Barker, *The Politics of Aristotle* (Oxford: The Clarendon Press, 1948). See also the discussion in his book *Social and Political Thought in Byzantium* (Oxford: The Clarendon Press, 1957), pp. 6–7.

in regime, tyrannicide, and other instabilities were regarded in the same manner as storms, earthquakes, and other natural catastrophes. There was a blending of the sacred and the secular, but the sacred was not debased by the secular.

Theocratic societies did not question the larger order within which they found themselves. Suffering was religiously meaningful. Kings or priests were the interpreters and lawgivers in the name of a wider context of religious practice. Among the ancient Jews we find a very clear conception of theocratic politics:

> Israel's monarchy is grounded not in the priesthood, but in apostolic prophecy. Israelite kings had the right to perform altar service and were charged with the maintenance of altars and temples. But they never bore the official title "priest"; their priestly function was but a by-role. The Israelite king succeeded to the task of the prophet-judge, not of the priest; the latter never bore secular authority in Israel. The ideal king of the future is a just judge, God-fearing and mighty; he has no priestly features. Modeled after the apostolic prophet-judge, the king is the elect of God. He does not incorporate any divine essence; he does not control the destiny of the cosmos through the cult; he is but the bearer of God's grace, appointed to office by his messenger-prophet. The king is thus another embodiment of the idea that it is God's will that rules on earth.[11]

Similarly in the case of China and Japan. In the Confucian tradition of government, political order was the creation of the early kings. "The early kings, by virtue of their high intelligence and perspicacity, revived the mandate of Heaven and ruled over the world. They were of one mind in making it their duty to bring peace and contentment to the world."[12]

If the king is the elect of God, human society is part of His universe, to be governed in accordance with His laws. This did not mean that kings, even despotic ones, had an easy time of it. Their responsibilities, while including human affairs, often transcended the world of man and spilled over into the world of nature. In many African kingdoms, for example, kings were held responsible for food supplies, rain, and other important natural phenomena. In

11. Yehezkel Kaufmann, *The Religion of Israel* (Chicago: University of Chicago Press, 1960), p. 266.

12. Ogyu Sorai, "The Confucian Way as a Way of Government," in *Sources of the Japanese Tradition,* edited by William Theodore de Bary (New York: Columbia University Press, 1958), p. 424.

the early Semitic kingdoms there were many cases of rulers being regarded as responsible for the deity in the coming of rains, for bad crops, and other natural disasters. "In Babylonia in some prehistoric period there existed a belief that the king was responsible for the state of agricultural land, and for the time occurrence of seasonal phenomena, and that belief exists sporadically today over the East."[13]

What are some of the general characteristics of theocracies? They have a system of kingship or priesthood, although leadership may be shared jointly. Many forms of leadership are thus possible, but leaders have two major qualities. First, they are in roles that are both personalized and institutionalized. Second, they are representatives of the deity. Their authority derives from that even if they are selected by the public at large.[14]

Theocracies are communities that are part of a natural and wider order both of nature and transcendence. There is thus no sharp distinction between the natural universe and the state, nor is there a sharp dividing line between the living and the dead, nor the real state and the transcendent state, that is, between the kingdom of man and the kingdom of God.

Laws tend to be linked to custom, ritual, and other religious practices, having their origins in prophecy, whether oracular or personal, or by decree. Changes come about in the effort to con-

13. S. H. Hooke, *Myth, Ritual, and Kingship* (Oxford: The Clarendon Press, 1958), p. 28.
14. R. Caillois puts it as follows: "Power like the sacred, seems to be an external sign of grace, of which the individual is the temporary abode. It is obtained through investiture, initiation, or consecration. It is lost through degradation, indignity, or abuse. It benefits from the support of the entire society which constitutes its depository. The king wears the crown, scepter, and purple reserved for the Gods. He has guards to protect him. He executes all types of coercion capable of forcing the rebellious to submit. But it must be pointed out that these means do not explain as much as they demonstrate the efficacy of power. To the degree to which people regard them as powerful, or consider them able to subjugate, or reveal reasons for being afraid, it is unnecessary to explain the motives for complaisance and docility. . . .
"Every king is God, descended from God, or ruler by the grace of God. He is sacred personage. It is consequently necessary to isolate him and to construct watertight compartments between him and the profane. His person harbors a holy force that creates prosperity and maintains the order of the universe. He assures the regularity of the reasons, the fertility of the soil and women. . . ." See Roger Caillois, *Man and the Sacred* (New York: The Free Press of Glencoe, 1959), pp. 90–91.

serve and strengthen the existing system rather than in attempting to transform it.

An important part of the sacred element in the community is maintained by religious practices and special classes of individuals who cater to ritual and custom in efforts to maintain the purity of the society and prevent the defilement of the sacred by the secular.

These characteristics should be sufficient to indicate the nature of theocracy. Most societies of the ancient world, including those of Greece and Rome, were theocratic, as more recently have been African political communities and those in the Middle East and Asia. What revolutions they had were to change regimes rather than fundamentally to alter the conception of authority and community. Their problems were related to the cosmos, and thus were no more disturbing than the larger mystery of life and the gods themselves.

Systems with political religion elevate the secular to the level of the sacred, and incorporate theocratic elements. They make the universe subservient to and an extension of man and his society. If in the theocracies, the cosmos and nature are not divorced from the state, they are larger than the state, and control it. In systems with political religion, man is the center of the universe. It is the reconciliation system that is the obverse of theocracy, not the mobilization type, although the latter contains elements of both.

THE RECONCILIATION SYSTEM

What I mean by a reconciliation system is most aptly expressed in the phrase "a government of laws and not of men." By this statement, which is the foundation stone of constitutional democracy, it is meant not only the requirement that men obey laws, a characteristic of all communities, but rather that law has a wider wisdom than any individual man. As such, its status is venerated for its own sake. Through laws, prudently known, man perfects his individuality and protects others from it. Although Plato does not consider law in *The Republic,* his concept of truth and harmony is itself a notion of an abstract law to be known through reason, that is, knowledge of the good. In so far as law is a standard as well as a framework, Plato begins the tradition of natural law in the Western world.

From then on, law is the constant preoccupation of secular theorists. How to shape it to human needs without destroying its insulation from the ordinary whim and fancy of men gave rise to great commentaries on law that are still the cultural tradition of the West—Justinian's and Gaius's Institutes, the works of the Glossators and the Commentators, Blackstone, Maine, Maitland, and Vinogradoff. Law as a framework embodying wisdom has been a constant object of study. The effort to resolve some of the paradoxes between an objective plane of law, at one with the rest of the universe, and with the ordinary and day-to-day laws made for the governance of the minutiae of daily life is a never ending dialogue over where natural law leaves off and positive law begins. It is a dialogue that in the medieval period came to include another division, between divine law and canon law, all of which needed to be sorted out into the respective spheres where their authority would be particular and useful.

This preoccupation with law in the West was one of the important ingredients for the development of a community that regarded the framework of law itself as the sole and ultimate commitment by which the community lived, breathed, and prospered. But it was not the only factor relevant to the development of a reconciliation system. The second was the separation of church and state. I shall try to show that the separation of church and state was in fact an essential element in developing such a system and, as well, how the notion of law was a necessary ingredient. This point cannot be emphasized too strongly, because I believe that the separation of church and state without a strong belief in the objective quality of law is in fact one basis for the growth of political religion. In the latter case (a government of men and not of laws), the legitimacy of the sovereign is substituted for the legitimacy of the law, with the result that politics becomes endowed with sacral characteristics. However, such matters will be examined when we discuss political religion. For the moment, we can explore more deeply the separation of church and state.

This doctrine itself is a curious one, and peculiarly Christian. Whatever the historical reasons, and I am sure there are many, Christianity, which originated in a condition of political subservience, saw its status enhanced by winning tolerance for itself. Not that it was content with mere tolerance and would not have transformed the community into a theocracy if it could have done so, but by and large it could be content with tolerance and live in a relatively harmonious relationship with secular authorities. Divine law and natural law were never quite the same, but were regarded as complementary. Revealed truth and rationality were not opposites but rather different sides of the same coin. The great achievement of St. Thomas was in effect the strengthening of the accord between church and state and providing it with an intellectual synthesis.

St. Thomas gave Christianity a profounder basis for what had already been established in principle. It was found first in the Pauline doctrine of rendering unto Caesar the things that are Caesar's. It was Pope Gelasius who made a fundamental point of this at the end of the fifth century:

> The Emperor, is the son of the Church, not its director. In matters of religion it is his to learn and not to teach. He has the privileges of his power which he has obtained by the will of God for the sake of public administration. . . .
>
> Before the time of Christ, some did have the offices of both king and priest, and in heathen times the devil copied this and the pagan emperors held the office of Pontifex Maximus. But Christ who was both king and priest never entrusted both powers to the same hands, but separated the two offices and the functions and dignities proper to each, and therefore, as Christian emperors stand in need of priests for eternal life, so the priests for the course of temporal things employ the directions of emperors.
>
> There are two authorities by which principally this world is ruled, the sacred authority of the bishops, and the royal power. . . .[15]

The most important consequence of this doctrine, which was reinforced rather than weakened by the historic battles men fought over it, was the conflict between church and state—the separation of temporal and spiritual jurisdictions. The fortunes of the one could, and did, vary independently of the other. No matter how religious a monarch, not even during the height of the doctrine of the divine right of kings was the principle undermined.

What was significant about this? It provided a philosophical

15. Quoted in Charles Howard McIlwain, *The Growth of Political Thought in the West* (New York: Macmillan, 1932), pp. 164–165.

basis for limiting the power of the executive. For the concept of checks and balances implies a faith that such a system helps to restore the governance of men to a natural harmony in which the individual's true nature is one of freedom within civil society. Civil society ruled by law is in turn reinforced by spiritual sanction on an individual basis. Indeed, Protestantism helped to reinforce this doctrine so that right conduct, guided by a Christian ethic, and individual freedom, tempered by representative government, were mutually reinforcing elements. The result was a high degree of self-restraint in behavior—such self-restraint being the essence of the liberal democratic polity.

Even now, when religion itself has declined and the burdens of civil society are immense, the concept of limited government has remained in the West. Such is the fear of arbitrary power in government that the idea of parliament and law, as well as a belief in constitutions and social compacts, becomes the sole symbolic instrument of civic rule. What there is of the sacred in Western secular government is in the framework itself. All other ideologies have declined. A constitutional framework, although it cannot be heroic, gives men the opportunity to make of their society what they will, within the framework of law. Law through representative government is to an important extent the political content of our civilization. It is the means by which we amend our way of life, without abdicating individual rights. It is necessarily undramatic, and to a large extent without glamour. As well, change under such circumstances is slow. The competition of individuals and groups, a pluralistic universe with relativistic values, is its main characteristic. Indeed, all values can change except two. One is the dignity of the individual, which can only be preserved through the dignity of law. The second is the principle of representative government.

What are some of the more practical virtues of such a system? Perhaps two are the most important. A government of laws allows that amendment that enhances law by tempering and ameliorating the difficulties its citizens face. In that respect, when it functions well it has resolved the twin problems of stable society and succession in public office. As well, it allows for secular values germane to industrialization. Having been established, the framework can persist even though the sacred "sword," as distinct from the secular one, has declined. However, it has not accomplished this without difficulty. The decline of religion has imposed on the Western democratic polity the singular problem of how to provide alternative sources of meaning, faith, and spiritual sustenance that all men need in some degree. Our crisis can thus be seen as arising out of unsatisfied moral ambitions. And our political framework mirrors faithfully this weakness. Precisely because our problems lie in the moral sphere, those new nations that have developed a system of political religion now appear to be morally less ambiguous than we are. Even though the political religions in the new nations have not reemerged in the classic form of theocracies, but in the form of secular beliefs, they define political and moral aims as one and the same. What loses is the idea of individualism. The peculiar genius of our civilization, that is, the relationship between individualism and law, is viewed as imprisoning, reactionary, and parochial—a Western notion.

At stake, then, is the survival of democracy itself. Reconciliation systems are undergoing a crisis intensified by the secularization of the religious sphere. The logic of this argument would be a return to religious belief as the way out of our difficulty. Whatever the merits and logic of this course of action, it is highly unlikely. New solutions need to be found. The resulting internal danger is that reconciliation systems might turn to political religions to reinforce their own position or in an illusory effort to eradicate enemies both within and without. This was the Nazi solution in Germany, and the Fascist solution in Italy. It is one of the permanent sources of common in Western Europe.

THE MOBILIZATION SYSTEM

Political religion that arose in the West is itself a response to the loss of faith that characterizes present reconciliation systems. What I have been suggesting can be rephrased as follows: By placing no reliance on church religion, one of the stabilizing elements that originally supported the political framework in reconciliation systems, the sacred, is employed in many new nations to develop a system of political legitimacy and to aid in mobilizing the community for secular ends. This makes constitutional democracy irrelevant to their experience. Having made political doctrine into political belief, efforts are made to formalize that faith as a means by which to achieve major aims.[16] In none of the new nations has

16. But if the aims were achieved, they would lose their significance. So it is that political religions need to have aims not all of which can be achieved. One such aim is the transformation of human beings into some higher order

this entirely succeeded, but particularly in Ghana, Mali, Guinea, Egypt, and Indonesia efforts at formalization have been made.

The mobilization system contains an implicit assumption: that which divides men from one another is due to unnatural causes— colonialism, neocolonialism, classes which derive their differences from hostile relationships centering around property. Men must be freed from these unnatural differences by both acts of leadership and exceptional public will. Harmony in the political sphere derives from the messianic leader who points out the dangers and noxious poisons of faction. Many such leaders are charismatic who represent the "one." They personify the monistic quality of the system.

To achieve such oneness, mobilization systems begin by politicizing all political life. As a result, politics as such disappears. This is in keeping with monistic political belief. Conflict is not only bad but also counterrevolutionary. It runs counter to the natural evolution of human society, and ideas of opposition downgrade and confuse the power of positive thinking. Ideas not only are dangerous, challenging the legitimacy of the regime or the charisma of the leader, but they also represent an unscientific vestige wherever they run counter to those of the regime. Hence the most counterrevolutionary groups of all are dissident intellectuals.

Mobilization systems are characterized by what Durkheim called repressive law. Punitive and symbolic, it is political crimes which are punished with great severity. Such regimes are humorless. Their model of society is an organic one. Although it does not always fit exactly, Marxism or some variant thereof is appealing because it satisfies these conditions theoretically and Leninism supports them organizationally. Such systems represent the new puritanism. Progress is its faith. Industrialization is its vision. Harmony is its goal. These are the factors that lie behind modern political religion.[17]

of being. The Soviet argument is that capitalism is in the long run a corrupting element in human society, and individuals who show capitalistic vestiges are to that extent corrupt. New nations tend to have similar views with regard to tribal societies. The latter, having fallen from grace by being corrupted by colonialism, remain corrupt.

17. See Edward Shils, "The Concentration and Dispersion of Charisma: Their Bearing on Economic Policy in Underdeveloped Countries," in World Politics, 11 (1958).

The new nations with political religion regard themselves as being without sin. This stems from the notion of rebirth, that is, the rise of new political units from colonial status, with all the purity of the newly born. Their objects are regeneration and emancipation of the citizenry from backwardness and other handicaps, such as racial discrimination. Rebirth lends itself to messianic government, which makes a rule of law and not of men virtually impossible. Regeneration regards individualism as backward-looking and restrictive, and this makes public checks on political authority extremely difficult.

In perhaps the best description of what I have been trying to convey, Talmon points out that

the decline of religious authority implied the liberation of man's conscience, but it also implied something else. Religious ethics had to be speedily replaced by secular, social morality. With the rejection of the Church, and of transcendental justice, the State remained the sole source and sanction of morality.[18]

The original impulse of political Messianism was ethical, not economic. In the new nations today it becomes ethical, but is now expressed in economic objectives. In his distinction between liberal and totalitarian democracy, Talmon suggests that both traditions

affirm the supreme value of liberty. But whereas one finds the essence of freedom in spontaneity and the absence of coercion, the other believes it to be realized only in the pursuit and attainment of an absolute collective purpose. It is outside our scope to decide whether liberal democracy has the faith that totalitarian democracy claims to have in final aims. What is beyond dispute is that the final aims of liberal democracy have not the same concrete character. They are conceived in rather negative terms, and the use of force for their realization is considered as an evil. Liberal democratics believe that in the absence of coercion men and society may one day reach through a process of trial and error a state of ideal harmony. In the case of totalitarian democracy, this state is precisely defined, and is treated as a matter of immediate urgency, a challenge for direct action, an imminent event.[19]

18. Talmon, *op. cit.*, p. 4.
19. *Ibid.*, p. 2.

The reasons for the rise of political religions among the new nations are not hard to find. Faith is a source of authority. The new nations face the problem involved in the creation of over-arching loyalties that transcend the more primordial ones of ethnic membership, religious affiliation, linguistic identification. That such loyalties are stubborn and not easily replaceable can easily be demonstrated in such new countries as India, Indonesia, and Nigeria. Where hitherto racially compartmentalized groups are to be found, the problem is immeasurably more difficult, as in the Federation of Rhodesia and Nyasaland.

Nor are such loyalties blind and unreasoning. Race, ethnicity, religion, and language are the means whereby people identify themselves, organize their community, find meaning for their sentiments, and express their beliefs. All the critical elements of man in society appear to be touched in some important manner by each of these matters. If such affiliations are to be increasingly less significant, a public must find itself linked up by a common in-terest in the wider polity through which their identity, their sen-timents, and their beliefs are enlarged and strengthened rather than minimized and destroyed. The point is that political religion seeks to do these things and render massive change heroic and joyful, infectious and liberating. But this is by no means simple to do, and in the development of a political religion conflicts are engendered that can be as fierce and time-consuming as the religious wars of the past, even if they are less dramatic.

The task, therefore, of building the polity is a difficult one, and one of the functions of political religion is to supply meaning and purpose to what might otherwise become a void. One cannot simply destroy primordial attachments and replace them with nothing.

Another major problem facing the new nations, in addition to breaking down parochial attachments (and it is closely related to that), is the problem of constituting authority. A system that en-joys a constitutional framework can achieve this only after a certain consensus about primordial loyalties has already gained ac-ceptance in the wider community. Without such consensus polit-ical authority remains the most sensitive political problem in the new nations. Some older countries have never been able to over-come these difficulties. France never institutionalized her constitu-tional order sufficiently. Primordial loyalties still flourish. Political authority, never fully integrated within the framework of law, demeaned the framework itself in spite of the very elaborate legal structure of France as a modern state.

In the new nations, political leaders now in power have only recently been in the business of challenging colonial authority and weakening men's obedience to political rule. To some extent, when popular enthusiasm and revolutionary ardor began to wane, these political leaders inherit an instability of regime and authority that is partly of their own making. Endowing their roles with sacred elements makes their authority stronger and the regime more secure. Moreover, since everything is known about the leaders, their past, their family, their daily routine, they can hardly be remote and distant. Quite the contrary, they characteristically remain friendly and fraternal. If such familiarity is not, however, to result in disrespect for authority, the sacred role needs to utilize familiarity and turn it about. The public comes to be grateful for the spreading of the sacred largesse. They are purified by the divine. They see that the "Man of the People" remains with the people, but they never confuse him with ordinary men. Authority then becomes stabilized in the role of the Leader and his manipulation of power, and friendliness is a token of majesty.

The third major problem the people of new nations face is the material development of their country. Everyone desires the things of this world, and a political religion can survive on austerity only up to a point. It must have its practical consequences. Here political religion is always less powerful than church religion because the former promises a different reward than the latter. That is, the political religion says that the political kingdom will provide abundance in material things—things, moreover, that have an immediate feel about them. They are cars, houses, food, clothes, television sets, transistor radios. Church religions, by promising more intangible rewards, have a better time of it in this respect.

The political religion thus requires a more specific ideological component than church religions, and it has built into it a particular kind of rationality as well—the rationality of economic life. This is both its handicap and its advantage. It is a handicap in so far as political religions will rarely have the same extrarational pull on a long-term basis that church religion does. It does not have the same sticking power. It is an advantage inasmuch as it turns men's minds to practical tasks, and with the rationality necessary to achieve them. To the extent that development becomes successful, it becomes possible to consider the decline of political religion and in its place the rise of a constitutional order. That is the great hope the West retains about the U.S.S.R. It is also the hope we bear for the new nations.

Political religion in new nations then comes to center upon three main objects: The development of a single system of central authority, the material development of the country, and the institutionalization of rationalistic values. All three are intimately connected as processes. All can be aided in important ways by political religion.

We can now consider the substance of political religion. What are its characteristics? How can it be recognized? How does it become transformed into something else? I shall try to show some specific examples of what I call political religion, and indicate how it functions. We can then see why political religion has the capacity for carrying out these functions.

III

I SUGGEST the general characteristics of political religion as follows. First, the state and the regime take on sacred characteristics. The sacred even extends to ordinary laws. What I mean can best be described in terms of Durkheim's distinction between repressive and restitutive law, as I have already suggested. Repressive law punishes on a symbolic level. The sacred quality of the community, having been violated, must be revenged. Death for treason is an example of repressive law. In communities with a small degree of political religion, it is hard to find cases of men being put to death for theft. In communities with a large degree of political religion, death for theft is not uncommon.[20]

20. Sekou Touré's comment is a good example:
"If you like, we may say that the Party is the brain of our society, while the State is the executive part of it, the part which works according to the spirit and the intentions of the Party.

"The State settles the great problems of a social, economic, financial, or administrative character, in the light of the objectives which the Party has decided to attain.

"It is thus that the Party, which has decided to create a new society for the greatest happiness of man, comes up presently against several difficulties. In the present society there are thieves, murderers through social imprudence. The thief and the murderer constitute a social danger. They make the members of the society feel worried and unsafe; they injure the property and the life of other people. Neither of them concerns himself in any way with the properties and the lives around him; they feel no respect for the social surroundings in which they live and operate, they have no sense of solidarity with all the men who make up society. The role of the State is to protect society from the evil deeds of such men.

Second, the sacred characteristic becomes essential to maintaining solidarity in the community. This has the effect of giving sacrosanct qualities to the new state. From this, in turn, a regime derives its legitimacy that is reinforced in a variety of ways. One way is characterized by a renewed interest in a semimythical past, to produce antecedents for the regime. Another is a persistent attack on a particular enemy. For example, the attack on colonialism is enlarged to include neocolonialism, which becomes a higher form of villainy against which political religions in new nations must be ever vigilant.

The mythical past, in addition to stressing continuity between an earlier period and the present, also serves to "periodize" a time of disgrace and misfortune. In new nations this is the period of colonialism. Both the new era and the golden past serve as reminders of the suffering and degradation through which the public passed, and stress the achievement of independence. The "birth" of the nation is thus a religious event, forming a fund of political grace that can be dispensed over the years.

The agent of rebirth is normally an individual—an Nkrumah, a Touré who, as the leader of the political movement, is midwife to the birth of the nation. Sometimes this is expressed in songs and chants and at other times in political prayers.[21]

In our eyes, the thief is an evil being. Whether he steals several millions or only a pin, his behavior comes from a mentality which we intend to destroy. Whoever he may be, whatever the conditions in which his theft has been committed, we shall punish him with the utmost severity. No one will be excepted." See *Towards Full Re-Africanization* (Paris: *Présence Africaine*, 1959), p. 46.

"That is why, at the suggestion of the Party, the Government has decided to deal with them with the utmost severity. In future, no pity will be shown to thieves. We shall impose extreme penalties on them. We have said that, if you caught a thief in the act of breaking open your door you could shoot him.

21.

> "Sekou Touré
> Grand-Merci à toi, Touré
> La libération de la Guinée
> Ne nous surprend guerre
> L'affame ne sent-il pas de loin
> Le fumet du plat salutaire
> Sekou Touré
> O don Divin à la Guinée
> Salut à toi, soit beni
> O toi, bienfaiteur de la Guinée
> Apôtre de la bonne cause
> O l'enfant prodigue."

From the poem "Independance," by Diely Mamoudou Kande, printed in *Présence Africaine* (December, 1959–January, 1960), p. 95.

Political leadership centers upon the individual with characteristics of revealed truth. From leader to party to state is a single
line embodied in the twin notions of personal authority and collective responsibility. The goals of the society are demanding, and are
laid down from above. By achieving them, men become honorable
and moral, reborn, and closer to perfection. Sometimes this is
considered to extend beyond a country's own borders. The former
chairman of the Convention People's Party, and Minister of
Presidential Affairs, in an officially distributed pamphlet wrote:

> Today . . . barely three years after the birth of Ghana, to millions
> of people living both inside and outside the continent of Africa,
> Kwame Nkrumah is Africa and Africa is Kwame Nkrumah.
> When the question is asked: "What is going to happen to
> Africa?" it is to one man that everyone looks for the answer:
> Kwame Nkrumah. To the imperialists and colonialists his name
> is a curse on their lips; to the settlers his name is a warning that
> the good old days at the expense of the Africans are coming
> to an end; to Africans suffering under foreign domination, his
> name is a breath of hope and means freedom, brotherhood and
> racial equality; to us, his people, Kwame Nkrumah is our father,
> teacher, our brother, our friend, indeed our very lives, for with-
> out him we would no doubt have existed, but we would not have
> lived; there would have been no hope of a cure for our sick
> souls, no taste of glorious victory after a life-time of suffering.
> What we owe him is greater even than the air we breathe, for
> he made us as surely as he made Ghana.[22]

As well, the party is the state. Those who do not accept this
unity are suspect. Nkrumah himself has written:

> The Convention People's Party is Ghana and Ghana is the Con-
> vention People's Party. There are some people who not only
> choose to forget this, but who go out of their way to teach others
> to forget it also. There are some persons, both staff and students
> [of the University College of Ghana], who mistakenly believe
> that the words "academic freedom" carry with them a spirit of
> hostility to our Party and the Government, the same Party of
> the workers and the farmers, and the same Government whose
> money founded the University and maintains it and who pro-

22. Tawia Adamafio, A Portrait of the Osagyefo Dr. Kwame Nkrumah
(Accra: Government Printer, 1960), p. 95.

vides them with their education in the hope that they will one
day repay their countrymen by giving loyal and devoted service
to the Government of the People.

The Convention People's Party cannot allow this confusion
of academic freedom with disloyalty and anti-Government ideas.

In the future we shall attach the greatest importance to the
ideological education of the youth. The establishment of the
Young Pioneers will be a step further in this direction. The
Youth Section of the Party will be fully mobilized under the
close guidance of the Youth Bureau of the National Secretariat.
We shall make our party ideology fully understood in every
section of the community.

We must regard it as an honor to belong to the Convention
People's Party. And I repeat we must work loyally and with
singleness of purpose for that is the essence of the true Party
spirit, the spirit that routed imperialism from our soil and the
spirit which we must recapture for the struggle that lies ahead.[23]

The party contains an elect. Control is centralized. There is
purification in belongingness, comfort in comradeship, democracy
in loyalty, brotherhood in membership.[24]

Similarly in the case of Guinea. There the structure of the party

23. Kwame Nkrumah, "What the Party Stands For," in *The Party*, C.P.P.
Monthly Journal, Vol. 1, No. 1 (September, 1960).

24. The messiah-like qualities of the president have been to some extent
ritualized and made more permanent, both in ceremony and in thought, than
was true in the past. Religion itself has not confronted this development, but
has more or less found a different level in those interstices between the metaphysics of national philosophy and the transcendental and personal beliefs of
individuals.
The case of Mali is quite similar. However, a very high proportion of the
population is Moslem. There is an acceptance of Islam by the government,
and traditional religious and social beliefs are modified through deliberate government policy. Recently I attended a wedding in Mali that illustrates this
point. The traditional extended clan unit had been recognized by the government, although the chief was, as was the case with most traditional chiefs
who had previously worked with the French, removed from office. A very
old man from a royal lineage was elected in his place. He carried the ceremonial sword, and all groups gave respect to it. The actual leader of the
ceremony was an important government official very high in the party, the
Union Soudanaise. The various traditional sections of the clan, women, elders,
children, men, danced and participated in the ceremony not only in their
traditional role but, as well, as members of the clan women's brigade, the
youth organizations, the party section, as the case might be. The blessings
invoked were to fall on the marriage partners, but also on the clan, and also
on the party and the state, simultaneously. Here, then, is an example of the
blending of old and new, church and political religions within the context of
older cultural and social groups.

extends into each village. There is a hierarchy of councils. At the top:

> . . . Le Parti assume le rôle dirigeant dans la vie de la nation qu'il dispose de tous les pouvoirs de la nation: les pouvoirs politique, judiciare, administratif, économique et technique sont entre les mains du Parti Démocratique de Guinée. C'est donne lui qui désigné le Chef de l'État par la voie du souffrage universel direct.[25]

Or, again, Sekou Touré:

> We have often said that, in our eyes, there are no soldiers, no civil servants, no intellectuals; there are only supporters of the Party. It is among the supporters of the Party that the standards of the value, of faithfulness, of course, of unselfishness are. It will be the supporters who establish [sic] make possible the prosperity of Guinea, as they made possible its independence. *If the Party wants the State to run as it desires, it should fortify its basic organization and ensure that democracy remains the essential and permanent principle of its activity.*[26]

Spreading the political religions abroad has also been attempted. The effort to establish a mobilization system failed in the Congo, but in that tragedy there are revealed some of the relationships between political coreligionists. In one of his famous "Dear Patrice" letters to Lumumba, Nkrumah wrote that

> in any crisis I will mobilize the Afro-Asian *bloc* and other friendly nations as in the present attempt to *dethrone* you. Whenever in doubt consult me. Brother, we have been in the game for some time now and we know how to handle the imperialists and the colonialists. The only colonialist or imperialist I trust is a dead one. If you do not want to bring the Congo into ruin, follow the advice I have given.[27]

These represent examples of the development of political religion through the single-party democracy emerging in Guinea and Ghana. There are, of course, many other examples to be found elsewhere, Indonesia, China, Mali, to mention only a few. China

25. Sekou Touré, *Cinquième Congrès National du Parti Démocratique de Guinée*, Rapport de Doctrine et de Politique Général (Conakry, Imprimene Nationale, 1959), p. 38.

26. *Ibid.*, p. 89 (my italics).

27. Quoted in Colin Legum, *Congo Disaster* (Baltimore: Penguin Books, 1961), p. 154 (my italics).

is, of course, exceptional. But so, in degree at least, are her problems. Mostly the mobilization systems are not communist. The failure to distinguish between the more general phenomenon of political religion in the mobilization system and the particular brand of political religion and structural form of Soviet or Chinese communism often leads Americans to broad errors of judgment about the new mobilization system.

The characteristics of political religion in mobilization systems can be summarized as follows. There are similarities between political religions and church religions. There are saints and villains. There are prophets and missionaries. To each individual the possibility of a political calling replaces the possibility of a religious calling. There is mysticism and authority. The real question, however, is whether or not the similarities mentioned above (and many others could be found) are nevertheless sufficient to establish political religion as an equivalent to church religion. Are their resemblances only superficial? Is it not a mistake to consider the artifacts of ritual and symbolic manipulation as the substance of religion itself, resulting in a misunderstanding of both religion and politics? One could argue indeed that this view debases the first and glorifies the second.

This may be correct, and I have, of course, considered this question in developing my analysis. What it raises, of course, is a larger view of religion. I should like to show that both church and politics can be seen as agents of the same fundamental phenomenon and that religion lies behind both churches and regimes.

IV

TO consider the question of religion further requires a short digression, as well as a restatement of some of the arguments put forward so far.

As I am using the term, religion is that which is concerned with the sacred, that is, special ideas and objects that, socially understood, are exceptionally venerated.[28] Although it is mysterious, all men are privileged to share in it.

28. A fuller definition of religion, to which I subscribe, is found in Bellah: "By religion I mean, following Paul Tillich, man's attitudes and actions with respect to his ultimate concern. This ultimate concern has to do with what is ultimately valuable and meaningful, what we might call ultimate value; and the ultimate threats to value and meaning, what we might call ultimate frustration. It is one of the social functions of religion to provide a meaningful

I said earlier that the oldest and most familiar system is the theocracy where leadership and authority are part of the seamless web of both politics and religion. There, the transcendental values expressed through the deity are transmitted by a king. Such a king is both ecclesiastical and secular simultaneously—so much so that it is impossible to separate, in any given act, the one aspect from the other. Many traditional African systems were like this, which is one of the reasons that many observers have commented on the profoundly religious nature of African societies. So, to some extent, was prewar Japan. Nor was Czarist Russia entirely different in this respect. All such systems had powerful secular elements within them. So does any organized church. But the distinction between sacred and secular was not always meaningful within these societies themselves.

The origins of theocratic systems are necessarily complex, but there is a good reason why they emerge out of mobilization systems and take the form of theocracy which I call a modernizing autocracy. The reason is that messianic or charismatic leadership in the mobilization system remains shaky, despite manifest popularity of political leaders. The leader never fully legitimizes his regime. The regime never is entirely successful in consolidating the authority of the leader. Over time, charisma turns into something else, as Weber originally pointed out. To control the transformation of

set of ultimate values on which the morality of a society can be based. Such values when institutionalized can be spoken of as the central values of a society.

"The other aspect of ultimate concern is ultimate frustration. As long as frustrations are seen as caused by determinate factors such as moral breach, the normal person can deal with them as they arise and they have no character of ultimacy. However, those frustrations which are inherent in the human situation, but which are not manageable or morally meaningful, of which death is the type case, may be called ultimate frustrations. The second function of religion is to provide an adequate explanation for these ultimate frustrations so that the individual or group which has undergone them can accept them without having core values rendered meaningless, and can carry on life in society in the face of these frustrations. This is done through some form of assertion that the ultimate values are greater than, can overcome, the ultimate frustrations and is symbolized in many ways—as the victory of God over death, of Eros over Thanatos, of Truth over illusion.

"The 'object' of ultimate concern, namely that which is the source of ultimate value and ultimate frustration must be symbolized if it is to be thought about at all. We may speak of these symbols as denoting the 'sacred' or the 'divine.'" See Robert N. Bellah, *Tokugawa Religion* (New York: The Free Press of Glencoe, 1957), pp. 6–7.

charisma with all its attendant dangers is to ritualize it and, by doing so, institutionalize both the role of the leader and the political habits required of the public.[29]

States created through nationalism have taken a form not dissimilar to theocracies in that they attempt to create new systems of transcendental values that have the twin effects of establishing legitimacy for the state and the moral underpinnings for those roles necessary to political objectives. "Religiosity" in the political sphere is used, however, to create a system of instrumental means and secular objectives rather than theocratic ones. In this respect political religion is at least partly employed for nonreligious objectives.

The symbolism of birth, regeneration, the personalization of leadership, and many other characteristics to be found in the formation of religious movements have the effect of casting out defilement and shame. The question still remains, however—To what extent are political religions in actual fact religions?

The discussion that follows turns on the following premises: There are certain fundamental needs of individuals that can be met only by their acceptance of transcendental beliefs. The needs, as I see them, are three: (1) the necessity of accepting death, (2) the necessity of establishing individual personality, and (3) the necessity of identifying objectives. The classic puzzle posed by these three needs results from their paradoxical relationship. If we are all doomed, as it were, as individuals, why the necessity to find purpose in living? Why the passionate commitment to life? Why the importance of knowing who and what we are?

These are the problems to which religion addresses itself. It is obvious that our commitments to life are not nullified by the inevitability of our death. Religion provides us with some form of immortality through a transcendental haven for souls. Political religion accomplishes the same end through the continuity of present society with the past and a secure political future. Individuals in a political community are made to feel themselves a product of lives lived before them within the context of the nation. This in turn is translated into family and kinship commitment as secured in the state. This is one of the reasons why family

29. For further observation on the ritualization of charisma see my book *Ghana in Transition* (New York: Atheneum Press, forthcoming), Chapter 15.

and kinship systems remain the building blocks of all political systems and, equally, why the state takes precedence over any family. The search for immortality, then, is expressed in both church religions and political religion. Both provide a means of triumphing over death in the face of its inevitability.

With respect to our second and third needs, it is a function of religion to provide identity and purpose to individuals. Identity is a reference point by means of which individuals relate to one another. This is closely connected to purpose. All religions try to explain why we exist, establish a standard of right and justice, and score inequity and human cupidity as well. If anguish, hardship, and suffering are all part of life, religion shows that justice and meaning are positive corollaries of these.

In the case of political religion, identity is to be found in citizenship, and meaning in justice. Plato's answer to Job's question is political, and in its own curious way, empirical. It is to be found in those arrangements of the human conscience that postulate justice not only as a highest good but also as a practical expression of the state.

This is why the state as a legal expression is not merely that of society in legal terms. It is also the basis for requiring obligation to the community. Meaning is thus political in relation to identity. The society gives purpose to the individual. The individual relates himself to others in a societal context. The state bases itself on a higher right to express that purpose and exact from its citizens those obligations necessary to ensure success. It may do so in a variety of ways, some of which appear indeed to obliterate the individual. Identity, then, through citizenship, locates the individual in relation to his obligations.

Obligation is related to our third factor, that is, purpose. Where church religion expresses moral purpose in right conduct and worthy objectives—aims that cleanse, purify, and promote in the individual a personal sense of worth—so too with political religion. It combines both the ultimate and intermediate aims of individuals in a morally acceptable blend. Theocracy does this when the ultimate ends of the state and the moral aims are one and the same because of the specific content of theocratic beliefs. Political religions introduce change in the normative order and require individuals to change their moral personalities. Thus in the U.S.S.R. the political religion requires a new type of individual.

Motivation must be altered as egotism is denied. Selflessness and equalitarianism within the society are the moral imperatives. These are then translated into work discipline and, through alteration of the individual's motivational structure, efficiency. A given technological end thus coincides with the moral end, to create a new political puritanism. This is a particularly attractive aspect of political religion to leaders in those new nations with mobilization systems.[30]

Political religions, although similar to theocracies, go further. In contrast to mobilization systems, for example, a theocratic country like Pakistan sets more modest economic and moral goals for itself, demanding fewer role alterations from the population than is the usual case in mobilization systems. The sense of urgency is less. The concept of historical time more archaic.

More particularly, political religion in mobilization systems fits individual moral purposes and life chances to technological dynamism. Individual roles are acceptable only in so far as they enlarge that dynamism and share in it. Hence the roles that an individual plays are both morally and technologically functional. By this means, individual purpose and national purpose are the same, a situation that does not normally apply in anything like the same degree in theocracies. Older roles are either objectionable, defining their occupants as enemies, or they become sentimentalized, relegated to a pleasant museum along with old costumes, antique artifacts, and other symbols of the past. Indeed, by becoming sentimental they may become functionally serviceable.

Immortality, identity, meaning, and purpose are among the profound individual needs that both church religion and political religion satisfy. By satisfying them, sometimes in the same context, and sometimes in different spheres, they make possible purpose in the face of death and promote solidarity and cooperation.

If these elements do what we say they do, then both church religion and political religion should have similarities of both spirit and form. By satisfying such needs they provide the ultimate basis for authority. Both serve to demarcate groups of men, one from the other, along a significant criterion of membership. Both de-

30. For a brief discussion of the "new puritanism of socialism" see my article "Political Organization and Ideology" in Moore and Feldman, eds., *Labor Commitment and Social Change in Developing Areas* (New York: Social Science Research Council, 1960).

mand allegiance as a condition of membership. Both provide the main routes of escape from death and oblivion.

There is, however, an important difference between the two that requires further comment. Church religious belief is more universalistic than political belief. Church religion seeks a widening affiliation through universal human values. Politics tends to be limited by the state. This is a threat to political religions, and one they readily recognize. Hence political religions seek universal formulas that have as their object the breaking down of national boundaries. The kingdoms of man must be one. This is one reason for the Communist commitment to completing the revolution. It cannot rest until it has universalized itself empirically so as to realize itself religiously.

If political religions are to satisfy the needs of individuals as I have defined them, what are the means open to them? First, prophets are needed. These interpret immortality, identity, and purpose through their own personal gifts of grace. They need to be father and teacher as well as founder of the community. They are the present equivalent of ancestral gods in theocracies or those mythological figures associated with the founding of older societies.

Such prophets need to light a tinder of hope in the ordinary day-to-day level of human demands. In new nations this is provided by creating something new, a new polity for future generations. Hence, political religions are for the young and are interested in the future. They provide hope and a belief in progress. To create hope and progress is to reinforce the immortality gained through family, kinship, and society itself.

By following the prophet one joins a select group. Identity and comradeship, human relationships and group functions are then combined, and each person finds his place in the scheme of development.

Finally, purpose and individual dignity, useful roles and satisfying work are enhanced by the link they provide with the messianic leader. Roles become more than functionally satisfying; they also partake of grace.

However, to achieve this requires more than a prophet. It requires effective organization. Indeed, a prophet without an organized militant following is poorer than without honor—he is unsuccessful. In mobilization systems the political religion is turned into an ideology expressed through the mechanism of the single party. We have seen that leader, party, and the state become one and the same. The community is organized according to the translation of political values, by means of the leader, into a popular but controlled system of roles.

We can now begin to draw together some of the threads of this discussion.

If we contrast Ghana, Guinea, Mali, China, or Indonesia—that is, mobilization systems with political religion—with India and the Philippines—that is, reconciliation systems without it—we find that in all, personality counts for much. Nehru, for example, occupies an exceptional place in his country's politics. The difference is that in both India and the Philippines, the quality of religious intensity is lacking *in* politics, although church religion remains certainly a factor *of* politics. No country is without some personal quality in its leadership. But the practice of catering to immortality, meaning identity and purpose and thereby justice, through prophetic leadership is more pervasive in Guinea, Ghana, and Mali, or China.

Here, then, we have one difference among the new nations. Several consequences follow. Those that center religiosity in politics ordinarily regard church religion as archaic. Justice is phrased less in terms of equity than in terms of purpose, with purpose directed toward collective ends. The search for meaning and identity results in such concepts as "African personality," Nkrumaism, or Sukarno's five principles. An earnest effort is made to ascribe new meaning to group life.

Ultimate ends are bound up directly with the state. It is the state that will fulfill the psychological and social needs that lie behind religions, not the church. The means include modernity and development, industrialization and science. These in turn are elevated to the status of transcendental beliefs. There a difficulty arises because they in fact are not transcendental but concrete, and as such exert a secularizing influence upon the social body. This is ordinarily kept in check by identifying concrete ends with "science." Modernity and technology become the prevailing "laws" of human schemes.[31]

31. In many mobilization systems the leaders are supporters of church religions as well, that is, of nonpolitical religious groups and beliefs. They may be hostile to specific churches, however. In other words, political prophets can be religious men in the usual sense of the term.

This is, of course, in sharp contrast to the system built around a constitutional framework. The latter posits ends beyond the state itself, more universal, indeed derivative from church religion. The state is merely an organized means for reconciling the multiplicity of objectives among the members. In this the state cannot provide identity but only membership. It cannot provide meaning, for its policy is an amalgam of many group and individual purposes. Purpose is left to individuals, to seek it out as they can. There is a separate role for church religions as such.

In reconciliation systems justice and political morality are more largely a matter of individual and social conscience. Things as they are are often the measure of things as they should be.

Hence, one conclusion I draw from this discussion is that what divides new nations is less a matter of formal politics than it is a difference between the countries with political religion and the countries without it. The latter have a constitutional framework providing for what individuals press as their own objectives. If these objectives are cheap and demeaning, so will the society appear cheap and demeaned. If the citizenry has some loftier conception of its values, these too will be mirrored in its activities. For a constitutional framework is just that. It is a mirror held up to the working community, and in a very real sense it is what democracy is all about. Leaders in countries with political religion have a great deal of difficulty understanding this, or if they do, accepting it, for it requires patience both with one's self and one's fellows.

In the terms laid out above, political religion qualifies for the title of "religion." I said earlier that I believe church religion to be more ethically powerful than political religion. However, in mobilization systems the decline of church religion gives to political religion a singular opportunity to fill those spiritual lacunae that, arising from the basic needs of individuals to find immortality, define identity, and determine their fate, can no longer be satisfied in more ordinary ways.

With respect to political communities, the single-party system with a prophetic leader at its head who is the repository of final authority expresses itself in mobilizing the resources of the community to suit the ideological and organizational needs of newly developing countries. Bringing wide participation in social and material life together with militantly disciplined political control, it enhances stability and organization in the name of sacrifice and lofty objectives.

Can mobilization systems with their political religions transform themselves into reconciliation systems whose commitment is to a liberal framework of law? This is a question of great concern to the West. One tendency in favor of transformation to a reconciliation system lies in the fact that a mobilization system successful in promoting economic development must eventually confront its own successes. It will need to decentralize authority and increase its economic efficiency. This could have the effect of reducing the prophetic element and, as well, diffusing and spreading authority. One might even see the beginnings of this process in the Soviet Union. Evidence, admittedly slender, and subject as well to less sanguine explanations, can be found in Khrushchev's Twentieth and Twenty-second Congress speeches. Even if one grants this tendency, however, the question remains whether or not political religions themselves possess sufficient flexibility to tolerate structural changes from one type of system to another.

Another possible factor favorable to the decline of political religions is that they are successful only in so far as ultimate ends and material ends are considered synonymous. This they can do only when what might be called the "aspirational gap" between material ends and genuine potentialities is extremely wide. Material ends appear to embody happiness, prosperity, well-being, dignity, and achievement, and similar venerated ultimate ends. It is, of course, the wisdom of the rich to know that material ends embody nothing of the sort. True, an industrial society has some pride of achievement and a sense of technological and political superiority that rankles those who are poorer. But evidence in the West shows that in a society in which there is a decline in church religion, the public has been left emotionally starved and dangerously anomic, despite the high rate of material achievement. We therefore might expect that an increase in material prosperity will increase secularization and weaken both the organizational and the ideological strengths of political religion itself.

Another factor that can contribute to the decline of political religion is a generational one. Once a revolution has been consolidated, its revolutionary achievements become remote to the next generation. Only if its prophets are made to appear larger than life size can the religious aspect be institutionalized. If this is not successful, the revolutionaries may become less than folk heroes, and even comic and absurd. Prophetic statements lose the power of prophecy, and "young pioneers" are simply trying to get ahead like everyone else. Does political religion lose its creativity through the mere erosion of time and generation? This is one possibility, since it is an integral part of the mechanism of government. Beliefs may themselves become tarnished if the state becomes a center of antagonism. If revolt against church religion is iconoclastic, the revolt against political religion tends to be cynical.

Despite these possibilities, however, it still appears extremely unlikely that mobilization systems with political religion can become changed into reconciliation systems without it. For one thing, the pace of economic growth would need to be great enough so that contradictions between the sacred and the secular could not be resolved by other means more appropriate to maintaining autocratic rule and monolithic structure. Moreover, even if decentralization of authority occurred, one would need to find other factors germane to reconciliation systems that I have already discussed, particularly a growth in individualism, competitiveness, and values about a framework of representative government as exemplified in new political roles.

Mobilization systems are understandable responses to pressures upon political leaders from their followers. They define a range of problems as political that in both theocratic and reconciliation systems are mainly handled apart from government. They chip away at the entire tradition of individual liberty—a tradition that in many new nations is probably stronger than we ordinarily think. They pose the problem of modernization in terms of an organizational rather than an industrial revolution; and, in order to achieve modernization by organizational means, political religion stresses the values that will both have organizational value and, as well, institutionalize new roles more fitting to modern life. In order to be effective, such political religion makes monopolistic claims of authority and prescience. The difficulty with it lies in the fact that, once having become significant as the key to both modernization and authority, factors other than political religion (including pluralism in political beliefs, factionalism in parties and government, and the veneration of law as a framework for political life) are all conspicuously absent.

If the possibility of change to a reconciliation system is small, what other alternatives present themselves? One can consider here the possibility of a frank and open totalitarianism. In that case, even if cynicism and disbelief occur, no one dares speak of these, and indeed a kind of inverted realism emerges. This was most dramatically exhibited in the Moscow trials. The dependence on the state for immortality, identity, and purpose was complete because individuals had no recognized existence apart from the state. One needs only to look at the final statement of Bukharin at the Moscow trials to see the apotheosis of the state-awarded personality. This alternative probably sounds more likely than it really is. One factor militating against it in new nations is that totalitarianism there cannot be quite so efficiently organized as in Western totalitarianisms. That takes considerable technology. Much more likely as a prospect is the growth of new theocracies in which the state and the political religion become ends in themselves. Whereas the political religion of the U.S.S.R. seeks to express itself in values that, even if unfilled, nevertheless are universal in their relation to both the wider religious systems of the West and integrated with the actualities of industrialization, it is possible that we shall see in some of the new nations a parochial blending of religion and state not entirely dissimilar to the traditional societies that preceded them. Here, then, is a third and most likely possibility: the emergence of new theocracies. Present leaders who, children of the West as much as of their own traditions, can in time be elevated to a pantheon of their own creation. A reinterpretation of political religion will absorb its modernizing significance by expressing modernization in traditional theocratic terms. We can expect, then, ritual and dogma to increase as political religion declines.

Such matters are not to be ignored, despite the rhetoric of modernizing nationalists. To return to the point I raised at the beginning of this discussion, one could assume that the new nations would be able to industrialize rapidly; we might argue in favor of the effects of industrializing that such a mixture of roles and functions would be produced in which all industrial countries might eventually come to look more and more alike. This argument does not apply to most of the new nations, however, because, as we have said, industrialization is not readily achievable in the foreseeable future. Possibly the only major exception to this statement will be India, and even there the picture is by no means clear. Hence a form of neotraditionalism, expressed in modern theocracies, may well come to have a renewed significance. Modern theocracies can utilize modern techniques of government and administration, and regard the state as an educative body instilling right principles of conduct and outlook. Particular values embodying political obligation and community, presently associated with a dominant party and leader, may also provide the basis for both prophet and scripture. The very real possibility exists that mobilization systems can be transformed into neotraditionalistic theocracies in which both traditional theocratic religions and modern political ones combine.

Our conclusion, then, points to the following three possibilities: First, for reasons intrinsic to the nature of political religion, mobilization systems among the new nations will be unstable in the long run. Second, few mobilization systems will be transformed into either reconciliation or totalitarian types. Third, there is a real possibility that they will be changed into *modernizing autocracies* within the framework of neotraditionalism, using ritual to institutionalize political religion.

If we can expect the ritualization of political religion within a new form of theocratic state as a most likely prospect in many of the new nations, it would be interesting to speculate on some of the probable characteristics of potential modern theocracies. Tendencies can already be identified. Formal monarchies are not apt to be established, associated as they are with pre-emancipation and with ethnic and premodern local groups against which the new state is often in conflict. More than likely are presidential systems, or, more acurately, "presidential monarchies," with nondynastic aspects of presidential systems combined with the dynastic aspects of ceremonial and ritual functions associated with kingship. A presidential monarch can play an active political role utilizing concentrated power, and a ritualized religious role as well, representative of the symbolic qualities of the entire nation.

The nationalist single party comes to form the new group of guardians and warriors of the state. These carry on the modern functions of entrepreneurship through state enterprise and leadership. Composed of an elect, they are the purveyors of ritual. Among them are those whose job it is to interpret and explain matters of dogma and ritual to the public. If not high priests, they are nevertheless appointed keepers of the sacred texts.

The texts themselves are a blend of ideology and theology. Mixtures of mysticism and pragmatism, they tend to be nonprogrammatic so that innovation will not be offended by any strict doctrine. However, they provide guides to moral conduct and help define individual relationships to the state and the leader as well. Beyond ordinary ideology, they strive to enhance individual immortality by linking it to the leader who is founder of the state, provide purpose by defining it, and indicate a hopeful future state of affairs to be achieved through the political kingdom. One would expect that the norms of egalitariansm, mass participation in social life, opportunity, abundance, that is, the values expressed in the totalitarian democratic tradition of which Talmon speaks, will all be expressed. The language of these texts, some of which already exist and are mainly written by the leaders themselves, follow the terminology of socialism in an extremely wide and loose sense. Evidence is already available about these texts and the expressions they possess. For example, in the African case, we can cite two main types. One consists of the writings of the President of Guinea, whose militant socialist version of *negritude* has blended the communal and esthetic properties of African traditional life with modern socialist values and practices. Another is the effort in Ghana to establish Nkrumaism as a philosophical system combining aspects of socialism, with an emphasis on the African personality and certain traditional customs and social forms. Notably absent are concerns with two central features of socialist doctrine: property and class.

The enemies include capitalism (as distinct from investment capital), neocolonialism or neoimperialism, racial discrimination, traditionalism, and those individuals or groups that show antagonism to the leader, regime, or political religion. The notion of evil can also be extended to include those roles that are not functional to the performance of modernized social and political activities that the state supports. In this respect the political religion helps to distinguish "good" and "bad" roles and to tie them to the needs of the modernizing state.

It is, of course, impossible to do more than briefly sketch in some possible characteristics of the new theocracies. Not all the new states will follow this pattern. That should go without saying.

Those that do will show widely differing practices. For example, they may vary in the degree in which all significant groups come under the religious umbrella. Particularly in the case of the civil servants, a kind of "positive neutralism" within the state may surround the bureaucratic role, with the effect of exempting them from ritualized practices and religious observances. The same may also hold true for groups representing church religions. The monopolistic quality of political religion does not always need to be directed against church practices and beliefs. Indeed, it is more likely to direct itself against other political religions instead (unless the church religion becomes an inhibiting influence in the state).

Political ritualization can help to blend the new roles of leader, priest, elect, into an effective system, surrounded by a religious doctrine that is itself a mixture of modernizing values (as in socialism) and unique traditions (as in *negritude*). These stress change with continuity, and form the basis of authority in the society. The ritualization of these values is therefore one way to institutionalize new roles of the polity, and most particularly that of the "Presidential monarch."[32]

The importance of political religion lies precisely in the barriers it places in the way of smooth transition from societies in which politics is sacred to those in which it is not, and, correspondingly, in the change from mobilization systems to reconciliation types. Despite the forces working to erode political religion, it is clear that, once authority is in some measure dependent on it, its decline becomes a political problem because it affects the basic stability of the society and the legitimization of authority embodied in a particular regime. Hence mobilization systems tend to fight secularization whether it derives from the ultimate incompatibilities posed by elevating material ends to sacred rank, or from the growth of disillusionment and cynicism.

Perhaps we have been somewhat misled by certain of the tendencies toward wider association between peoples and nations, which is itself an important and obvious consequence of the decline of colonialism. I say "misled" because within the universalizing and fraternizing relations of the new nation-states there is also to be found a new parochialism. Under certain circumstances

32. For a detailed analysis of a modernizing autocracy, see my book *The Political Kingdom of Uganda: A Study in Bureaucratic Nationalism* (Princeton: Princeton University Press, 1961), *passim*.

such a perfectly respectable doctrine as neutralism may turn out to be a disguised way of withdrawing from more widely accepted responsibilities. If the values of the political religion become less than universal, and if the level of political life in the mobilization system becomes a source of shame and embarrassment to political leaders, then the iron-curtain phenomenon could appear in those new nations that desire an exemption from ordinary standards of judgment applied to them in other parts of the world. In other words, if a new nation should exhibit a second-rate countenance to the world, it may also find it necessary to invert the criteria of second-rateness. Disguised in the doctrine of each nation's finding its "own way" in wrestling with internal problems is the danger of self-delusion. Political religion does, after all, deal in illusions.

If these assumptions are correct, the likely possibility of change will become centered upon ritualization, a circumstance that limits the functional consequences of religion without destroying its relation to authority. Political leadership will derive from strongly ritualistic roles. Exactly what the specifications of these roles will be it is impossible to predict, but they would certainly have strong traditionalistic features at least superficially attached to them. We can see this occurring already in the titles taken by Nkrumah in Ghana, which include a number of traditional forms in addition to "Osagyefo" (Military Savior).

V

OBVIOUSLY the analysis we have sketched in above has proceeded on several levels. The difficulty has been how to weave together the relationship between those fundamental needs both religion and politics can satisfy in ordinary human beings while relating them to the dynamic properties of different structural types. Properly, then, this discussion ought to be regarded as the beginning of a study rather than as the end of it. There is no doubt in my mind that political religion is one way of assisting polities to define their aims and establish their priorities while allowing political leaders to remain exempt from ordinary criticisms and errors. That this is dangerous goes without saying. As well, such a process might have the effect of stifling creative thought and daring among those who have been brought up in the faith. Nevertheless, if this is an age in which religious faith has been sharply restricted as a guide to men's actions and purposes, it cannot be too surprising if the state steps in to fill the void—especially when there are so many other compelling reasons for the state to do so.

What should be clear about political religion is that it is an unsettling factor in a state—at least in the long run. Political religions are subject to even more severe and cynical disenchantment by their adherents than church religions. For the latter, in addition to their more transcendental concerns, are also a code for expressing individual terrors and moralities. True, not all religions deal specifically with moral questions. Ultimately, however, they express individual continuity, individual identity, and individual purpose.

Our hopes for democracy in the new nations are based on unreliable notions that man will eventually assert his personality against restrictive governments no matter what the odds against him. That in the long run no matter now abjectly a man is made to crawl before the state he will in the end assert himself against it. This is a comforting notion. It is lent some substance because in new nations it is difficult to insulate even relatively distant and faraway peoples from the echoes of liberal beliefs and from democratic and libertarian events. Perhaps if educational programs emphasize something more than a combination of technical information and ideological indoctrination (a growing trend), there will be resistance to the decretals put forward by political religionists.

What is more likely, however, is that real modernization will begin in most of the new nations when the political religions are turned in upon themselves and when the insularities and exemptions from judgment that so many political leaders demand are ended in a new round of secular questioning. This will take time. Meanwhile, Tocqueville's words on the French Revolution are relevant:

> They will say that a country governed by an absolute ruler in a *democracy* because he governs by such laws and maintains such institutions as are favorable to the great mass of the people. Such a government, it will be said, is *democratic*, a *democratic monarchy*.

But *democratic government, democratic monarchy* can only mean one thing in the true sense of these words: a government where the people more or less participate in their government. Its sense is intimately bound to the idea of political liberty. To give the democratic epithet to a government where there is no political liberty is a palpable absurdity, since this departs from the natural meaning of these words.

Such false or obscure expressions are adopted: (*a*) because of the wish to give the masses illusions, for the expression "democratic government" will always evoke a certain degree of appeal; (*b*) because of the embarrassing difficulty in finding a single term which would explain the complex system of an absolute government where the people do not all participate in public affairs but where the upper classes have no privileges either and where legislation aims to provide as much material welfare as possible.[33]

The phenomenon of which Tocqueville speaks is not entirely dissimilar to the mobilization systems among the new states. They are "presidential monarchies," and rather aristocratic ones. Their political religions express liberty in corporate discipline. Through corporate discipline the state provides immortality, meaning, and purpose. But even when such political religions are compelling for other reasons, they are less profound than church religions. The intermingling of the sacred and the secular makes the former more mundane. Political religions rarely incorporate the spirit and the wider meanings of human life, although they may make explicit and even ennoble the narrower meanings of social life. They cannot contemplate the concept of fate itself, even though determining the career and opportunities for an individual. They cannot give immortality even when they perpetuate the race, provide for the protection of the incumbents, and seek to provide for family and society.

Talmon argues that the

reign of the exclusive yet all-solving doctrine of totalitarian democracy runs counter to the lessons of nature and history. Nature and history show civilization as the evolution of historically and pragmatically formed clusters of social existence and social endeavor, and not as the achievement of abstract man on a single level of existence.[34]

33. See Tocqueville, *op. cit.*, pp. 102–103.
34. Talmon, *op. cit.*, p. 254.

I hope that he is right. But nature shows such multiplicity and diversity that claims in its name can give false comfort. More likely we shall witness pragmatically formed clusters of social belief, political practices, and patterns of leadership more in keeping with the undigested practices of uneven modernization. Here the problems of political ritualization, manipulation of symbols, and new theocracies are equally plausible solutions to problems of political religion, authority, and modernization.

The integrative revolution

Primordial sentiments and civil politics in the new states

CLIFFORD GEERTZ

I

In 1948, scarcely a year after Independence, Pandit Nehru found himself in the always unsettling position for an opposition politician finally come to power of being obliged to place in practice a policy he had long espoused but never liked. With Patel and Sitaramayya, he was appointed to the Linguistic Provinces Committee.

The Congress had supported the principle of linguistic determination of state boundaries within India almost since its founding, arguing, ironically enough, that British maintenance of "arbitrary"—that is, nonlinguistic—administrative units was part of a divide-and-rule policy. In 1920 it had actually reorganized its own regional chapters along linguistic lines so as better to secure its popular appeal. But with the echoes of partition perhaps still ringing in his ears, Nehru was deeply shaken by his experience on the Linguistic Committee, and with the candor that makes him virtually unique among the leaders of the new states, he admitted it:

[This inquiry] has been in some ways an eye-opener for us. The work of 60 years of the Indian National Congress was standing before us, face to face with centuries-old India of narrow loyalties, petty jealousies and ignorant prejudices engaged in mortal conflict and we were simply horrified to see how thin was the ice upon which we were skating. Some of the ablest men in the country came before us and confidently and emphatically stated that language in this country stood for and represented culture, race, history, individuality, and finally a sub-nation.[1]

But, horrified or not, Nehru, Patel, and Sitaramayya in the end were forced to endorse the claims of Andhra as a Telugu-speaking state, and the thin ice was broken. Within the decade India had been almost entirely reorganized along linguistic lines, and a wide range of observers, both domestic and foreign, were wondering aloud whether the country's political unity would survive this wholesale concession to "narrow loyalties, petty jealousies, and ignorant prejudices."[2]

The problem that opened Nehru's eyes in such wide astonishment is phrased in linguistic terms, but the same problems phrased in a wide variety of terms is, of course, literally pandemic to the new states, as the countless references to "dual" or "plural" or "multiple" societies, to "mosaic" or "composite" social structures, to "states" that are not "nations" and "nations" that are not "states," to "tribalism," "parochialism," and "communalism," as well as to pan-national movements of various sorts demonstrate.

When we speak of communalism in India we refer to religious contrasts; when we speak of it in Malaya we are mainly concerned with racial ones, and in the Congo with tribal ones. But the grouping under a common rubric is not simply adventitious; the phenomena referred to are in some way similar. Regionalism has been the main theme in Indonesian disaffection, differences in custom in Moroccan. The Tamil minority in Ceylon is set off from the Sinhalese majority by religion, language, race, region, and

1. Quoted in S. Harrison, "The Challenge to Indian Nationalism," *Foreign Affairs*, 34: 3, April, 1956.

2. For a very dim view, see S. Harrison, *India: The Most Dangerous Decades*, Princeton, N.J., Princeton University Press, 1960. For a lively Indian view that sees the "scheme of dividing India in the name of Linguistic States" as "full of poison" but yet necessary "to make easy the way to democracy and to remove racial and cultural tension," see B. R. Ambedkar, *Thoughts on Linguistic States*, Delhi, B. R. Ambedkar, ca. 1955.

social custom; the Shiite minority in Iraq is set off from the dominant Sunnis virtually by an intra-Islamic sectarian difference alone. Pan-national movements in Africa are largely based on race, in Kurdistan, on tribalism; in Laos, the Shan States, and Thailand, on language. Yet all these phenomena, too, are in some sense of a piece. They form a definable field of investigation.

That is, they would, could we but define it. The stultifying aura of conceptual ambiguity that surrounds the terms "nation," "nationality," and "nationalism" has been extensively discussed and thoroughly deplored in almost every work that has been concerned to attack the relationship between communal and political loyalties.[3] But as the preferred remedy has been to adopt a theoretical eclecticism that, in its attempt to do justice to the multifaceted nature of the problems involved, tends to confuse political, psychological, cultural, and demographic factors, actual reduction of that ambiguity has not proceeded very far. Thus a recent symposium on the Middle East refers indiscriminately to the efforts of the Arab League to destroy existing nation-state boundaries, those of the Sudan Government to unify a somewhat arbitrary and accidentally demarcated sovereign state, and those of the Azerin Turks to separate from Iran and join the Soviet Republic of Azerbaijan as "nationalism."[4] Operating with a similarly omnibus concept, Coleman[5] sees Nigerians (or some of them) as displaying five different sorts of nationalism at once—"African," "Nigerian," "Regional," "Group," and "Cultural." And Emerson[6] defines a nation as a "terminal community—the largest community that, when the chips are down, effectively commands men's loyalty, overriding the claims both of the lesser communities within it and those that cut across it or potentially enfold it within a still greater society . . . ," which simply shifts the ambiguity from the term "nation" to the term "loyalty," as well as seeming to leave

3. See, for example, K. Deutsch, *Nationalism and Social Communication*, New York, Wiley, 1953, pp. 1–14; R. Emerson, *From Empire to Nation*, Cambridge, Mass., Harvard University Press, 1960; J. Coleman, *Nigeria: Background to Nationalism*, Berkeley, University of California Press, 1958, pp. 419ff; F. Hertz, *Nationalism in History and Politics*, New York, Oxford University Press, 1944, pp. 11–15.

4. Walter Z. Laqueur (ed.), *The Middle East in Transition: Studies in Contemporary History*, New York, Praeger, 1958.

5. *Op. cit.*, pp. 425–426.

6. *Op. cit.*, pp. 95–96.

such questions as whether India, Indonesia, or Nigeria are nations to the determination of some future, unspecified historical crisis.

Some of this conceptual haze is burned away, however, if it is realized that the peoples of the new states are simultaneously animated by two powerful, thoroughly interdependent, yet distinct and often actually opposed motives—the desire to be recognized as responsible agents whose wishes, acts, hopes, and opinions "matter," and the desire to build an efficient, dynamic modern state. The one aim is to be noticed: it is a search for an identity, and a demand that that identity be publicly acknowledged as having import, a social assertion of the self as "being somebody in the world."[7] The other aim is practical: it is a demand for progress, for a rising standard of living, more effective political order, greater social justice, and beyond that of "playing a part in the larger arena of world politics," of "exercising influence among the nations."[8] The two motives are, again, most intimately related, because citizenship in a truly modern state has more and more become the most broadly negotiable claim to personal significance, and because what Mazzini called the demand to exist and have a name is to such a great extent fired by a humiliating sense of exclusion from the important centers of power in world society. But they are not the same thing. They stem from different sources and respond to different pressures. It is, in fact, the tension between them that is one of the central driving forces in the national evolution of the new states; as it is, at the same time, one of the greatest obstacles to such evolution.

This tension takes a peculiarly severe and chronic form in the new states, both because of the great extent to which their peoples' sense of self remains bound up in the gross actualities of blood, race, language, locality, religion, or tradition, and because of the steadily accelerating importance in this century of the sovereign state as a positive instrument for the realization of collective aims. Multiethnic, usually multilinguistic, and sometimes multiracial, the populations of the new states tend to regard the immediate, concrete, and to them inherently meaningful sorting implicit in such "natural" diversity as the substantial content of their in-

7. I. Berlin, *Two Concepts of Liberty*, New York, Oxford University Press, 1958, p. 42.
8. E. Shils, "Political Development in the New States," *Comparative Studies in Society and History*, 2: 265–292; 379–411, 1960.

dividuality. To subordinate these specific and familiar identifications in favor of a generalized commitment to an overarching and
somewhat alien civil order is to risk a loss of definition as an autonomous person, either through absorption into a culturally undifferentiated mass or, what is even worse, through domination by
some other rival ethnic, racial, or linguistic community that is
able to imbue that order with the temper of its own personality.
But at the same time, all but the most unenlightened members of
such societies are at least dimly aware—and their leaders are acutely
aware—that the possibilities for social reform and material progress
they so intensely desire and are so determined to achieve rest with
increasing weight on their being enclosed in a reasonably large,
independent, powerful, well-ordered polity. The insistence on
recognition as someone who is visible and matters and the will to
be modern and dynamic thus tend to diverge, and much of the
political process in the new states pivots around an heroic effort to
keep them aligned.

II

A MORE exact phrasing of the nature of the problem involved
here is that, considered as societies, the new states are abnormally
susceptible to serious disaffection based on primordial attachments.[9] By a primordial attachment is meant one that stems from
the "givens"—or, more precisely, as culture is inevitably involved
in such matters, the assumed "givens"—of social existence: immediate contiguity and kin connection mainly, but beyond them
the givenness that stems from being born into a particular religious
community, speaking a particular language, or even a dialect of a
language, and following particular social practices. These congru-
ities of blood, speech, custom, and so on, are seen to have an in-
effable, and at times overpowering, coerciveness in and of themselves. One is bound to one's kinsman, one's neighbor, one's fellow
believer, *ipso facto*; as the result not merely of personal affection,
practical necessity, common interest, or incurred obligation, but at
least in great part by virtue of some unaccountable absolute import
attributed to the very tie itself. The general strength of such
primordial bonds, and the types of them that are important, differ

9. E. Shils, "Primordial, Personal, Sacred and Civil Ties," *British Journal
of Sociology*, June, 1957.

from person to person, from society to society, and from time to time. But for virtually every person, in every society, at almost all times, some attachments seem to flow more from a sense of natural—some would say spiritual—affinity than from social interaction.

In modern societies the lifting of such ties to the level of political supremacy—though it has, of course, occurred and may again occur—has more and more come to be deplored as pathological. To an increasing degree national unity is maintained not by calls to blood and land but by a vague, intermittent, and routine allegiance to a civil state, supplemented to a greater or lesser extent by governmental use of police powers and ideological exhortation. The havoc wreaked, both upon themselves and others, by those modern (or semimodern) states that did passionately seek to become primordial rather than civil political communities, as well as a growing realization of the practical advantages of a wider-ranging pattern of social integration than primordial ties can usually produce or even permit, have only strengthened the reluctance publicly to advance race, language, religion, and the like as bases for the definition of a terminal community. But in modernizing societies, where the tradition of civil politics is weak and where the technical requirements for an effective welfare government are poorly understood, primordial attachments tend, as Nehru discovered, to be repeatedly, in some cases almost continually, proposed and widely acclaimed as preferred bases for the demarcation of autonomous political units. And the thesis that truly legitimate authority flows only from the inherent coerciveness such attachments are conceived somehow to possess is frankly, energetically, and artlessly defended:

The reasons why a unilingual state is stable and a multilingual state unstable are quite obvious. A state is built on fellow feeling. What is this fellow feeling? To state briefly it is a feeling of a corporate sentiment of oneness which makes those who are charged with it feel that they are kith and kin. This feeling is a double-edged feeling. It is at once a feeling of "consciousness of kind" which, on the one hand, binds together those who have it so strongly that it overrides all differences arising out of economic conflicts or social gradations and, on the other, severs them from those who are not of their kind. It is a longing not to belong to any other group. The existence of this fellow feeling is the foundation of a stable and democratic state.[10]

It is this crystallization of a direct conflict between primordial and civil sentiments—this "longing not to belong to any other group"—that gives to the problem variously called tribalism, parochialism, communalism, and so on, a more ominous and deeply threatening quality than most of the other, also very serious and intractable problems the new states face. Here we have not just competing loyalties, but competing loyalties of the same general order, on the same level of integration. There are many other competing loyalties in the new states, as in any state—ties to class, party, business, union, profession, or whatever. But groups formed of such ties are virtually never considered as possible self-standing, maximal social units, as candidates for nationhood. Conflicts among them occur only within a more or less fully accepted terminal community whose political integrity they do not, as a rule, put into question. No matter how severe they become they do not threaten, at least not intentionally, its existence as such. They threaten governments, or even forms of government, but they rarely at best—and then usually when they have become infused with primordial sentiments—threaten to undermine the nation itself, because they do not involve alternative definitions of what the nation is, of what its scope of reference is. Economic or class or intellectual disaffection threatens revolution, but disaffection based on race, language, or culture threatens partition, irredentism, or merger, a redrawing of the very limits of the state, a new definition of its domain. Civil discontent finds its natural outlet in the seizing, legally or illegally, of the state apparatus. Primordial discontent strives more deeply and is satisfied less easily. If severe enough, it wants not just Sukarno's or Nehru's or Moulay Hasan's head it wants Indonesia's or India's or Morocco's.

The actual foci around which such discontent tends to crystallize are various, and in any given case several are usually involved concurrently, sometimes at cross-purposes with one another. On a

10. Ambedkar, *op. cit.*, p. 11. Noting that the modern bilingual states of Canada, Switzerland, and (white) South Africa might be quoted against him, Ambedkar adds: "It must not be forgotten that the genius of India is quite different than the genius of Canada, Switzerland, and South Africa. The genius of India is to divide—the genius of Switzerland, South Africa and Canada to unite."

merely descriptive level they are, nevertheless, fairly readily enumerable:[11]

1] *Assumed Blood Ties.* Here the defining element in quasi-kinship. "Quasi" because kin units formed around known biological relationship (extended families, lineages, and so on) are too small for even the most tradition-bound to regard them as having more than limited significance, and the referent is, consequently, to a notion of untraceable but yet sociologically real kinship, as in a tribe. Nigeria, the Congo, and the greater part of sub-Saharan Africa are characterized by a prominence of this sort of primordialism. But so also are the nomads or seminomads of the Middle East —the Kurds, Baluchis, Pathans, and so on; the Nagas, Mundas, Santals, and so on, of India; and most of the so-called "hill tribes" of Southeast Asia.

2] *Race.* Clearly, race is similar to assumed kinship, in that it involves an ethnobiological theory. But it is not quite the same thing. Here, the reference is to phenotypical physical features— especially, of course, skin color, but also facial form, stature, hair type, and so on—rather than any very definite sense of common descent as such. The communal problems of Malaya in large part focus around these sorts of differences, between, in fact, two phenotypically very similar Mongoloid peoples. "Negritude" clearly draws much, though perhaps not all, of its force from the notion of race as a significant primordial property, and the pariah commercial minorities—like the Chinese in Southeast Asia or the Indians and Lebanese in Africa—are similarly demarcated.

3] *Language.* Linguism—for some yet to be adequately explained reasons—is particularly intense in the Indian subcontinent, has been something of an issue in Malaya, and has appeared sporadically elsewhere. But as language has sometimes been held to be the altogether essential axis of nationality conflicts, it is worth stressing that linguism is not an inevitable outcome of linguistic diversity. As indeed kinship, race, and the other factors to be listed below, language differences need not in themselves be particularly divisive: they have not been so for the most part in Tanganyika, Iran (not a new state in the strict sense, perhaps), the Philippines, or even in Indonesia, where despite a great confusion of tongues

11. For a similar but rather differently conceived and organized listing, see Emerson, *op. cit.*, Chapters 6, 7, and 8.

linguistic conflict seems to be the one social problem the country has somehow omitted to demonstrate in extreme form. Furthermore, primordial conflicts can occur where no marked linguistic differences are involved, as in Lebanon, among the various sorts of Batak-speakers in Indonesia, and to a lesser extent perhaps between the Fulani and Hausa in northern Nigeria.

4] *Region.* Although a factor nearly everywhere, regionalism naturally tends to be especially troublesome in geographically heterogeneous areas. Tonkin, Annam, and Cochin in prepartitioned Vietnam, the two baskets on the long pole, were opposed almost purely in regional terms, sharing language, culture, race, etc. The tension between East and West Pakistan involves differences in language and culture too, but the geographic element is of great prominence owing to the territorial discontinuity of the country. Java versus the Outer Islands in archipelagic Indonesia; the Northeast versus the West Coast in mountain-bisected Malaya, are perhaps other examples in which regionalism has been an important primordial factor in national politics.

5] *Religion.* Indian partition is the outstanding case of the operation of this type of attachment. But Lebanon, the Karens and the Moslem Arakenese in Burma, the Toba Bataks, Ambonese, and Minahassans in Indonesia, the Moros in the Philippines, the Sikhs in Indian Punjab and the Ahmadiyas in Pakistani, and the Hausa in Nigeria are other well-known examples of its force in undermining or inhibiting a comprehensive civil sense.

6] *Custom.* Again, differences in custom form a basis for a certain amount of national disunity almost everywhere, and are of especial prominence in those cases in which an intellectually and/or artistically rather sophisticated group sees itself as the bearer of a "civilization" amid a largely barbarian population that would be well advised to model itself upon it: the Bengalis in India, the Javanese in Indonesia, the Arabs (as against the Berbers) in Morocco, the Amhara in—another "old" new state—Ethiopia, etc. But it is important also to point out that even vitally opposed groups may differ rather little in their general style of life: Hindu Gujeratis and Maharashtrians in India; Baganda and Bunyoro in Uganda; Javanese and Sundanese in Indonesia. And the reverse holds also: the Balinese have far and away the most divergent pattern of customs in Indonesia, but they have been, so far, notable for the absence of any sense of primordial discontent at all.

But beyond such a mere listing of the sorts of primordial ties that tend, in one place or another, to become politicized it is necessary to go further and attempt also to classify, or somehow order, the concrete patterns of primordial diversity and conflict that in fact exist in the various new states and of which these ties are the components.

This seemingly routine exercise in political ethnography is a rather more delicate task than at first appears, however, not only because those communalistic challenges to the integrity of the civil state that are at the moment being openly pressed must be discerned, but also because those that are latent, lying concealed in the enduring structure of primordial identifications, ready to take explicit political form given only the proper sorts of social conditions must be revealed. The fact that the Indian minority in Malaya has not so far posed a very serious threat to the viability of the state does not mean that it might not do so if something odd happened to the world price of rubber or if Nehru's hands-off policy toward overseas Indians should be replaced by one more like that of Mao toward the overseas Chinese. The Moro problem, which provided postgraduate field training for select members of several generations of West Pointers, now merely simmers in the Philippines, but it may not do so forever. The Free Thai movement seems dead at the moment, but it could revive with a change in Thailand's foreign policy or even with Pathet success in Laos. Iraq's Kurds, whom General Kassem had ostensibly mollified, now show signs of restlessness again. And so on. Primordially based political solidarities have a deeply abiding strength in most of the new states, but it is not always an active and immediately apparent one.

Initially, a useful analytic distinction can be made with respect to this matter of classification between those allegiances that operate more or less wholly within the confines of a single civil state and those that do not but which run across them. Or, put somewhat differently, one can contrast those cases in which the racial, tribal, linguistic, and so on, reference group that is charged with a "corporate sentiment of oneness" is smaller than the existing civil state, and those where it is larger, or at least transgresses its borders in some fashion. In the first instance primordial discontent arises from a sense of political suffocation; in the second, from a sense of political dismemberment. Karen separatism in Burma, Ashanti in Ghana, or Baganda in Uganda are examples of the former; pan-Arabism, greater Somaliism, pan-Africanism, of the latter.

Many of the new states are plagued by both these sorts of problems at once. In the first place, most interstate primordial movements do not involve entire separate countries, as the pan-movements at least tend to do, but rather minorities scattered through several, for example: the Kurdistan movement to unite Kurds in Iran, Syria, Turkey, and the Soviet Union, perhaps the most unlikely-to-succeed political movement of all time; the Abako movement of Kasuvubu and his Republic of The Congo and Angola allies; the Dravidistan movement, in so far as it comes to see itself as extending across Palk Strait from South India into Ceylon; the movement—or perhaps it is so far only a formless sentiment—for a unified and sovereign Bengal independent of both India and Pakistan. And there are even a few classical irredentist-type problems scattered among the new states—the Malays in South Thailand, the Pushtu speakers along the Afghan border of Pakistan, and so on; and when political boundaries become more firmly established in sub-Saharan Africa there will be a great many more of them. In all these cases, there is—or there may develop—both a desire to escape the established civil state and a longing to reunite a politically divided primordial community.[12]

In the second place, interstate and intrastate primordial attachments often cross-cut one another in a complex network of balanced—if most precariously balanced—commitments. In Malaya one of the more effective binding forces that has, so far at least, held Chinese and Malays together in a single state despite the tremendous centrifugal tendencies the racial and cultural difference generates is the fear on the part of either group that should the Federation dissolve they may become a clearly submerged minority in some other political framework: the Malays through the turn of the Chinese to Singapore and China; the Chinese through the turn of the Malays to Indonesia. In a similar way, in Ceylon both the Tamils and Sinhalese manage to see themselves as minorities: the Tamils because 70 per cent of the Ceylonese are

12. The intensity, prevalence, or even the reality of such desires in each case is another matter, about which nothing is being asserted here. How much, if any, feeling in favor of assimilation to Malaya exists among the South Thailand Malays, the actual strength of the Abako idea, or the attitudes of Tamils in Ceylon toward the Dravidian separatists of Madras are matters for empirical research.

Sinhalese; the Sinhalese because the eight million of them in Ceylon are all there are, while in addition to the two million Tamils on the island there are 28 million more in South India. In Morocco, there has tended to be both a within-state split between Arab and Berber, and an extra-state split between partisans of Nasser's pan-Arabism and of Bourguiba's and Balafrej's *regroupement maghrebin*. And Nasser himself, until the Syrian debacle perhaps the new States' most accomplished virtuoso in the primordial arts, is absorbed in juggling pan-Arabist, pan-Islamic, and pan-African sentiments in the interests of Egyptian hegemony among the Bandung powers.

But whether the relevant attachments outrun state boundaries or not, most of the major primordial battles are for the moment being fought within them. A certain amount of international conflict focusing around, or at least animated by, primordial issues does exist among the new states. The hostility between Israel and her Arab neighbors and the quarrel of India and Pakistan over Kashmir are the most prominent cases, of course. But the embroilment of two older states, Greece and Turkey, over Cyprus is another; the impending clash between Somalia and Ethiopia concerning an essentially irredentist problem a third; the Indonesian difficulties vis-à-vis Peking with respect to the issue of "dual citizenship" for Chinese residents of Indonesia a mild fourth, and so on. As the new states solidify politically, such disputes may well grow both more frequent and more intense. But as of now they have not yet become—with the exception of the Israeli-Arab conflict and, sporadically, the Kashmir problem—paramount political issues, and the immediate significance of primordial differences is almost everywhere primarily domestic, though this is not to say that they are therefore without important international implications.[13]

13. Nor does the interstate significance of primordial sentiments lie wholly in their divisive power. Pan-American attitudes, weak and ill-defined as they may be, have provided a useful context of mild solidarity for the confrontation of leaders of major African countries—Arab and Negro alike—as at Casablanca in January, 1961. Burma's strenuous (and expensive) efforts to strengthen and revitalize international Buddhism, as in the Sixth Great Council and Yegu in 1954, have served to link her more effectively with the other Theravada countries—Ceylon, Thailand, Laos, and Cambodia. And a vague, mainly racial, feeling of common "Malayness" has played a positive role in the relations between Malaya and Indonesia and Malaya and the Philippines (though not, as yet, between Indonesia and the Philippines).

The construction of a typology of the concrete patterns of primordial diversity that are found within the various new states is severely hampered, however, by the simple lack of detailed and reliable information in the overwhelming majority of the cases. But, again, a gross and merely empirical classification can nonetheless fairly easily be devised, and should prove useful as a rough-and-ready guide to a wilderness otherwise uncharted, and facilitate a more incisive analysis of the role of primordial sentiments in civil politics than is possible in terms of "pluralism," "tribalism," "parochialism," "communalism," and the other clichés of commonsense sociology:

1] One common and, relatively speaking, simple pattern seems to be that of a single dominant and usually, though not inevitably, larger group set over against a single strong and chronically troublesome minority: Cyprus with Greeks and Turks; Ceylon with Sinhalese and Tamils; Jordan with Jordanians and Palestinians, though in this last case the dominant group is the smaller.

2] Similar in some ways to this first pattern, but more complex, is that of one central—often enough in a geographic sense as well as a political—group and several mediumly large and at least somewhat opposed peripheral groups: the Javanese versus the Outer Island peoples in Indonesia; the Irrawaddy Valley Burmese versus the various hill tribes and upland valley peoples in Burma; the central plateau Persians and the various tribes in Iran (though, again, this is not strictly a new state); the Atlantic Plain Arabs encircled by the diverse Berber tribes of the Rif, the Atlas, and the Sous; the Mekong Lao and the tribal peoples in Laos; and so on. How far such a pattern is to be found in black Africa is unclear. The one case where it might have crystallized, with the Ashanti in Ghana, the power of the central group seems to have, at least temporarily, been broken. And whether in a new state the Baganda will be able to maintain their dominant position vis-à-vis the other Uganda groups through their greater education, political sophistication, and so on, and despite their comprising but about a fifth of the population, remains to be seen.

3] Another pattern that forms an internally even less homogeneous type is a bipolar one of two nearly evenly balanced major groups: Malays and Chinese in Malaya (though there is also a smaller Indian group); or Christians and Moslems in Lebanon (though here both groups are actually aggregates of smaller sects); or Sunnis and Shiis in Iraq. Perhaps the two regions of Pakistan, although the Western region is far from wholly homogeneous within itself, gives that state a somewhat bipolar primordial pattern. Vietnam before partition tended to take this form—Tonkin versus Cochin—this problem now having been solved with the assistance of the great powers. Even Libya, which has scarcely enough people to develop decent group conflicts, has something of this pattern with the Cyrenecia-Tripolitania contrast.

4] Next, there is the pattern of a relatively even gradation of groups in importance, from several large ones through several medium-sized ones to a number of small ones, with no clearly dominant ones and no sharp cut-off points. India, the Philippines, Nigeria, Kenya are perhaps examples.

5] Finally, there is simple ethnic fragmentation, as Wallenstein has called it, with multiple small groups, into which somewhat residual category it is necessary to toss much of Africa, at least until more is known about it.[14] One proposal, issuing from the nothing if not experimental Leopoldville Government, suggesting a grouping of the Congo Republic's estimated 250 or so separate tribal-linguistic groups into eighty autonomous tribal regions, which would then be organized into twelve federated states, gives something of an indication of the extent to which such fragmentation can go, and the complexity of primordial allegiances it may involve.

The world of personal identity collectively ratified and publicly expressed is thus an ordered world. The patterns of primordial identification and cleavage within the existing new states are not fluid, shapeless, and infinitely various, but are definitely demarcated and vary in systematic ways. And as they vary, the nature of the individual's problem of social self-assertion varies with them, as it does also according to his position within any one type of pattern. The task of securing recognition as someone who is somebody to whom attention must be paid appears in a different form and light to a Sinhalese in Ceylon than it does to a Javanese

14. I. Wallerstein, "The Emergence of Two West African Nations: Ghana and the Ivory Coast," unpublished Ph.D. thesis, Columbia University, 1959.

in Indonesia or a Malay in Malaya, because to be a member of a major group set over against one minor one is a quite different matter than to be a member of such a group over against a plurality of minor ones or another major one. But it appears also in a different form and light to a Turk in Cyprus than to a Greek, to a Karen in Burma than to a Burmese, to a Tiv in Nigeria than to a Hausa, because membership in a minor group places one in a different position than does membership in a major one, even within a single system.[15] The so-called pariah communities of "foreign" traders that are found in so many of the new states—the Lebanese in West Africa, the Indians in East Africa, the Chinese in Southeast Asia and, in a somewhat different way, the Marwaris in South India—live in an altogether different social universe, so far as the problem of the maintenance of a recognized identity is concerned, than do the settled agricultural groups, no matter how small and insignificant, in the same societies. The network of primordial alliance and opposition is a dense, intricate, but yet precisely articulated one, the product, in most cases, of centuries of gradual crystallization. The unfamiliar civil state, born yesterday from the meager remains of an exhausted colonial regime, is superimposed upon this fine-spun and lovingly conserved texture of pride and suspicion and must somehow contrive to weave it into the fabric of modern politics.

III

THE reduction of primordial sentiments to civil order is rendered more difficult, however, by the fact that political modernization tends initially not to quiet such sentiments but to quicken them. The transfer of sovereignty from a colonial regime to an independent one is more than a mere shift of power from foreign hands to native ones; it is a transformation of the whole pattern of political life, a metamorphosis of subjects into citizens. Colonial governments, like the aristocratic governments of premodern Europe in whose image they were fashioned, are aloof and un-

15. For a brief discussion of this problem with respect to Indonesia, see C. Geertz, "The Javanese Village," in G. W. Skinner (ed.), *Local, Ethnic and National Loyalties in Village Indonesia,* Yale University, Southeast Asia Studies, Cultural Report Series, No. 8, 1959, pp. 34–41.

responsive; they stand outside the societies they rule, and act upon them arbitrarily, unevenly, and unsystematically. But the governments of the new states, though oligarchic, are popular and attentive; they are located in the midst of the societies they rule, and as they develop act upon them in progressively more continuous, comprehensive, and purposeful manner. For the Ashanti cocoa farmer, the Gujerati shopkeeper, or the Malayan Chinese tin miner, his country's attainment of political independence is also his own attainment, willy-nilly, of modern political status, no matter how culturally traditional he may remain nor how ineffectively and anachronistically the new state may in practice function. He now becomes an integral part of an autonomous and differentiated polity that begins to touch his life at every point except the most strictly private. "The same people which has hitherto been kept as far as possible from government affairs must now be drawn into them," the Indonesian nationalist Sjahrir wrote on the eve of World War II, defining exactly the character of the "revolution" that was in fact to follow in the Indies over the next decade—"That people must be made politically conscious. Its political interest must be stimulated and maintained."[16]

This thrusting of a modern political consciousness upon the mass of a still largely unmodernized population does indeed tend to lead to the stimulation and maintenance of a very intense popular interest in the affairs of government. But, as a primordially based "corporate feeling of oneness," remains for many the *fons et origo* of legitimate authority—the meaning of the term "self" in "self-rule"—much of this interest takes the form of an obsessive concern with the relation of one's tribe, region, sect, or whatever to a center of power that, while growing rapidly more active, is not easily either insulated from the web of primordial attachments, as was the remote colonial regime, or assimilated to them as are the workaday authority systems of the "little community." Thus, it is the very process of the formation of a sovereign civil state that, among other things, stimulates sentiments of parochialism, communalism, racialism, and so on, because it introduces into society a valuable new prize over which to fight and a frightening new force with which to contend.[17] The doctrines of the nationalist

16. S. Sjahrir, *Out of Exile*, New York, John Day, 1949, p. 215.
17. As Talcott Parsons has pointed out, power, defined as the capacity to mobilize social resources for social goals, is not a "zero-sum" quantity within

propagandists to the contrary notwithstanding, Indonesian regionalism, Malayan racialism, Indian linguism, or Nigerian tribalism
are, in their political dimensions, not so much the heritage of
colonial divide-and-rule policies as they are products of the replacement of a colonial regime by an independent, domestically an-
chored, purposeful unitary state. Though they rest on historically
developed distinctions, some of which colonial rule helped to
accentuate (and others of which it helped to moderate), they are
part and parcel of the very process of the creation of a new polity
and a new citizenship.

For a telling example in this connection one may look to Ceylon,
which, having made one of the quietest of entries into the family
of new states is now the scene of one of its noisiest communal up-
roars. Ceylonese independence was won largely without struggle; in
fact, without even very much effort. There was no embittered
nationalist mass movement, as in most of the other new states, no
loudly passionate hero-leader, no diehard colonial opposition, no
violence, no arrests—no revolution really, for the 1947 transfer of
sovereignty consisted of the replacement of conservative, moderate,
aloof British civil servants by conservative, moderate, aloof British-
educated Ceylonese notables who, to more nativistic eyes at least,
"resembled the former colonial rulers in everything but the color
of their skin."[18] The revolution was to come later, nearly a decade
after formal independence, and the British governor's valedictory
expression of "profound satisfaction that Ceylon has reached its
goal of freedom without strife or bloodshed along the path of
peaceful negotiation,"[19] proved to be somewhat premature: in 1956

---

a social system, but, like wealth, is generated by the working of particular, in
this case political rather than economic, institutions. "The Distribution of
Power in American Society," *World Politics*, 10:123–143, 1957. The growth
of a modern state within a traditional social context represents, therefore,
not merely the shifting or transfer of a fixed quantity of power between groups
in such a manner that aggregatively the gains of certain groups or individuals
match the losses of others, but rather the creation of a new and more efficient
machine for the production of power itself, and thus an increase in the general
political capacity of the society. This is a much more genuinely "revolutionary"
phenomena than a mere redistribution, however radical, of power within a
given system.

18. D. K. Rangenekar, "The Nationalist Revolution in Ceylon," *Pacific
Affairs*, 33: 361–374, 1960.

19. Quoted in M. Weiner, "The Politics of South Asia," in G. Almond
and J. Coleman, *The Politics of the Developing Areas*, Princeton, N.J., Princeton University Press, 1960, pp. 153–246.

wild Tamil-Sinhalese riots claimed more than a hundred lives, in 1958, perhaps as many as two thousand.

The country, 70 per cent Sinhalese, 23 per cent Tamil, has been marked by a certain amount of group tension for centuries.[20] But such tension has taken the distinctively modern form of an implacable, comprehensive, and ideologically instigated mass hatred mainly since the late S. W. R. D. Bandaranaike was swept into the premiership on a sudden wave of Sinhalese cultural, religious and linguistic revivalism in 1956. Himself Oxford-educated, vaguely Marxist and essentially secularist in civil matters, Bandaranaike undermined the authority of the English-speaking (and bi-ethnic Colombo) patriciate by appealing openly, and one suspects somewhat cynically, to the primordial sentiments of the Sinhalese, promising a "Sinhala-only" linguistic policy, a place of pride for Buddhism and the Buddhist clergy, and a radical reversal of the supposed policy of "pampering" the Tamils, as well as rejecting Western dress for the traditional "cloth and banian" of the Sinhalese countryman.[21] And if, as one of his more uncritical apologists claims, his "supreme ambition" was not "to set up an outmoded, parochial, racialist government," but to "stabilize democracy and convert his country into a modern welfare state based on Nehru-style socialism,"[22] he soon found himself the helpless victim of a rising tide of primordial fervor, and his death, after thirty hectic and frustrating months in power, at the hands of an obscurely motivated Buddhist monk was merely that much more ironic.

The first definite move toward a resolute, popularly based, social reform government led, therefore, not to heightened national unity, but to the reverse—increased linguistic, racial, regional, and religious parochialism, a strange dialectic whose actual workings

20. About half the Tamils are stateless "Indian Tamils"—that is, individuals transported to Ceylon in the nineteeth century to work on British tea estates, and now rejected as citizens by India on the ground that they live in Ceylon, and by Ceylon on the ground that they are but sojourners from India.

21. Commenting on the spectacular failure of Sir Ivor Jennings's 1954 prediction that Bandaranaike was unlikely to win the leadership of the nationalist movement because he was a "political Buddhist," having been educated as a Christian, Rangenekar shrewdly remarks, "In an Asian setting a Western-educated politician who renounces his Westernization and upholds indigenous culture and civilization wields a much greater influence than the most dynamic local thoroughbred can ever hope to do." Rangenekar, *op. cit.*

22. *Ibid.*

have been well described by Wriggins.[23] The institution of universal suffrage made the temptation to court the masses by appealing to traditional loyalties virtually irresistible, and led Bandaranaike and his followers to gamble, unsuccessfully as it turned out, on being able to tune primordial sentiments up before elections and down after them. The modernizing efforts of his government in the fields of health, education, administration, and so on, threatened the status of consequential rural personages—monks, ayurvedic doctors, village schoolteachers, local officials—who were thereby rendered that much more nativistic and insistent upon communal tokens of reassurance in exchange for their political support. The search for a common cultural tradition to serve as the content of the country's identity as a nation now that it had become, somehow, a state, led only to the revivification of ancient, and better forgotten, Tamil-Sinhalese treacheries, atrocities, insults, and wars. The eclipse of the Western-educated urban elite, within which class loyalties and old-school ties tended to override primordial differences, removed one of the few important points of amicable contact between the two communities. The first stirrings of fundamental economic change aroused fears that the position of the industrious, frugal, aggressive Tamils would be strengthened at the expense of the less methodical Sinhalese. The intensified competition for government jobs, the increasing importance of the vernacular press, and even government-instituted land-reclamation programs—because they threatened to alter population distribution and so communal representation in the parliament—all acted in a similarly provocative manner. Ceylon's aggravated primordial problem is not a mere legacy, an inherited impediment to her political, social, and economic modernization; it is a direct and immediate reflex of her first serious—if still rather ineffective—attempt to achieve such modernization.

And this dialectic, variously expressed, is a generic characteristic of new state politics. In Indonesia, the establishment of an indigenous unitary state made the fact that the thinly populated but mineral-rich Outer Islands produced the bulk of the country's foreign-exchange earnings, while densely populated, resource-poor

23. H. Wriggins, "Impediments to Unity in New Nations—the Case of Ceylon," unpublished MS.

Java consumed the bulk of its income, painfully apparent in a way it could never become in the colonial era, and a pattern of regional jealousy developed and hardened to the point of armed revolt.[24] In Ghana, hurt Ashanti pride burst into open separatism when, in order to accumulate development funds, Nkrumah's new national government fixed the cocoa price lower than what Ashanti cocoa growers wished it to be.[25] In Morocco, Riffian Berbers, offended when their substantial military contribution to the struggle for independence was not followed by greater governmental assistance in the form of schools, jobs, improved communications facilities, and so on, revived a classic pattern of tribal insolence—refusal to pay taxes, boycott of market places, retreat to a predatory mountain life—in order to gain Rabat's regard.[26] In Jordan, Abdullah's desperate attempt to strengthen his newly sovereign civil state through the annexation of Cis-Jordan, negotiation with Israel, and modernization of the army provoked his assassination by an ethnically humiliated pan-Arab Palestinian.[27] Even in those new states where such discontent has not progressed to the point of open dissidence, there has almost universally arisen around the developing struggle for governmental power as such a broad penumbra of primordial strife. Alongside of, and interacting with, the usual politics of party and parliament, cabinet and bureaucracy, or monarch and army, there exists, nearly everywhere, a sort of parapolitics of clashing public identities and quickening ethnocratic aspirations.

What is more, this parapolitical warfare seems to have its own characteristic battlegrounds; there are certain specific institutional

24. H. Fieth, "Indonesia," in G. McT. Kahin (ed.), *Government and Politics of Southeast Asia*, Ithaca, N.Y., Cornell University Press, 1959, pp. 155–238; and G. McT. Kahin (ed.), *Major Governments of Asia*, Ithaca, N.Y., Cornell University Press, 1958, pp. 471–592. This is not to say that the crystallization of regional enmities was the sole motivating force in the Padang rebellion, nor that the Java-Outer Islands contrast was the only axis of opposition. In all the quoted examples in this essay, the desire to be recognized as a responsible agent whose wishes, acts, hopes, and opinions matter is intertwined with the more familiar desires for wealth, power, prestige, and so on. Simple primordial determinism is no more defensible a position than economic determinism.

25. D. Apter, *The Gold Coast in Transition*, Princeton, N.J., Princeton University Press, 1955, p. 68.

26. W. Lewis, "Feuding and Social Change in Morocco," *Journal of Conflict Resolution*, 5:43–54, 1961.

27. R. Nolte, "The Arab Solidarity Agreement," American University Field Staff Letter, Southwest Asia Series, 1957.

contexts outside the customary arenas of political combat into which it has a strong inclination to settle. Though primordial issues do, of course, turn up from time to time in parliamentary debates, cabinet deliberations, judicial decisions and, more often, in electoral campaigns, they show a persistent tendency to emerge in purer, more explicit, and more virulent form in some places where other sorts of social issues do not ordinarily, or at least so often or so acutely, appear.

One of the most obvious of these is the school system. Linguistic conflicts, in particular, tend to emerge in the form of school crises—witness the fierce dispute between Malay and Chinese teachers' unions over the degree to which Malay should replace Chinese in Chinese schools in Malaya, the three-way guerrilla war between partisans of English, Hindi, and various local vernaculars as instruction media in India, or the bloody riots staged by Bengali-speaking university students to block the imposition of Urdu by West on East Pakistan. But religious issues, too, tend to penetrate educational contexts quite readily. In Moslem countries there is the enduring question of the reform of traditional Koranic schools toward Western forms; in the Philippines there is the clash between the American-introduced tradition of the secular public school and the intensified clerical effort to increase the teaching of religion in such schools; and in Madras there are the Dravidian separatists announcing sanctimoniously that "education must be free from political, religious or communal bias," by which they in fact mean that it "must not stress Hindu writings such as the epic Ramayana."[28] Even largely regional struggles tend to engulf the school system: in Indonesia the rise of provincial discontent was accompanied by a competitive multiplication of local institutions of higher learning to the point where, despite the extreme shortage of qualified instructors, there is now a faculty in nearly every major region of the country, monuments to past resentments and perhaps cradles for future ones; and a similar pattern may now be developing in Nigeria. If the general strike is the classical political expression of class warfare, and the *coup d'état* of the struggle between militarism and parliamentarianism, then the school crisis is

28. P. Talbot, "Raising a Cry for Secession," American University Field Staff Letter, South Asia Series, 1957.

perhaps becoming the classical political—or parapolitical—expression of the clash of primordial loyalties.

There are a number of other poles around which parapolitical vortices tend to form, but so far as the literature is concerned they have been more noted in passing than analyzed in detail. Social statistics, for example. In Lebanon there has not been a census since 1932, for fear that taking one would reveal such changes in the religious composition of the population as to make the marvelously intricate political arrangements designed to balance sectarian interests unviable. In India, with its national language problem, just what constitutes a Hindi speaker has been a matter of some rather acrimonious dispute, because it depends upon the rules of counting: Hindi enthusiasts use census figures to prove that as many as a half of India's people speak "Hindi" (including Urdu and Punjabi), while anti-Hindiists force the figure down as low as 30 per cent by considering such matters as script differences, and evidently even religious affiliation of the speaker, as linguistically significant. Then, too, there is the closely related problem of what, in connection with the strange fact that according to the 1941 census of India there were 25 million tribal peoples but in the 1951 one only 1.7 million, Weiner has aptly called "genocide by census redefinition."[29] In Morocco, published figures for the percentage of the population that is Berber run all the way from 35 to 60 per cent, and some nationalist leaders would like to believe, or have others believe, that the Berbers are a French invention altogether.[30] Statistics, real or fancied, concerning the ethnic composition of the civil service are a favorite weapon of primordial demagogues virtually everywhere, being particularly effective where a number of local officials are members of a group other than the one they administrate. And in Indonesia a leading newspaper was

29. M. Weiner, "Community Associations in Indian Politics," unpublished MS. The reverse process, "ethnogenesis by census redefinition," also occurs, as when in Libreville, the Gabon capital, Togolese and Dahomeans are lumped statistically into a new category, "the Popo," or in Northern Rhodesia copperbelt towns Henga, Tonga, Tambuka, and so on, are "by common consent" grouped together as Nyasalanders, these manufactured groupings then taking on a real "ethnic" existence. I. Wallerstein, "Ethnicity and National Integration in West Africa," Cahiers d'etudes africaines, 3: 129–139 October, 1960.

30. The 35 per cent figure can be found in N. Barbour (ed.), A Survey of North West Africa, New York, Oxford University Press, 1959, p. 79; the 60 per cent figure in D. Rustow, "The Politics of the Near East," in Almond and Coleman, op. cit., pp. 369–453.

banned, at the height of the regionalist crisis, for printing, in mock·
innocence, a simple bar graph depicting export earnings and government expenditure by province.

Dress (in Burma hundreds of frontier tribesmen brought to
Rangoon for Union day to improve their patriotism are cannily
sent home with gifts of Burmese clothing), historiography (in
Nigeria a sudden proliferation of tendentious tribal histories
threatens to strengthen the already very powerful centrifugal tendencies plaguing the country), and the official insignia of public
authority (in Ceylon, Tamils have refused to use automobile
license plates marked with Sinhala characters, and in South India
they have painted over Hindi railroad signs) are other as yet but
impressionistically observed spheres of parapolitical controversy.[31]
So, also, is the rapidly expanding complex of tribal unions, caste
organizations, ethnic fraternities, regional associations, and religious sodalities that seems to be accompanying urbanization in
virtually all the new states, and has made the major cities in some
of them—Lagos, Beirut, Bombay, Medan—caldrons of communal
tension.[32] But, details aside, the point is that there swirls around
the emerging governmental institutions of the new states, and
the specialized politics they tend to support, a whole host of self-
reinforcing whirlpools of primordial discontent, and that this parapolitical maelstrom is in great part an outcome—to continue the
metaphor, a backwash—of that process of political development
itself. The growing capacity of the state to mobilize social resources
for public ends, its expanding power, roils primordial sentiments
because, given the doctrine that legitimate authority is but an
extension of the inherent moral coerciveness such sentiments
possess, to permit oneself to be ruled by men of other tribes, other
races, or other religions is to submit not merely to oppression but
to degradation—to exclusion from the moral community as a lesser
order of being whose opinions, attitudes, wishes, and so on, simply

31. On Burmese dress, see H. Tinker, *The Union of Burma*, New York,
Oxford University Press, 1957, p. 184. On Nigerian tribal histories, see Coleman, *op. cit.*, pp. 327–328. On Ceylonese license plates, see Wriggins, "Cey·
lon's Time of Troubles, 1956–8," *Far Eastern Survey*, 28: 33–38 (1959). On
Hindi railroad signs, see Weiner, "Community Associations . . . ," *op. cit.*

32. For a general discussion of the role of voluntary associations in the
urbanization process in modernizing societies, see Wallerstein, "The Emergence of Two West African Nations," *op. cit.*, pp. 144–230.

do not fully count, as those of children, the simple-minded and the insane do not fully count in the eyes of those who regard themselves as mature, intelligent, and sane.

Though it can be moderated, this tension between primordial sentiments and civil politics probably cannot be entirely dissolved. The power of the "givens" of place, tongue, blood, looks, and way-of-life to shape an individual's notion of who, at bottom, he is and with whom, indissolubly, he belongs is rooted in the non-rational foundations of personality. And, once established, some degree of involvement of this unreflective sense of collective self-hood in the steadily broadening political process of the national state is certain, because that process seems to touch on such an extraordinarily wide range of matters. Thus, what the new states—or their leaders—must somehow contrive to do as far as primordial attachments are concerned is not, as they have so often tried to do, wish them out of existence by belittling them or even denying their reality, but domesticate them. They must reconcile them with the unfolding civil order by divesting them of their legitimizing force with respect to governmental authority, by neutralizing the apparatus of the state in relationship to them, and by channeling discontent arising out of their dislocation into properly political rather than parapolitical forms of expression. This goal, too, is not fully achievable or at least has never yet been achieved—even in Mr. Ambedkar's Canada and Switzerland (the less said of South Africa in this connection, the better) with their admitted "genius to unite." But it is relatively so, and it is upon the possibility of such relative achievement that the hope of the new states to turn the attack upon their integrity and their legitimacy by un-fettered primordial enthusiasms rests. As with industrialization, urbanization, restratification, and the various other social and cultural "revolutions" these states seem feted to undergo, the containment of diverse primordial communities under a single sovereignty promises to tax the political capacity of their peoples to its utmost limits—in some cases, no doubt, beyond them.

IV

THIS "integrative revolution" has, of course, already begun, and a desperate search for ways and means to create a more perfect union is everywhere underway. But it has merely begun and just

got under way, so that if one surveys the new states on a broadly
comparative basis, one is confronted with a bewildering picture of
diverse institutional and ideological responses to what, for all its
variation in outward form, is essentially a common problem—the
political normalization of primordial discontent. The new states
are, today, rather like naïve or apprentice painters or poets or
composers, seeking their own proper style, their own distinctive
mode of solution for the difficulties posed by their medium. Imi-
tative, poorly organized, eclectic, opportunistic, subject to fads,
ill-defined, uncertain, they are exceedingly difficult to order typo-
logically, either in classical categories or invented ones, in the same
paradoxical way that it is usually so much more difficult to classify
immature artists firmly into schools or traditions than it is mature
ones who have found their own unique style and identity. Indonesia, India, Nigeria, and the rest share, in the matter at hand,
only a predicament; but a predicament that is one of the main
stimuli to political creativity for them, pressing them on to a rest-
less experimentation in order to find ways to extricate themselves
from it and triumph over it. Again, this is not to say that all this
creativity will ultimately be successful; there are *manqué* states as
there are *manqué* artists, as France perhaps demonstrates. But it is
the recalcitrance of primordial issues that, among other things,
keeps the process of incessant political, and even constitutional,
innovation going, and gives to any attempt at systematic classification of new state polities a radically provisional, if not simply premature, quality.

An attempt to order the various governmental arrangements
now emerging in the new states as means for coping with problems
arising from linguistic, racial, and so on, heterogeneity must begin,
therefore, with a simple empirical review of a number of such arrangements, a mere setting out in model form of existing experiments. From such a review it should be possible to derive a sense
of at least the *ranges* of variation involved, a notion of the general
dimensions of the social field within which these arrangements are
taking shape. Typologizing becomes, in this approach, a matter,
not of devising constructed types, ideal or otherwise, which will
isolate fundamental constancies of structure amid the confusion
of phenomenal variation, but of determining the limits with which
such variation takes place, the domain over which it plays. Here, a
sense of such ranges, dimensions, limits, and domains can perhaps

best be conveyed, in a kaleidoscopic sort of way, by the rapid presentation of a series of snapshot pictures of the "integrative revolution" as it seems to be proceeding in several selected new states showing different concrete patterns of primordial diversity and different modes of political response to those patterns. Indonesia, Malaya, Burma, India, Lebanon, Morocco, and Nigeria, culturally distinct and geographically scattered, are as appropriate subjects as any for this type of flying survey of divided nations en route— *ex hypothesi*—to unity.[33]

INDONESIA

Until about the beginning of 1957, the regional tension between Java and the Outer Islands was kept in bounds by a combination of the continuing momentum of revolutionary solidarity, a broadly representative multiparty system, and a characteristically Indonesian bisection of paramount executive power in an institution called the Dwi-Tunggal—loosely, "dual leadership"—in which the two veteran nationalist leaders, Sukarno, a Javanese, and Moham-

33. As, with the partial exception of Indonesia, all the following summaries are based on the literature rather than on field research, a full bibliography of sources would obviously be too lengthy for inclusion in an essay. I therefore list below only those works upon which I have relied rather heavily.

The best general survey including the countries discussed is Almond and Coleman, *op. cit.*, and for Asia I have found the two previously cited symposia edited by Kahin, *Governments and Politics of Southeast Asia* and *Major Governments of Asia*, most useful. Emerson, *op. cit.*, also offers some valuable comparative materials.

INDONESIA: H. Fieth, *The Wilopo Cabinet, 1952–1953*, Ithaca, N.Y., Southeast Asia Program of Cornell University, Monograph Series, 1958; H. Fieth, *The Indonesian Elections of 1955;* Ithaca, N.Y., Southeast Asia Program of Cornell University, Interim Reports Series, 1957; G. McT. Kahin, *Nationalism and Revolution in Indonesia*, Ithaca, N.Y., Cornell University Press, 1952. G. Pauker, "The Role of Political Organization in Indonesia," *Far Eastern Survey*, 27: 129–142, 1958; G. W. Skinner, *Local, Ethnic and National Loyalties in Village Indonesia*, *op. cit.*

MALAYA: M. Freedman, "The Growth of a Plural Society in Malaya," *Pacific Affairs* 33: 158–167, 1960; N. Ginsburg and C. F. Roberts Jr., *Malaya*, Seattle, University of Washington Press, 1958; J. N. Parmer, "Malaya's First Year of Independence, *Far Eastern Survey*, 27: 161–168, 1958; T. E. Smith, "The Malayan Elections of 1959," *Pacific Affairs*, 33: 38–47, March, 1960.

BURMA: L. Bigelow, "The 1960 Elections in Burma," *Far Eastern Survey*, 29:70–74, 1960; G. Fairbairn, "Some Minority Problems in Burma," *Pacific Affairs*, 30:299–311, 1957; J. Silverstein, "The Federal Dilemma in Burma," *Far Eastern Survey*, 28:97–105, J. Silverstein, "Politics in the Shan State: The Question of the Secession from the Union of Burma," *The Journal of Asian*

med Hatta, a Sumatran, shared primacy as president and vice-president of the Republic. Since then, the solidarity has faded, the party system collapsed, and the Dwi-Tunggal split. Despite the effective military suppression of the regional rebellion of 1958, and despite Sukarno's feverish attempts to focus the government on his person as the incarnation of "the spirit of '45," the political equilibrium thus lost has not been restored, and the new nation has become an almost classic case of integrative failure. With every step toward modernity has come increased regional discontent; with each increase in regional discontent has come a new revelation of political incapacity; and with each new revelation of political incapacity has come a loss of political nerve and a more desperate resort to an unstable amalgam of military coercion and ideological revivalism.

It was the first (and, thus far, the only) general elections of 1955 that, by completing the general outlines of a parliamentary system, made it inescapably apparent to reflective Indonesians that they had either to find some way of solving their problems within the framework of the modern civil order they had almost reluc-

Studies, 18:43–58, 1958; H. Tinker, *op. cit.*

INDIA: Ambedkar, *op. cit.*; S. Harrison, *India, op. cit.*; R. L. Park, and I. Tinker (eds.), *Leadership and Political Institutions in India*, Princeton, N.J.; Princeton University Press, 1959; *Report of the States Reorganization Commission*, New Delhi, Republic of India, 1955; M. Weiner, *Party Politics in India*, Princeton, N.J., Princeton University Press, 1957.

LEBANON: V. Ayoub, "Political Structure of a Middle East Community: A Druze Village in Mount Lebanon," unpublished Ph.D. Thesis, Harvard University, 1955; P. Rondot, *Les Institutions politiques du Liban*, Paris, Institut d'Etudes de L'Orient Contemporain, 1957; N. A. Zaideh, *Syria and Lebanon*, London, Ernest Benn, 1957; N. A. Zaideh, "The Lebanese Elections, 1960," *Middle East Journal*, 14:367–381, 1960.

MOROCCO: D. Ashford, *Political Change in Morocco*, Princeton, N.J., Princeton University Press, 1961; N. Barbour (ed.), *A Survey of Northwest Africa*, New York, Oxford University Press, 1959; H. Favre, "Le Maroc A L'Epreuve de la Démocratisation," unpublished MS., 1958; J. and S. Lacouture, *Le Maroc A L'Epreuve*, Paris, Editions du Seuil, 1958; W. Lewis, "Rural Administration in Morocco," *Middle East Journal*, 14:45–54, 1960; W. Lewis, "Feuding and Social Change in Morocco," *The Journal of Conflict Resolution*, 5:43–54, 1961.

NIGERIA: J. Coleman, *op. cit.*; *Report of the Commission Appointed to Enquire into the Fears of Minorities and the Means of Allaying Them*, London, Her Majesty's Stationery Office, 1958; H. and M. Smythe, *The New Nigerian Elite*, Stanford, Calif., Stanford University Press, 1960.

For current events I have found the American University Field Staff letters, particularly those on Indonesia (W. Hanna), Malaya (W. Hanna), India (P. Talbot), Morocco (C. Gallagher), and Nigeria (R. Frodin), very useful.

tantly created or face a rising crescendo of primordial discontent
and parapolitical conflict. Having been expected to clear the air,
the elections only stirred it. They shifted the political center of
gravity away from the Dwi-Tunggal toward the parties. They
crystallized the popular strength of the Communist Party, which
not only gained some 16 per cent of the total vote, but drew nearly
90 per cent of its support from Java, thus fusing regional and ideological tensions. They dramatized the fact that the interest of some
of the more important centers of power in the society—the army,
the Chinese, certain Outer Island export traders, and so on—were
not adequately represented in the formal political system. And
they shifted the basis of qualification for political leadership away
from revolutionary distinction toward mass appeal. At once the
elections demanded that, if the existing civil order were to be
maintained and developed, a whole new set of relationships among
the president, vice-president, parliament, and cabinet be worked
out; that an aggressive, well-organized totalitarian party hostile to
the very conception of democratic, multiparty politics be contained; that important groups outside the parliamentary framework
be brought into effective relation to it; and that a new basis for
elite solidarity other than the shared experiences of 1945–1949 be
found. Given extremely intractable economic problems, a cold-war
international environment, and a large number of long-standing
personal vendettas among the highly placed, it would perhaps have
been surprising had this multiple demand been met. But there is
no reason to believe that given the requisite political talents, it
could not have been.

In any case, it was not. By the end of 1956 the always delicate
relationship between Sukarno and Hatta became so strained that
the latter resigned, an action that in essence withdrew the stamp
of legitimacy from the central government so far as many of the
leading military, financial, political, and religious groups in the
Outer Islands were concerned. The duumvirate had been the symbolic, and to a great extent the real, guarantee of the recognition
of the various Outer Island peoples as full and equal partners
with the so much more numerous Javanese in the Republic, a
quasi-constitutional warranty that the Javanese tail would not be
permitted to wag the Indonesian dog. Sukarno, part Javanese
mystic and part inveterate eclectic, and Hatta, part Sumatran puri-
tan and part shirt-sleeve administrator, supplemented one another
not only politically but primordially. Sukarno summed up the

syncretic high culture of the elusive Javanese; Hatta, the Islamic mercantilism of the less subtle Outer Islanders. The major political parties—particularly the Communists, fusing Marxist ideology with traditional Javanese "folk religion," and the Moslem Masjumi, which having gained nearly half of its popular vote in the more orthodox regions outside Java became their major spokesman —aligned themselves accordingly. Thus, when the vice-president resigned and the president moved to become, under his conception of a back-to-1945 (that is, pre-elections) "guided democracy," the sole axis of Indonesian national life, the Republic's political balance was upset and the advance toward regional disaffection entered its radical phase.

Since then, spasmodic violence has alternated with a frantic search for political panaceas. Abortive coups, misfired assassination attempts, and unsuccessful insurrections have followed one after the other, punctuated by an astounding wealth of ideological and institutional experiments. New Life movements have given way to Guided Democracy movements, and Guided Democracy movements to "Back to the 1945 Constitution" movements, while governmental structures—national councils, state planning commissions, constitutional conventions, and so on—have multiplied like weeds in a neglected garden. But from all this nervous tinkering and breathless sloganeering no form competent to contain the country's diversity has appeared, because such random improvisation represents not a realistic search for a solution to the nation's integrative problems but a desperately laid smoke screen behind which to hide a growing conviction of impending political catastrophe. For the moment, a new, *de facto* duumvirate divides leadership—Sukarno, calling ever more shrilly for a renewal of the "revolutionary spirit of unity," and Lieutenant General A. H. Nasution, Defense Minister and former Army Chief of Staff (and another colorless Sumatran professional), directing the military in its expanded role as a quasi-civil service. But their relationship to each other, as well as the extent of their effective power, remains, like just about everything else in Indonesian political life, undetermined.

MALAYA

In Malaya, the striking thing is the degree to which the over-all integration of the diverse groups in a rigidly multiracial society is taking place not so much in terms of state structure as such, but of that much more recent political invention, party organization. It is the Alliance, a confederation of the United Malays National Organization, the Malayan Chinese Association, and the less important Malayan Indian Congress, within which primordial conflicts are being informally and realistically adjusted and where the strong centrifugal tendencies, as intense as perhaps any state—new, old, or middle-aged—has ever faced, are, so far, being effectively absorbed, deflected, and contained. Formed in 1952, at the height of the terrorist "emergency," by conservative, English-educated, upper-class elements in the Malay and Chinese communities (the Indians, never quite certain which way to jump, joined a year or two later), the Alliance is one of the most remarkable examples of the successful practice of the art of the impossible in the whole sphere of new-state politics—a federated, noncommunal party of subparties themselves frankly, explicitly, and on occasion enthusiastically communal in appeal, set in a context of primordial suspicion and hostility that would make the Habsburg Empire seem like Denmark or Australia. On the mere surface of things, it ought not to work.

The important question is, anyway, whether it will continue to work. Malaya has been independent only since mid-1957, has benefited from relatively favorable economic conditions, from—the Communist insurrection aside—a fairly smooth transfer of sovereignty and the continuing *présence anglaise* this has made possible, and the ability of a conservative, somewhat rationalistic oligarchy to convince the mass of the population that it is a more suitable vehicle for their aspirations than the left-wing, emotionally populist sort of leadership that characterizes most of the other new states. Is Alliance rule merely the lull before the storm as was United National Party rule, which it rather resembles, in Ceylon? Is it destined to weaken and disintegrate when the social and economic seas roughen as did the Indonesian Dwi-Tunggal–multiparty system? Is it, in a word, too good to last?

The omens are mixed. In the first general election, held prior to revolution, the Alliance captured 80 per cent of the popular vote and 51 of the 52 elected seats in the federal legislative council, to become virtually the sole legitimate heir to the colonial regime; but in the 1959 elections, the first held subsequent to independence, it lost a good deal of ground to more simply communal

parties, its popular vote falling to 51 per cent and its seats to 73 of
103. The Malay sector, the UMNO, was weakened by the unexpected sweep of the pious, rural, heavily Malay northeast by an
intensely communal party calling for an Islamic theocratic state,
"the restoration of Malay sovereignty," and "Greater Indonesia."
The Chinese and Indian wings were undercut by Marxist parties
in the large towns along the tin- and rubber-rich central west coast,
where large numbers of new, lower-class Chinese and Indian voters
had entered the rolls under the liberalized post-independence citizenship laws, the Marxism adapting itself, here as elsewhere, to
primordial loyalties with little difficulty. Buffeted by these losses—
which first became apparent in the state elections held a couple of
months prior to the federal ones—the Alliance in fact came very
close to splitting altogether. The losses of the UMNO tempted
younger, less conservative elements in the MCA to press for a
greater number of Chinese candidacies, for an explicit condemna-
tion by the Alliance of Malay racialism, and for a review of state
educational policy with respect to the language problem in Chinese
schools. Hothead elements in the UMNO responded in kind, and
though the rift was patched, or patched over, in time for the elections, several of the younger leaders of the MCA resigned, and the
UMNO girded itself to expel primordial "agitators" in its own
midst.

Thus, although as in Indonesia, the holding of general elections
brought latent primordial issues into such a focus that they had to
be faced directly rather than concealed behind a facade of nationalist rhetoric, in Malaya political talents seem so far to have been
rather more competent to this task. Though the Alliance is less
absolutely dominant and perhaps somewhat less integrated than
it was in the immediate post-independence period, it is still quite
comfortably in power and still an effective civil framework within
which very intense primordial issues can be adjusted and contained
rather than allowed to run free in parapolitical confusion. The
pattern that seems to be developing, and perhaps crystallizing, is
one in which a comprehensive national party, with its three sub-
parts or subparties, comes almost to comprise the state and is
multiply assailed by a field of small parties—by class parties for
being too communal, and communal parties for not being communal enough (and by both for being "undemocratic" and "reactionary")—each of which is trying to knock chips off one or

another part of it by attacking the points of strain that develop within it as it functions and by appealing more openly to primordial sentiments. The intricate inner working of the Alliance as it endeavors to hold the vital center against efforts from all directions to undermine its basic source of strength—a matter-of-fact, *quid-pro-quo*, all-in-the-same-boat political understanding among Malay, Chinese, and Indian leaders—is thus the quintessence of the integrative revolution as it is proceeding in Malaya.[34]

BURMA

In Burma, the case is almost diametrically opposite to the Malayan.[35] Although again, and unlike Indonesia, a comprehensive national party (U Nu's "clean faction" of the Anti-Fascist People's Freedom League) governs a formally federal state with only weak, if bitter, opposition, its power is mainly based on a direct appeal to the cultural pride of the Burmans (that is, speakers of Burmese), while the minorities, some of whom helped keep the country in a multisided civil war for the first few years after independence, are catered to by a rather intricate and highly peculiar constitutional system that protects them in theory against the Burman dominance that the party system tends to produce in fact. Here the government itself is to a very great extent the obvious agency of a single, central primordial group, and it is faced, therefore, with a very serious problem of maintaining legitimacy in the eyes of members of peripheral groups—more than one-third of the population—who are naturally inclined to see it as alien, a problem it has attempted to solve largely by a combination of elaborate legal gestures of reassurance and a good deal of aggressive assimilationism.

Briefly, the constitutional system designed to allay minority

34. If it is finally realized, the projected Malaysian Federation linking Malaya with Singapore, Brunei, North Borneo, and Sarawak will, of course, present this pragmatic approach the adjustment of primordial conflict with a whole new range of problems, perhaps even more difficult than those it has already faced, to deal with.

35. The following paragraphs were written prior to the second, seemingly more permanent, Army takeover in Burma, a takeover at least in part stimulated by growing primordial conflicts, especially with respect to the Shans. It remains to be seen what approach the Army takes to the ethnic diversity problem in Burma and whether it proves any more successful in this regard than U Nu and the AFPFL.

fears consists of—to date—six juridically nonuniform "states," demarcated largely along regional-linguistic-cultural lines and possessing dissimilar formal powers. Some states have a—surely nominal—right of secession; others not. Each state has somewhat different electoral arrangements, and controls its own elementary schools. The elaboration of state governmental structure varies from the Chin, which has hardly any local autonomy whatever, to the Shan, where traditional "feudal" chiefs have been able to maintain a goodly number of their traditional rights; while Burma proper is not viewed as a constituent state within the Union at all, but as virtually indistinguishable from it. The degree to which territorial boundaries match primordial realities varies—with the Karen the most chronically discontented and the small Kayah State evidently resting on the politically convenient invention of a "Red Karen" race. From each of these states a delegation is elected to the upper house of the bicameral Union legislature, the Chamber of Nationalities, which is heavily weighted in favor of the minority peoples. In the Union government this chamber is overshadowed by the popularly chosen lower house, the Chamber of Deputies, but as each state delegation to it sits, along with the lower-house representatives from its state, to form the State Council that governs the state, it has significant local importance. Further, the head of the state (that is, of the State Council) is appointed at the same time to be minister for the state in the Union government, and constitutional amendments demand two-thirds approval of both houses, so that the minorities are given at least a formal check on the powers of the government and the lower chamber to which it is responsible. And finally, the presidency of the Union, a largely ceremonial office, is rotated, by informal agreement rather than explicit constitutional provision, among ethnic groups.

It is within this finely wrought constitutional structure, which so artfully blurs the distinction between the Union and its constituent members at precisely the time it seems to be formalizing it most exactly, that the vigorously assimilationist policies of the AFPFL are pursued. This tradition of "Burmanization," or of what some minority groups more bluntly call "AFPFL imperialism," traces back to the very beginnings of the nationalist movement in the Buddhist student clubs at the turn of the century, and by the thirties the Thakins were calling for an independent nation in which Burmese would be the national language, Burman dress would be the national costume, and the classical role of the (predominantly Burman) Buddhist monkhood as teacher, guide, and counselor to the secular government would be restored. Since independence and the accession of the pietistic Thakin Nu to the premiership, the government has moved strenuously to bring about these ends, the noticeable relaxation of the assimilative pressure during the year and a half of military rule, being followed by an even more intense assertion of such pressure following U Nu's landslide re-election on a Buddhism-as-a-state-religion platform in 1960. (In Burma proper his "clean" AFPFL captured outright about 80 per cent of the lower-house seats; in the states and the disaffected Arakan area about a third.)

As a result, most of the political adjustments of primordial interests in Burma have tended to be cast, in form at least, in juristic terms, to be carried out in a rather odd and artificial vocabulary of constitutional legalism. The Karens' conviction that the official boundaries of their state were too circumscribed to compensate for the loss of the special privileges they enjoyed under the colonial regime helped send them into revolt; their submission following military defeat by Union forces was in turn sealed and symbolized by their acceptance of those boundaries, plus a number of additional legal penalties imposed as object lessons: an explicit denial of the right of secession, the reduction of their representation in both houses of parliament, and the revocation of an earlier decision to unite the Kayah State with the Karen. Similarly, the primordial discontent of the Arakanese and the Mons—which has also periodically flared into open violence—has been expressed in demands for Arakanese and Mon states, which U Nu has at length been forced to support despite his oft-reiterated opposition to the formation of any more states. In Shan State the traditional chiefs have brandished their constitutional right to secession and a states' rights doctrine they claim is written into the constitution as bargaining weapons in their higgle with the Union over the amount and kind of compensation to be paid them for the surrender of various of their traditional powers. And so on. This irregular and unorthodox constitutional framework, which is so nicely exact in language and so usefully vague in meaning that "not even [Burmese] lawyers seem able to tell whether the Union

is in fact a federal or a unitary state,"[36] allows the single-party,
Burman-centered AFPFL regime to pursue its strongly assimilationist policies in almost all aspects of actual government, while
maintaining at least minimal loyalty from the non-Burman
Burmese, something it did not have a decade ago—though if its
ethnic enthusiasm is not contained, it may not have it a decade
hence either.

INDIA

India, that vast and various labyrinth of religious, linguistic,
regional, racial, tribal, and caste allegiances is developing a many-
sided political form to match for baffling irregularity her Daedalian
social and cultural structure. Waddling in (in E. M. Forster's
gently mocking image) at this late hour to take her seat among
the nations, she is beset by virtually the entire range of primordial
conflicts complexly superimposed one upon the other. One peels
off Punjabi linguism and finds Sikh religious communalism,
scratches Tamil regionalism and finds anti-Brahman racialism,
views Bengali cultural arrogance from a slightly different angle
and sees Greater Bengal patriotism. No general and uniform political solution to the problem of primordial discontent seems possible
in such a situation, only a loose assemblage of diverse, locally
adapted, *ad hoc* solutions, related to one another only incidentally
and pragmatically. The policies suitable for the tribal dissidence of
the Assam Naga are not generalizable to the caste-based disaffection of peasant landlords in Andhra. The central government
stance taken toward Orissa princes cannot be taken toward
Gujerati industrialists. The problem of Hindu fundamentalism in
Uttar Pradesh, the heartland of Indic culture, takes a rather different form in Dravidian Mysore. So far as primordial issues are concerned, Indian civil politics amounts to a disconnected series of
attempts to make the temporary endure.

The major institutional vehicle through which these attempts
are being made is, of course, the Indian National Congress.
Though, like the Malayan Alliance and the Burmese AFPFL, the
Congress is a comprehensive national party that has largely pre-
empted the governmental apparatus of the new state and become
its most important centralizing force, it has done so neither as a

36. Fairbairn, *op. cit.*

confederation of frankly primordial subparties nor as an agency of majority group assimilationism. The first of these courses is precluded by the multifarious nature of the primordial pattern—the sheer number of different groups involved—and the second by the absence of any one clearly central group within this pattern. As a result, the Congress, its slightly North Indian complexion aside, has tended to become an ethnically neutral, resolutely modernist, somewhat cosmopolitan force on the national level at the same time that it has built up a multiplicity of separate, and to a large extent independent, parochial party machines to secure its power on the local level. The image the Congress presents is thus a double one: in one focus, lecturing Hindi zealot and Tamil xenophobe alike, stands Nehru, "a reflective, cultivated, modern intellectual, full of wistfulness, skepticism, dogmatism, and self-doubt in the presence of his own country";[37] in the other, deliberately manipulating (among other things) the local realities of language, caste, culture, and religion to keep the party dominant, stand a whole set of less pensive regional bosses—Kamaraj Nadar in Madras, Chavan in Bombay, Atulya Ghosh in Maharashtra, Patnaik in Orissa, Kairon in Punjab, and Sukhadia in Rajahstan.

The States Reorganization Act of 1956—itself, as has been mentioned, the culmination of a process begun within the Congress several decades before independence—gave this pattern of civil hub and primordial rim its official institutionalization. The division of the country into linguistically demarcated subunits is, in fact, part and parcel of the general approach of attempting to insulate parapolitical forces from national concerns by sequestering them in local contexts. Unlike those of Burma, the states of India have real and explicitly—perhaps too explicitly—spelled out constitutional powers in every field from education and agriculture to taxation and public health, so that the political process centering around the state assemblies and the formation of state governments is far from being an inconsequential matter. It is on the state level that perhaps the bulk of the bitter hand-to-hand clashes that form the everyday substance of Indian domestic politics are coming to take place, and where the adjustments of parochial interests are coming to be effected, in so far as they are effected at all.

37. E. Shils, *The Intellectual between Tradition and Modernity: The Indian Situation*, Comparative Studies in Society and History, Supplement I, The Hague, Mouton, 1961, p. 95.

Thus, in the 1957 elections, even more than in those of 1952, the Congress found itself engaged in a multifront war, fighting different election battles in the various states, against different sorts of opponents capitalizing on different sorts of discontents—against the Communists in Kerala, Bengal, and Andhra; against communal religious parties in Punjab, Uttar and Madhya Pradesh, and Rajasthan; against tribal unions in Assam and Bihar; against ethnolinguistic fronts in Madras, Maharashtra, and Gujerat; against feudal-prince restorationist parties in Orissa, Bihar, and Rajasthan; against the Praja Socialists in Bombay. Not all these struggles pivoted around primordial issues but virtually all—even those involving leftist "class" parties—seem to have been significantly influenced by them.[38] In any case, as none of these opposition parties was able to spread beyond the few strongholds where the particular veins they tapped proved comparatively rich, the Congress as the only genuinely national party was able to maintain overwhelming control of both the central and—with a few exceptions—the state governments, even though it captured less than half the popular vote.

How, out of this conglomerate hodgepodge of courthouse machinations arises the rather cerebral, dispassionate, moralistic central Congress government to serve as a kind of extraordinary committee for the conduct of foreign policy, as a comprehensive social and economic planning commission and as a symbolic expression of all-India national identity is something of an Eastern mystery. Most observers put it down, rather without analysis, to Nehru's charismatic force as a nationalist hero. His position as apostolic heir to Gandhi and avatar of independence bridges the gulf between his own cosmopolitan intellectualism and the provincial horizons of the mass of his people. And it is perhaps for this reason, as well as for his matchless ability to keep local bosses loyal, in line, and reasonably unambitious, that the problem of succession—"after Nehru, who?"—has in India even more of a fundamentally disquieting quality than in most of the other new states where succession is also nearly always a prominent anxiety. The fact that India

38. "The success of the Kerala Communist Party as the first regional Communist Party in India to capture control of a state government can be explained, above all, by its ability to manipulate the regional patriotism of all Kerala at the same time that it manipulated politically strategic class lobbies within linguistic boundaries."—Harrison, *India, op. cit.*, p. 193. In Bombay, both the Communists and the Praja Socialists joined in the Maharashtra linguistic front; in opposed Gujarat, the Gujerati one.

has been held together up to now, Ambedkar says flatly, is due to the force of Congress Party discipline—"But how long is the Congress to last? The Congress is Pandit Nehru and Pandit Nehru is Congress. But is Pandit Nehru immortal? Anyone who applies his mind to these questions will realize that the Congress will not last until the sun and the moon."[39] If the Burmese integrative problem is to restrain primordial enthusiasm at the center, the Indian seems to be to restrain it at the periphery.

LEBANON

Lebanon may be—as Hitti has pointed out—not much larger than Yellowstone Park, but it is a good deal more astonishing. Although its population is almost entirely Arabic-speaking and shares a generally "Levantine" ethos, it is rigidly partitioned into seven major Moslem (Sunni, Shi'a, and Druze) and Christian (Maronites, Greek Orthodox, Greek Catholic, and Armenian Orthodox) sects and about that many minor ones (Protestants, Jews, Armenian Catholics, and so on), a confessional heterogeneity that not only forms the principal public framework of individual self-identification, but is woven directly into the whole structure of the state. Seats in the parliament are allotted on a strictly sectarian basis according to demographic proportions that are fixed by law and that have remained essentially unchanged in the five elections held since independence. Paramount executive authority is not merely bisected, but trisected, with the president of the country conventionally a Maronite, the prime minister a Sunni, and the chairman of parliament a Shi'i. Cabinet posts are carefully doled out on a confessional basis, and a similar balance is maintained in the civil service from ministry secretaries, district administrators, and diplomatic posts all the way down to rank-and-file clerical jobs. The judicial system is equally a maze of religious pluralism, with both the laws themselves and the courts applying them varying as to sect, final authority in personal law cases sometimes lying outside the boundaries of the country altogether.[40] Arab province and Christian outpost, modern commercial entrepôt and last relic of

39. Ambedkar, op. cit., p. 12. The Chinese attack may, of course, provide an even more powerful cement than Nehru—a common enemy.
40. See Professor Rheinstein's remarks, p. 224, below.

the Ottoman Millet system, Lebanon is almost as much an entente as a state.

The sort of politics this entente supports are equally wondrous. Political parties, though formally present, play as yet but a marginal role. The struggle for pelf and power pivots instead around strong local leaders, who tend to be either important absentee landlords or, in the freehold sections of the country, heads of large and prominent extended families. Each of these faction chiefs, whose following is bound to him in essentially traditional rather than ideological terms, then forms alliances with similar faction chiefs from other locally represented sects, yielding in the election campaign a Tammany Hall sort of "one Irishman, one Jew, one Italian" ticket-balancing.

This process is encouraged by the device of having the entire electorate in any one district vote in all the local races regardless of sect, so that, for example, a Maronite voting in a district where there are also Sunni, Greek Orthodox, and Druze seats at stake chooses among the Sunni, Greek Orthodox, and Druze candidates as well as among his own—the Maronite ones—and vice versa. This, in turn, leads to the forming of composite lists through which the candidates in each sect attempt to link themselves with popular candidates in other sects so as to attract the necessary external votes. As lists are rarely split, because the possibility of a candidate making effective alliances rests on his ability to bring loyal voters with him (and because the average voter has little knowledge of candidates of other sects on which to base rational judgments of their worth, anyway), this means that although, for any given seat, Maronite competes against Maronite, or Sunni against Sunni, and so on, it is actually lists that are elected. The electoral process thus acts to align certain leaders from the various sects over against certain other such leaders in such a way that political ties tend to cross-cut sectarian ones. Members of different sects are driven into each others' arms in interconfessional coalitions; members of the same sect are driven apart into intraconfessional factions.

Such calculated forging (and breaking) of alliances between significant political personalities is not confined merely to campaign tactics, but extends over the whole of political life. Among the strongest leaders the same principles come into play with respect to the higher national offices; so that, in example a leading

Maronite who considers himself as a possible president will attempt to align himself in public life with a leading Sunni who is aiming for the premiership, and so on, both in order to gain Sunni support and to prevent his immediate Maronite rivals for the presidency from making so effective an alliance themselves. Similar patterns operate throughout the system, at every level and in every aspect of government.

As such coalitions are so opportunistically rather than ideologically put together, they frequently dissolve overnight, as seeming bosom companions suddenly fall out and mortal enemies unite amid a storm of accusations and counteraccusations of betrayal, corruption, incompetence, and ingratitude. The pattern is thus fundamentally an individualistic, even egoistic, one, despite its grounding in traditional religious, economic, and kinship groupings, with each would-be political power scheming to advance his career by a skillful manipulation of the system. Both places on tickets led by strong figures and votes themselves are bought (during the 1960 elections the amount of money in circulation rose 3 million Leb.); rivals are slandered and, on occasion, physically attacked; favoritism, nepotic or otherwise, is accepted procedure; and spoils are considered the normal reward of office. "There is no right in Lebanon," Ayoub's Mount Lebanon Druzes say, "there is only silver and the 'fix.' "[41]

Yet out of all this low cunning has come not only the most democratic state in the Arab world, but the most prosperous; and one that has in addition been able—with one spectacular exception—to maintain its equilibrium under intense centrifugal pressures from two of the most radically opposed extrastate primordial yearnings extant: that of the Christians, especially the Maronites, to be part of Europe, and that of the Moslems, especially the Sunnis, to be part of pan-Arabia. The first of these motives finds expression mainly in a so-called "isolationist" view of Lebanon as a special and unique phenomenon among the Arab states, a "nice piece of mosaic" whose distinctiveness must be jealously conserved; the second takes the form of a call for reunion with Syria. And in so far as Lebanese politics escapes the merely personal and traditional and becomes involved with general ideas and issues, it is in these terms that it tends to polarize.

The one spectacular exception to the maintenance of equilib-

41. Ayoub, *op. cit.*, p. 82.

rium, the 1958 civil war and American intervention, was in great part precipitated by just this sort of atypical ideological polarization. On the one hand President Sham'un's unconstitutional attempt to succeed himself and, presumably, to align Lebanon more closely with the West in order to enhance Christian power against the rising tide of Nasserism, excited the ever-present Moslem fears of Christian domination; on the other, the sudden outburst of pan-Arab enthusiasm stimulated by the Iraqi revolution and Syria's turn toward Cairo led to the equally ever-present Christian fear of drowning in a Moslem sea. But the crisis—and the Americans—passed. Sham'un was, at least temporarily, discredited for "dividing the country." The pan-Arabist fever was, also at least temporarily, checked by a renewed conviction, even within Sunni circles, that the integrity of the Lebanese state must at all costs be preserved. Civil rule was quickly restored, and by 1960 a new election could be held peacefully enough, bringing back most of the old familiar faces to the old familiar stands.

It seems, therefore, that Lebanese politics, as they are now constituted, must remain personalistic, factional, opportunistic and unprogrammatic if they are to work at all. Given the extreme confessional heterogeneity and the penetration of this heterogeneity throughout the entire organization of the state, any increase in ideologized party politics tends very quickly to lead to an unstable Christian-Moslem polarization over the pan-Arab issue and to the breakdown of the cross-sect links that in the course of normal political maneuvering divide the sects and unite, if somewhat precariously, the government. Machiavellian calculation and religious toleration are opposite sides of the same coin in Lebanon; in the short run, anyway, the alternative to "silver and 'the fix' " may very well be national dissolution.

MOROCCO

Across the whole of the Middle East—except for Nile-bound Egypt—runs an ancient social contrast between, as Coon puts it, "the tame and the insolent, the domestic and the independent"— between those living within the political, economic, and cultural orbit of the great generative cities and those living, if not precisely outside that orbit, along its fringes and providing "the supply of rebels who, since the beginning of the Bronze Age, have kept the urban civilizations refreshed and in motion."[42] Between the central power of the shahs and sultans and the stubborn libertarianism of the outlying tribes there existed (and to a great extent still exists) a delicate balance. When the state was strong, the tribes were obliged to give it at least grudging recognition and to check their anarchic impulses; when it was weak, they ignored it, plundered it, or—one or another of them—even overthrew it to become in turn the carriers and defenders of the urban great tradition. For the better part of the time, however, neither fully effective despotism nor mere tribal rampage prevailed. Rather, an uneasy truce between center and perimeter was maintained, tying them together in "a loose system of give and take" under which "mountaineers and nomads come to town freely, their fastnesses are left alone, and they let the caravans of travelers, traders, and pilgrims cross [their territories] without hindrance or inconvenience over and above the normal rigors of travel."[43]

In Morocco, this contrast has always been particularly strong, in part because so much of the terrain is mountainous, in part because of the gradual superimposition, after the seventh century, of an Arabic culture migrant from the East upon a relatively large indigenous Berber population, and in part because of the country's relatively great distance from the primary foci of Middle Eastern civilization in Egypt and Mesopotamia.

The complex early history of the region aside, the establishment of the Arabized, Islamic reformist Sherifian dynasty toward the end of the seventeenth century and the subsequent royal efforts to reduce the field of Berber customary law in favor of Koranic law, to repress saint worship and cultic practices, and to purify Islamic belief of local pagan accretions, crystallized the distinction between *bled al makhzen*—"the land of government"—and *bled as siba*—"the land of insolence." Claiming direct descent from the Prophet (the meaning of the term "sherif"), the dynasty, which rules until today, attempted to assert both spiritual and temporal power over the more Arabized population of the Atlantic Plain as well as over the more Berberized ones of the encircling Rif and Atlas mountains; but though the spiritual claim—that of imamship—has been commonly accepted, the temporal has been more of a some-

42. C. Coon, *Caravan*, London, Cape, 1952, p. 295.
43. *Ibid.*, pp. 264–265.

time thing, particularly in the peripheral upland regions. Thus arose perhaps the most striking and distinctive feature of the Moroccan political system: the attachment of the urban and peasant populations of the plain to the sultan as autocratic head of a rather developed patrimonial bureaucracy (the Makhzen) of ministers, notables, soldiers, magistrates, clerks, policemen, and tax collectors; and the attachment of the tribal peoples to his person as "Lord of the Believers," but not to his secular government or its representatives.

By the time of the establishment of the French and Spanish protectorates in 1912, the sultanate had become so seriously weakened by a combination of internal corruption and external subversion that it was unable to exert effective control not merely over the mountains but in the plain as well. Though for a decade or so the seignoral proconsulship of Marshal Lyautey held the tribes in check and, in a somewhat paternalistic way, reinvigorated the Makhzen bureaucracy, after his departure his successors initiated the so-called "Berber Policy" dedicated to drawing a sharp distinction between Arab and Berber, and isolating the latter from the influence of the Makhzen entirely. Special Berber schools, designed to produce a "Berber elite," were set up, missionization increased; and—most important—the symbolic supremacy of Koranic law (and thus of the sultan as imam) was undermined by the placing of the mountain tribes under the French criminal code and officially recognizing the judicial competence of customary law tribal councils in civil disputes. Coinciding with the rise of the intense Islamic puritanism of the Egyptian and Afghan-Parisian reformers Abduh and Al-Afghani among the notables of the Arabized towns, and particularly those around the ancient Qarawiyin University at Fez, the Berber Policy and its implied threat to Islam stimulated the growth of nationalism under the banner of defending the faith against European-sponsored secularization and Christianization. Thus—even if under rather seriously altered conditions—the national movement in Morocco has also taken the classic form of attempting to strengthen the integrative power of a generally Mid-Eastern urban civilization against the centrifugal tendencies of tribal particularism.

The exile of Sultan Mohammed V by the French in 1953 and his wildly triumphant return as a national hero in 1955 put the cap on this political and cultural revival of the Makhzen, and inaugurated, after independence was achieved, a new-state regime perhaps most aptly described as a "modernizing autocracy."[44] With the French and the Spanish gone, the Rabat Sultanate has become again the double-pronged pivot of the system. The major nationalist party, the Istiqlal, its independent power undercut by the lack, thus far, of national elections of a genuine parliament, has become the incumbent of a somewhat modernized but still essentially patrimonial Makhzen. Led by conservative Arabized notables of the lowland cities and towns (and again most especially of Fez—"la ville sainte de l'Islame . . . la métropole de l'arabisme . . . [et] la vraie capitale du Maroc"),[45] it has acted as the administrative arm of the throne, a "college of viziers" dominating the royal-appointed Councils of Government, the party-rationalized civil bureaucracy, and the reinstated (and reformed) Islamic judicial system. But as the attitude toward Istiqlal among the tribesmen has been, like their attitude to earlier palace official-doms, at best lukewarm and at worst actively hostile, the relationship between the sultan and at least the more intact, peripheral tribes has remained essentially personal. Loyal to the king and resistant to his government, the tribes have been, since the transfer of sovereignty as they were before it, the main source of primordial threats to national integration.

Since 1956, heartland-hinterland crises have come thick and fast. The absorption into the Royal Army of the irregular military force formed from among the tribes during the sultan's exile—the so-called "Liberation Army"—has proved to be a most ticklish task leading to open clashes; only after the king firmly removed the Royal Army from Istiqlal influence and attached it directly to the palace under his son, Prince Moulay Hasan, as chief of staff, was the tension in part eased. In the fall of 1956, a Berber chieftain from the Middle Atlas, an intimate of the king and a bitter opponent of the Istiqlal, resigned his post as interior minister in the royal cabinet, and returned to the mountains to preach primordialism to the tribes ("It is the tribes who have made the glory of Morocco"), calling for the dissolution of all political parties ("It is contrary to the interests of the country to confer responsibility on men who totally ignore the tribes") and a national rally

44. For this concept and its analytic implications, see D. Apter, *The Political Kingdom in Uganda*, Princeton, N.J., Princeton University Press, 1961, pp. 20–28.

45. Favre, *op. cit.*

around the figure of Mohammed V. ("We have in this nation both weak and strong. United on the same mountains and under the same skies, they are equal before the king.")[46] His effort soon ceased—at least openly—evidently upon the advice of the king; but a few months later an even more traditionalistic Berber, the governor of the mountainous eastern province of Tifilalet, went into semirevolt, simultaneously refusing to obey "a party which hinders us from living as we wish," and declaring his undying loyalty to the sultan. The king soon secured his peaceful submission and placed him in forced residence near the imperial palace; but in late 1958 and early 1959 sporadic uprisings also occurred in the north and northeast, they too being contained within narrow limits largely through the agency of the king's personal popularity, diplomatic skill, military strength, and religious charisma.

Yet the modernizing aspect of the new Moroccan state is as real as the autocratic, and probably more enduring. The restlessness of the tribes does not represent merely "the past and the province against the future and the nation,"[47] but the concern of the traditional,"land of insolence" groups to find a secure and accepted place in that future and nation. The development, first clandestinely and then—as the various parapolitical expressions of tribal dissatisfaction collapsed—openly, of a new national political party, the Popular Movement, as the vehicle of rural aspirations, is but one of the more obvious signs that mere hostility to urban culture and unbending resistance to central authority is coming to be replaced among the outlying peoples by a fear of being relegated to second-class citizenship within a modern civil order. Under the leadership of the former head of the Liberation Army, Ahardane, and with the vaguest of programs—"Moslem socialism" and a new union around the king as imam, not just for Morocco, but for the whole Maghrib—the new party has at best but one foot in that order. But as a rapid sequence of very serious political mutations— the holding of local elections; the breakaway of the left wing of Istiqlal to form a proletarian party; the sudden, premature death of Mohammed V, and the succession of his less popular son— have cast a cloud of uncertainty over the future of monarchical

46. Quotations in this sentence from Lahcen el-Youssi and in the following from Addi ou Bihi taken from Lacouture, *op. cit.*, p. 90.
47. *Ibid.*, p. 93.

government in the last couple of years, the new state may well find itself increasingly hard pressed to satisfy and contain the subtle fusion of traditional *siba* sentiments and modern political ambitions neatly summed up in Ahardane's stiff-necked slogan, "We have not acquired independence in order to lose liberty."[48]

NIGERIA

The distinctive feature of Nigerian political life as it has evolved since the Second World War has been what Coleman has called "the regionalization of nationalism."[49] Whereas in most of the other new states the final phases of the pursuit of independence saw a progressive unification of diverse elements into an intensely solidary opposition to colonial rule, open dissidence emerging only after devolution and the inevitable waning of revolutionary comradeship, in Nigeria tension between various primordial groups increased in the last decade of dependency. After 1946 the Nigerian struggle for freedom was less a matter of defying foreign authority and more a matter of drawing boundaries, founding capitals, and distributing powers in such a way as to dampen and contain sharpening ethnoregional hostilities prior to the disappearance of that authority. It was marked not so much by growing insurgency in order to force the British to leave as by feverish negotiation, in both Lagos and London, in order to create a *modus vivendi* among the Yoruba, Ibo, and Hausa-Fulani so that they could leave.

The arrangement ultimately devised (in a 240-page, fine-print constitution) was a radically federal one, composed of three powerful constituent regions—the Northern, the (south-) Eastern, and the (south-) Western—each with its own capital, its own parliament, cabinet, and high court, and its own budget. Each region is dominated by a particular ethnic group—respectively, the Hausa, Ibo, and Yoruba; a particular political party—the Northern Peoples' Congress (NPC), the National Council of Nigeria and the Cameroons (NCNC), and the Action Group (AG); and a particular political personality—Alhaji Sir Ahmadu Bello, the Sardauna ("Sultan") of Sokoto, Dr. Nnamdi Azikiwe and Chief Obafemi Awolowo. Perched, somewhat insecurely, on top of these regional strongholds is the federal government at

48. Quoted in Ashford, *op. cit.*, p. 322.
49. Coleman, *op. cit.*, pp. 319–331.

Lagos as the arena in which the sort of two-against-one coalition politics one would naturally expect from this type of three-person game takes place and out of whose changeful processes the authoritative leadership to fill the vacuum at the center of the system will presumably at length emerge.

The sort of form that leadership will take, who will provide it, and how, in the workings of this Swiss-clock governmental mechanism, it will actually manage to be produced remain, however, entirely obscure. In the meantime, the triangular pattern of primordial identification continues to crystallize in the country at large, as the tribal societies of traditional Nigeria gradually regroup themselves into the regional-linguistic (and in the Moslem North, religious) folk societies of modern Nigeria. But though increasingly important as the country's ethnic skeleton, this pattern does not exhaust the full variety of ingrained "consciousness of kind," because in each region there remain a large number of smaller groups outside the core Hausa, Yoruba, and Ibo areas at least somewhat resistant to assimilation to these broader subnational entities. And it is in these marginal areas—the southern half of the North, the eastern edge of the West, and the southern and eastern borders of the East—that the most vital electoral competition between major ethnic groups tends to take place, as each party attempts, with some success, to capitalize on minority resentments within their opponents' strongholds. What appears at the center as a three-way subnational competition, and at the regional capitals as (more and more) a one-party ethnocracy, represents in the countryside a much more complex and diversified network of tribal alliances and oppositions.[50] It is a tiered system in which local loyalties remain mostly organized in traditional terms,

50. The whole picture is further complicated, not only by the fact that tribal identifications within the three major groups have not altogether given way before the wider ethnolinguistic loyalty, but also that not all members of such larger units are located in their home regions, having migrated or spilled over into the others where they sometimes form, particularly in the towns, an important oppositional minority. The whole problem of the allegiance of an individual living outside his "home region" is an extremely ticklish one for all new states in which integrative problems have been coped with by creating territorial substates tinged with primordial significance, as Nehru's continual insistence that, for example, a Bengali living in Madras is a citizen of the state level, of Madras, not of Bengal, and that all notions of a "national homeland" for ethnic groups living elsewhere in India must be stamped out demonstrates. The additional fact that some such groups are more mobile than others (in Nigeria, the Ibo; in India, the Marwari and so on) only intensifies this problem.

provincial ones have become organized in party-political terms, and national ones are just beginning to become organized at all.

Thus, although the regionalization of nationalism process led to the establishment of a party system and constitutional structure in which Nigeria's several hundred primordial groups, ranging from the nearly six million Hausa to tribal fragments of only a few hundred, have been able, thus far, to live in at least reasonable amity, it also created a void at the very heart of national political life and left the country more or less acephalous. Since independence (in October, 1960), political attention has consequently turned toward the federal capital at Lagos as parties and their leaders jockeyed for starting positions from which to launch their campaigns to correct this condition. After an initial attempt to form a governing alliance between the economically and politically more advanced Eastern and Western regions against the more traditional North stumbled over the entrenched hostility between the mobile, aggressive Ibo intelligentsia and the stolid, wealthy Yoruba business class—and between the mercurial Dr. Azikiwe and the lofty Chief Awolowo—the North and East formed such an alliance, isolating the West. Azikiwe resigned the Eastern premiership to become governor general, in theory a merely symbolic office, but which he may well make into something more; the Sardauna of Sokoto, choosing to remain lion of the North in his regional premiership, sent his lieutenant, Alhaji Sir Abubakar Tafawa Balewa, to serve in his stead as federal prime minister; and Awolowo, odd man out in this first of what will probably be a series of two-against-one coalitions, resigned his post as Western premier to become leader of the opposition in the federal parliament.

Posts taken, the maneuvering has begun. The federal parliament has decided to form—if the regional parliaments agree—a fourth state, the Midwest, out of the minority area of the Western Region; Awolowo has shifted from a markedly right- to a markedly left-wing ideological position in an attempt to shake the somewhat tory government and ride the antineocolonialism horse to power, splitting the Action Group in the process; tensions within the NCNC between the increasingly accommodative old guard and the still radical Young Turks has increased, and so on. But all this has more confused issues than clarified them; complicated matters rather than simplified them. Independent (as this is written) for less than a year, Nigeria, the newest of the new states considered here, offers but the most unformed materials upon which to base an assessment of its essential character and probable future. Possessed of what would appear to be an extraordinarily unwieldy set of political institutions hurriedly put together in the last hectic years of constitution making before independence, lacking a comprehensive national party, a supereminent political leader, an overarching religious tradition or a common cultural background, and—seemingly—of several minds about what to do with freedom now that it has, almost as a matter of course, received it, it has an unusually tentative, up-in-the-air quality, even for a new state.

V

CENTER-AND-ARC regionalism and dual leadership in Indonesia, single-party interracial alliance in Malaya, aggressive assimilationism wrapped in constitutional legalism in Burma, a cosmopolitan central party with provincial machines fighting a multifront war against every sort of parochialism known to man (and a few known only to Hindus) in India, sectarian slate making and logrolling in Lebanon, Janus-faced autocratic rule in Morocco, and unfocused check-and-balance scrimmaging in Nigeria—are these systems as merely unique as they appear? From this array of efforts after political order, does any evidence emerge for the claim that the integrative revolution is a general process?

Over the cases reviewed here, at least, one common developmental tendency does stand out: the aggregation of independently defined, specifically outlined traditional primordial groups into larger, more diffuse units whose implicit frame of reference is not the local scene but the "nation"—in the sense of the whole society encompassed by the new civil state. The leading principle in terms of which this lumping is mainly carried out varies—region in Indonesia, race in Malaya, language in India, religion in Lebanon, custom in Morocco, and quasi-kinship in Nigeria. Whether it involves becoming an Outer Islander in addition to a Minangkabau, a Kachin over and above a Duleng, a Christian as well as a Maronite, or a Yoruba rather than only an Egba, the process, though variously advanced, both as between countries and within them, is general. It is a progressive extension of the sense of

primordial similarity and difference generated from the direct
and protracted encounter of culturally diverse groups in local
contexts to more broadly defined groups of a similar sort interacting within the framework of the entire national society, an
extension Freedman has described particularly well for Malaya:

> Malaya was and remains a culturally plural society. Paradox-
> ically, from a purely structural point of view, its plural nature
> is more marked today than ever before. Nationalism and polit-
> ical independence in their early phases have tended to define,
> on a pan-Malayan basis, ethnic blocs which in former times
> were merely categories. Then the social map of Malaya was, so
> to speak, made up of a kaleidoscope of small culturally defined
> units rearranging themselves in accordance with local conditions.
> "The Malays" did not interact with "the Chinese" and "the
> Indians." Some Malays interacted with some Chinese and some
> Indians. But as "Malays," "Chinese" and "Indians" come to be
> realized as structural entities on a nation-wide scale, they can
> begin to have total relations with one another.[51]

The emergence of a nation-wide system of "ethnic-blocs" engaged in "total relations with one another" sets the stage for a
direct clash between personal identity and political integrity in the
new states. By generalizing and extending tribal, racial, linguistic,
or other principles of primordial solidarity, such a system permits
the maintenance of a profoundly rooted "consciousness of kind,"
and relates that consciousness to the developing civil order. It
allows one to continue to claim public acknowledgment of one's
existence and import in terms of the familiar symbols of group
uniqueness, while at the same time becoming more and more
drawn into a political society cast in a wholly different mold than
the "natural" community those symbols define. But, on the other
hand, it also simplifies and concentrates group antagonisms, raises
the specter of separatism by superimposing a comprehensive political significance upon those antagonisms, and, particularly, when
the crystallizing ethnic blocs outrun state boundaries, stirs international controversies. The integrative revolution does not do away
with ethnocentrism; it merely modernizes it.

Yet modernizing ethnocentrism does render it more easily reconciled to the presence of developed national political institutions. The effective operation of such institutions does not require

51. Freedman, *op. cit.*

the simple replacement of primordial ties and identifications by civil ones. In all probability, such a replacement is a sheer impossibility. What it does demand is an adjustment between them, an adjustment such that the processes of government can proceed freely without seriously threatening the cultural framework of personal identity, and such that whatever discontinuities in "consciousness of kind" happen to exist in the general society do not radically distort political functioning. At least as they have been conceived here, primordial and civil sentiments are not ranged in direct and implicitly evolutionary opposition to one another in the manner of so many of the theoretical dichotomies of classical sociology—*Gemeinschaft* and *Gesellschaft*, mechanical and organic solidarity, folk and urban society; the history of their development does not consist simply of the expansion of the one at the expense of the other. Their marked tendency to interfere with one another in the new states stems not from any natural and irremovable antipathy between them but rather from dislocations arising from the differing patterns of change intrinsic to each of them as they respond to the disequilibrating forces of the mid-twentieth century. Their clash is an outcome of the contrasting sorts of transformation that traditional political institutions and traditional modes of self-perception undergo as they move along their separate paths toward modernity.

On the self-perception side, the nature of the modernizing process is virtually uninvestigated; it is not usually even recognized that such a process exists. The already mentioned aggregation of narrowly circumscribed tribal, linguistic, religious, and so on, groups into larger more generalized ethnic blocs set within the context of a common social frame is certainly a crucial part of it. A simple, coherent, broadly defined ethnic structure, such as is found in most industrial societies, is not an undissolved residue of traditionalism but an earmark of modernity. But how this reconstruction of the system of primordial affiliation takes place, the stages through which it passes, the forces that advance or retard it, the transformations in personality structure it involves, all are largely unknown. The comparative sociology (or social psychology) of ethnic change remains to be written.

With respect to the political side, it can hardly be said that the problem is unrecognized, for the notion of a civil society, of the nature of citizenship and the diffuse social sentiments on which it rests, has been a central concern of political science since Aristotle. But it remains none the less vague; much easier to point to than describe; much easier to sense than to analyze. What the civic sense more than anything else seems to involve is a definite concept of the public as a separate and distinct body and an attendant notion of a genuine public interest, which though not necessarily superior to, is independent of and at times even in conflict with, both private and other sorts of collective interest. When we talk about the changing forms of civil politics in the new states or elsewhere, it is the vicissitudes of just this sense of the public and the public interest, its waxings and wanings, its alterations in mode of expression, to which we refer. Again, however, though we have at least a general idea of the nature of civility and the range of forms through which it is materialized in industrial states, very little is known about the processes by which the present patterns have come to be what they are. A genuine civil sense is often even denied—incorrectly in my opinion—to traditional states at all. In any case, the stages through which a modern sense of political community arises out of a traditional one has been at best but impressionistically traced, and thus both the roots and the character of civility remain obscure.

A satisfactory understanding of the reasons for the chronic tension in the new states between the need to maintain a socially ratified personal identity and the desire to construct a powerful national community demands, therefore, a more circumstantial tracing of the stages through which their relationship to one another passes as each proceeds along the special lines of its own development. And it is in the histories of those states as they unfold before our eyes that such a tracing is most readily to be accomplished. The diverse constitutional, quasi-constitutional, or simply *ad hoc* experiments in government that characterize at least those new states described here represent, among other things, an attempt to establish a pattern of politics in which the looming headlong clash of primordial and civil loyalties can be averted. Whether ethnic differentiation is given its political expression in terms of territorial subunits, political parties, government posts, executive leadership, or, as is most common, one or another combination of these, the effort is everywhere to find a formula that will keep the pace of modernization of the nation's sense of selfhood in step with the parallel modernization not only of its political, but of its economic, stratificatory, domestic, and so on, institutions as well. It is by watching the integrative revolution happen that we shall understand it. This may seem like a mere wait-and-see policy, inappropriate to the predictive ambitions of science. But such a policy is at least preferable, and more scientific, to waiting and not seeing, which has been largely the case to date.

In any case, the success of the efforts to find a formula for balance in the midst of change now taking place in the new states is nowhere assured. A high degree of governmental immobilism resulting from the attempt to reconcile divergent primordial groups is everywhere apparent. The mere prejudices that must be tolerated in order to effect such reconciliations are often repugnant. But as the alternatives to such attempts as these to construct a civil politics of primordial compromise would seem to be either Balkanization, *Herrenvolk* fanaticism, or the forcible suppression of ethnic assertion by a leviathan state, can they be viewed, especially by members of a society that has notably failed to resolve its own most troublesome primordial problem, with either indifference or contempt?

Equality, modernity,
and democracy in the new states

LLOYD FALLERS

SOCIAL STRATIFICATION has fascinated students of modern Western societies and they have written about it with great perceptiveness and at great length. Equality and inequality and their place in modern society have been major themes in the work of such diverse figures as Burke and Marx, Tocqueville and Weber. In recent decades, the study of stratification has become one of the most highly developed branches of professional sociology.

The reason for this great concern, quite clearly, is that the question of equality has played a peculiarly prominent role in the recent history of the West. It has dominated the ideologies of countless political movements and the personal aspirations of millions of individuals. Indeed, it would perhaps not be exaggerating to say that, from the point of view of most modern Westerners, including most social scientists, the progress of equality has been

The writer is deeply grateful to Marshall Hodgson, Milton Singer, Margaret Fallers, and the members of the Committee for the Comparative Study of New Nations for careful reading and criticism of successive drafts of this essay. They are, of course, in no way responsible for its remaining flaws.

the central theme of recent history. For many, modernity and equality have seemed to be nearly synonymous; so also have equality and political democracy.

This very fascination with the subject, however, and the constant effort to refine our concepts and methods for studying it, may deceive us as we turn our attention to what seem to be analogous events and processes in the contemporary non-Western world. Concepts that have proved useful in the interpretation of the Western experience—concepts like "class," "feudal," "aristocracy," "democratic," "middle class," "proletarian," and "peasant"—may not have the same explanatory power when applied to processes that are different in important respects. That equality is also a central issue in the lives of contemporary non-Western peoples is apparent from the most cursory examination of the rhetoric of their leaders (though even here we must be wary; the Western experience has influenced non-Western politicians as well as Western social scientists, with the result that ideas and aspirations not entirely familiar to Western experience may be expressed in words that sound deceptively familiar). If we are to understand the *kind* of issue equality is in the new states, we must try to stand a bit outside the Western experience and ask ourselves just how far, and in what respects, equality, democracy, and modernity have been related at different times and places.

As a contribution toward a broadening of perspective in these matters, we shall try to outline some of the more general consequences of economic and political modernization for stratification systems. In doing this, it will be useful to include some explicit discussion of the Western case in order to achieve greater clarity concerning the relationship between the concepts we commonly use in thinking about stratification and the peculiarities of the Western historical experience out of a consideration of which these concepts have grown. This will inevitably involve oversimplification, for it is of course impossible within the scope of a short essay to do justice to the rich variety and complexity of the past few hundred years of Western history. Indeed, the very expression "the Western case" will no doubt be offensive to students of this historical complexity. There are, indeed, important differences among Western countries, particularly, for our present purposes, between those that modernized early and those that did so later. There are also differences between "old Europe" and its cultural outliers in America and Australasia (though these are hardly as great as many have assumed). Whatever the difficulties, the attempt at generalization seems justifiable and useful. Most historians would probably agree that there is sufficient unity among Western societies and cultures to give a measure of common pattern to their systems of social stratification, when contrasted with those of the other societies and cultures we shall consider. If, in a preliminary comparison of the modernization of the West with the contemporary situation of some non-Western societies, we misconstrue this common pattern, we shall at least have raised issues that may stimulate more adequate comparative discussion.

These caveats must apply also to our discussion of the non-Western areas whose systems of stratification, both traditional and modern, we shall compare with Western ones. We shall try to outline, briefly and schematically, the stratification systems of traditional India, the Ottoman Empire, and sub-Saharan Africa, and also those of the new states that in recent times have emerged in those areas. Three examples do not, of course, exhaust the wide range of forms stratification may take, but they do provide sufficient variation to make possible a preliminary exercise in comparative analysis.

The general theme we shall pursue is that the systems of stratification that emerge from the process of political and economic modernization are the products of the interaction between the forces of generic modernity (which of course we must define) and the traditional societies and cultures upon which, and within which, modernity works. This statement will seem obvious, and even trite, to all except those who see in modernization an all-consuming solvent of the past. That modern societies are different from others—that there will be features common to modern societies, East and West (and South), that set them off from their traditional predecessors—is of course assumed; or at any rate the discovery of some of the elements of the generically modern is one of the aims of this inquiry. But it will be argued that the outcome of the process of modernization will also be heavily conditioned by the nature of a society's traditional heritage—that, for example, modern Western society, including its stratification system, is what it is in part because of the special character of the late medieval European society and culture out of which it grew.

To anticipate the results of our comparative inquiry: The particular relationship between equality and political democracy that has been a feature of the modernization of stratification in the West appears to be the result of a pattern of interaction between tradition and modernity that is far from universal. While a kind of egalitarian politics seems to be one of the products of modernization everywhere, political democracy appears to be the result of more special circumstances. On the other hand, our inquiry will not suggest that these circumstances are so special that only the Western world is able to bring them together. Other societies and cultural traditions, undergoing modernization under different historical conditions, seem to exhibit features that suggest that they are capable of responding to political modernity in a broadly analogous way.

In pursuing this comparative investigation, we shall discuss in turn the various traditional societies and the forces of modernization that have impinged upon them. First, however, it will be useful to outline the conception of social stratification we shall use as a guide to more systematic analysis.

A comparative view of stratification

MUCH of the work on social stratification, as we have noted, has taken as its point of departure the data of a particular system or family of systems—usually Western. Consequently, it has been usual to begin with some prominent feature of one of these systems, say, with the differential relationship of persons to the means of production or with the differential prestige of occupational roles. Other students of the subject have stressed the cultural differences that distinguish the various strata of society, while still others have been interested in ideologies about equality and inequality. Each of these ways of looking at the field is, of course, "valid" enough in the sense that each leads us to a deeper understanding of some particular aspect of how the multifaceted phenomenon that is stratification works in the particular society in question. But if we wish to pursue comparative studies, it seems preferable to begin with a broader and more analytical view of the sort developed in Parsons' essays and implicit in much of the work of Weber.[1] Although we cannot, of course, hope to begin with a closed and final set of concepts that will be equally applicable to every situation and problem, we can start by considering some of the basic aspects and dimensions of stratification.

THE PRIMARY ROOTS OF STRATIFICATION

Surely one of the fundamental bases for stratification phenomena everywhere is man's tendency to judge his fellows and himself as more or less worthy in the light of some moral standard. Thus a people's stratification system is rooted in its culture, and particularly in its culturally elaborated image of the "admirable man," the man whom everyone would like to be. Such images provide a spur to individual ambition—and to group ambition, too, since the unit of stratification is seldom in any simple sense a single person—thus providing a means by which individuals' and groups' energies and intelligence may be enlisted on behalf of society's goals. This is true in an important sense even when position in a stratification system is ascribed, for the qualities required of, say, a medieval European baron or an Indian Brahman are not, strictly speaking, inherited, either biologically or jurally. "Living up" to the demands of such a position always requires exertion on the part of the incumbent; and thus, even in such cases, there is an element of active pursuit of culturally defined standards.

Stratification is equally, however, rooted in social structure in the sense of the network of routinized relations, based upon mutual understandings and expectations about behavior, among persons and groups in society, for in this network of relations there is always some differentiation of roles, and thus the same image of excellence cannot be held before everyone. In addition to age, sex, and kinship roles there tends to be, certainly in the societies

1. Talcott Parsons, "An Analytical Approach to the Theory of Social Stratification," *American Journal of Sociology*, 45:841–862, 1940; "A Revised Analytical Approach to the Theory of Social Stratification," in Reinhard Bendix and S. M. Lipset (eds.), *Class, Status and Power: A Reader in Social Stratification*, New York, The Free Press of Glencoe, 1953, pp. 92–129; Max Weber, *Essays in Sociology*, edited by H. Gerth and C. Wright Mills, New York, Oxford University Press, 1947. A concern with stratification runs as a minor theme through all of Weber's sociological writing.

with which we are concerned here, a division of labor with regard to economic, political, and religious tasks. As a counterpart to, and sustaining, these differentiated roles in society, culture must therefore present, not just an undifferentiated image of the "admirable person," but also images of the "admirable woman," the "admirable son," the "admirable priest," and so on. This does not, of course, mean that by thus providing differentiated images of excellence to correspond with the differentiation of roles, the culture thereby relinquishes over-all judgment among persons in general. Some dominant image of the "admirable person" tends to remain, and this image involves a selection and relative evaluation among differentiated roles themselves in terms of the degree to which they embody the features defined by the over-all image of excellence.

Thus, the study of stratification may appropriately begin with a cataloguing of the array of differentiated roles, with a delineation of cultural definitions of virtue and excellence in human behavior, and with a study of the interaction between these in terms of both cultural differentiation and over-all differential evaluation of roles. This, however, is only the beginning, for the place of actual persons and groups in all this cannot be regarded as a passive one. If persons are assigned to different roles, and if culture evaluates these roles differentially, holding up some as more worthy than others, then the processes by which persons are allocated among roles may be expected to engage the interests and anxieties of persons and groups. Persons and groups may be expected to strive actively to achieve or defend their positions and, in the process, to manipulate, and even create, elements of the culture that evaluates them. A recognition of this "dynamic" element in stratification systems makes it useful to distinguish "secondary" structural and cultural aspects of such systems. By the "secondary structural aspect" of stratification we mean the structures and processes by which persons are allocated among roles, as distinguished from the "primary" differentiation of roles, or division of labor. By "secondary culture" we mean ideas and beliefs *about* stratification—about how and why persons are allocated among roles as they are and about the justice or injustice of this process—as contrasted with the "primary" definitions of excellence and the relative worth of roles.

SECONDARY CULTURAL ASPECTS

It is in relation to the secondary culture of stratification that we may most appropriately consider the famous concepts "ascription" and "achievement." These concepts certainly describe an important range of variation in cultural definitions of the proper allocation of roles, and one that has been particularly widely discussed in connection with the process of modernization and the progress of equality and democracy, it generally being assumed that these involve a movement from ascription to achievement. It has perhaps been recognized less commonly that neither occurs "pure" in the natural state and that consequently each tends to be accompanied by additional cultural complexities not encompassed by the concepts themselves. We have already noted that persons who occupy high ascribed roles do not really "inherit" the roles themselves; rather they inherit the right to strive for such roles on favorable terms, often in competition with others. The notion of *noblesse oblige*, for example, expresses the obligation incumbent upon the legitimate occupant of an ascribed role to perform certain definite kinds of behavior. From the point of view of the person assigned by ascription to a low position, the situation is still more complex. For him there is probably always some difficulty in accepting as immutable a definition of himself as unworthy by nature, no matter what he may do. This is not, of course, to argue that he cannot, in some sense, come to accept his position. It does mean that a culture that presents to certain persons very much greater opportunity to occupy the most admired roles must offer cogent reasons why this should be so, and probably must also offer consolation in some form to those thereby deprived of such highly valued opportunity.

In addition to the dominant, public view of how the allocation of persons to highly valued roles should and does take place, there also tends to develop a complex of more private, but yet quite standardized, subcultures that express the hopes and fears of groups of persons variously placed in the stratification system. A revealing example is provided by the tendency of middle-class people in the West to combine great public devotion to the principle of achievement and equality of opportunity with an equally great, but less publicly expresssed, concern with genealogy and the symbols of aristocracy. This paradox is particularly marked in the highly achievement-oriented society of modern United States, where genealogy is nevertheless a major preoccupation. In a sense the very emphasis upon the importance of achievement stimulates the growth of a "counterculture" expressing persons' desire to be "more equal than others." Everyone wants at least an equal opportunity to achieve higher roles, but also wants to be protected from competition from below. In India, where, according to the theory of Hindu high culture, caste position is immutable, lowly placed castes find consolation in myths explaining that they were once Brahmans, too, but that at some time in the past were illegitimately demoted by caste enemies.[2] Perhaps belonging to the same family of phenomena are the more or less formalized dramatic and gamelike performances in which low-ranking persons sometimes express ambivalently, in imitation that shades over into caricature, both their acceptance and resentment of the culture that places others above them in relative worth.[3]

Out of these complex crosscurrents of cultural attitudes toward inequality there may crystallize, under certain circumstances, relatively compact bodies of belief and value expressing the special position in the stratification system of particularly cohesive groups of persons. Presumably the growth of such subcultures is facilitated by the existence of relatively closed social groups of the sort to which Max Weber applied the term *Stand,* usually translated as "status group," thus giving analytical meaning to the German word for the estates of medieval European society. Such subcultures may pertain to broad horizontal strata within society or they may be associated with occupational, or even territorial, groups. Under some circumstances, as Weber noted, they may produce very explicit and highly articulated ideologies that, borne by aggressive social groups, may reshape substantially the cultural orientation of whole societies. This is, of course, a matter of central importance in the theory of modernization, involving as it does the problems of innovation and class-consciousness, and we shall there-

2. McKim Marriott, *Caste Ranking and Community Structure in Five Regions of India and Pakistan,* Poona, Deccan College Monograph Series 23, 1960, pp. 16–17.

3. Gerald Berreman, "Caste in India and the United States," *American Journal of Sociology,* 66: 120–127, 1960; George C. Homans, *English Villagers of the Thirteenth Century,* Cambridge, Mass., Harvard University Press, 1941, pp. 366–367.

fore have to return to it later on in our discussions of particular societies. Here it is sufficient to note that the development of compact subcultures is one, but *only* one, of the forms the secondary culture of stratification may take.

SECONDARY STRUCTURAL ASPECTS

These cultural phenomena do not, of course, occur apart from the structure of social relations in which the persons who are their bearers are involved. We have spoken briefly of the primary structure of role differentiation and have suggested that beyond this, in order to understand the ways in which stratification actually works, we must examine the "secondary" processes and structures by which persons are allocated among the roles thus differentiated.

One aspect of all this is commonly conceptualized by writers on stratification by means of the image of the pyramid. The shape of the pyramid is meant to indicate the relative numbers of roles at the various levels that are available for allocation. (The height of the pyramid and the numbers and kinds of "levels" differentiated may indicate either the primary cultural evaluation of various roles or the secondary cultural image of the system as a whole, depending upon the interests of the writer.) The important point for our present purposes is that the structural situation—the relative numbers of different roles that are available—may greatly influence persons' opportunities to occupy the more highly valued positions, quite apart from any cultural values concerning achievement and ascription. In traditional peasant societies, elites tend to be small and common folk to be numerous, with relatively few "middle-class" persons in between. In this situation, even though the elite may be very much open to talent—as it is in traditional societies rather more often than has commonly been supposed—actual opportunities for mobility may be few. On the other hand, an increase in the number of middle-class roles available may greatly alter the structure of opportunity without any substantial change in the culture of stratification.

To an important degree, this may be an economic matter where the number of roles in question is determined essentially by the supply of goods and services of kinds that serve either as facilities for the performance of such roles or as symbols expressive of them. Thus changes in the supply and control of such goods and services may exert what is, in the short run at least, a relatively unilateral influence upon stratification. It is to such changes, and the changes in the degrees and kinds of role differentiation that frequently accompany them, that Marx draws our attention in support of his contention that the organization of the economy lies at the heart of social stratification, and indeed of society in general. Viewed in wider perspective and over the longer term, however, such processes take their place, along with processes of a more cultural nature, as only one among a number of "forces" making up the complex of social and cultural change.

Political systems, in terms of which legitimate authority to make binding decisions is distributed, influence, and are influenced by, stratification systems, much as economic systems are. Political roles are themselves the objects of differential evaluation and the exercise of political power may influence the allocation of roles of other kinds. But politics is not synonymous with stratification any more than economics is, and hence democracy is not synonymous with equality.

There are still other structural features that influence the process of role allocation, among the most important being family and kinship structures. Stratification is probably never a purely individual matter, but rather always involves kinship groups of some kind, which is one reason why an element of status ascription is present in even the most achievement-oriented societies. Egalitarian ideologists have recognized this, hence their frequent attempts to eliminate the family. In traditional societies, kinship solidarities are commonly widely ramifying (although of course this phrase may cover a wide range of phenomena). With modernization, the kinship unit of stratification tends to shrink, principally because in modern societies occupational roles, played outside domestic contexts in functionally specialized economic, political, or religious organizations, tend to become the main focus of stratification. With this loss of direct articulation between kinship groups and the division of labor, the allocation of roles becomes a much more complex matter—comes to be mediated much more by special educational structures and a labor market external to the family, and much less by training within the domestic or extended kinship group. Kinship solidarities, including quite widely ramifying ones, do not, however, automatically disappear under such circumstances; a tendency toward kinship ascription of status

persists in all modern societies, influencing, sometimes quite profoundly, both the allocation of occupational roles and their cultural evaluation. We shall have to discuss later on some of the
differences in traditional kinship structures and their consequences
for the modernization of stratification.

These remarks should suffice to indicate in a preliminary way our
view of the main dimensions of stratification systems. We may
now turn to a closer examination of the patterns of stratification
characteristic of the traditional societies and cultures that were the
antecedents of the new states.

The traditional societies

ALMOST all the new states have grown out of peasant societies, and it is therefore part of our task to inquire into the forms
stratification characteristically takes in such societies. The term
"peasant society" is in some respects an unfortunate one because it
refers directly to only one segment of the society's population; we
use it principally in order to avoid such terms as "feudal society,"
whose historical connotations are too specific for our purposes. The
term does have the merit, however, of drawing attention to certain
important characteristics of the societies with which we wish to
deal, including some important common features of their stratification systems. With all their real differences, the societies that in
most cases preceded the new states shared a broad pattern of social
and cultural differentiation whose main features are revealed by an
examination of the peasant village in relation to the rest of society.
This pattern may be contrasted, on the one hand, with that characteristic of what we may call "tribal societies" and, on the other,
with that typically found in societies in which modernization has
made substantial inroads.

The peasant village, as Kroeber has said, is what it is because of
its relationship to the social and cultural superstructure above it;
it is "a part-society with a part-culture."[4] Standing alone, it would
no longer be a *peasant* village. In contrast, the communities that
make up a tribal society are functionally more autonomous. In
Durkheim's famous image of the "segmental society"—an analogy
he drew from the segmental worms—each local unit tends to be

4. A. L. Kroeber, *Anthropology*, New York, Harcourt, Brace, 1948, p. 284.

similar to the others and to be functionally complete in itself.[5] The analogy, of course, is not entirely satisfactory; analogies from biological to social systems seldom are. Tribal communities—those of most North American Indians and the pagan peoples of the Philippines, for example—are often bound together in a kind of interdependence by relations of trade and exchange of personnel through marriage, but there is something in the analogy, nevertheless: the communities that make up a tribal society do commonly have a kind of potential functional autonomy that makes it possible for them, for example, to multiply simply by fission.[6] The political order of the tribal society is often what Easton has called a "contingent" political order, a kind of miniature "international" order among essentially (or at least potentially) sovereign units.[7] Above all, the tribal community tends to be *culturally* more self-sufficient. There is little cultural differentiation, either within or among communities, and no overarching elite who might be the bearers of a differentiated elite culture. Each local community "contains" the whole culture.

The peasant community, however, has none of these kinds of self-sufficiency. Peasant villages may sometimes be little differentiated from one another, but they are bound together into a larger whole by a differentiated, superordinate elite, whom the villagers support through the payment of taxes or tribute and to whom they owe political allegiance. Most important, the elite are custodians of a distinct subculture, an elite or "high" culture, usually embodied in the scriptures and associated literature of one of the world religions. In relation to the culture of the elite, the peasant is a rustic whose culture is a "folk" version of the elite culture.[8] It is the association of the elite with the higher, "purer" version of the common culture that legitimates its economic and political

5. Émile Durkheim, *The Division of Labor in Society*, New York, The Free Press of Glencoe, 1947, p. 175.

6. Meyer Fortes, "The Structure of Unilineal Descent Groups," *American Anthropologist*, 55:17–41, 1953.

7. David Easton, "Political Anthropology," in Bernard J. Siegel (ed.), *Biennial Review of Anthropology*, Stanford, Calif., Stanford University Press, 1959, p. 237. Sir Henry Maine expressed a similar idea: "Ancient jurisprudence . . . may be likened to international law filling . . . the interstices between the great groups which are the atoms of society." *Ancient Law*, London, Oxford World's Classics, 1931, p. 138.

8. Robert Redfield, *Peasant Society and Culture*, Chicago, University of Chicago Press, 1956, pp. 60–66.

supremacy in the eyes of the peasant. It is the relative crudity, in the eyes of the elite, of the villagers' folk version of the common culture that makes him truly a peasant.

Thus, the secondary structural and cultural aspects of stratification assume an importance in peasant societies that they do not possess in tribal ones. Cultural differentiation gives peasant systems a dimension of "depth," an added "distance" from "top" to "bottom"; and this, in turn, gives the secondary structural question of the placement of persons in the system an added prominence. It creates, or at any rate makes more important, the problem of social mobility. It also raises the problem of the legitimacy of the system and its placement of persons and thus stimulates the growth of ideologies, both public and private, about how the system does and should work. It is all this which makes the peasant society typically "more highly stratified" than the tribal society.

We may also briefly contrast peasant societies with modern ones, though we shall say more about this later on when we consider the process of modernization of stratification as such. If the peasant society is in important respects more differentiated, both structurally and culturally, than the tribal one, it remains less differentiated, in equally important respects, than the society to which we give the name "modern." In contrast with those characteristic of modern societies, the elites of peasant society tend to be relatively unspecialized, to consist generally only of rulers and those learned in religion. And while handicrafts may reach extremely high levels of skill and aesthetic expressiveness, and trade may become an important calling, they remain essentially domestic occupations, carried out in the context of the household of the practitioner or his elite patron, despite the important role that corporate bodies such as guilds have sometimes played in promoting the interests of craftsmen and traders and in controlling entry into these occupations. Even government is commonly carried out in a domestic idiom, the polity being treated rather like an extension of the ruler's household and public officials as his domestic servants.[9] Lacking are those functionally specialized political and economic organizations, so characteristic of modern societies, that are separated from the households of their members and in which the

9. The evolution from personal servant to public official is traced in great detail in T. F. Tout, *Chapters in the Administrative History of Medieval England*, Manchester, The University Press, 1920–1933.

latter play purely occupational roles in exchange for basic income.
Also lacking is the cultural commitment to constant innovation
that lends a certain instability to both the cultural and structural
aspects of stratification in modern societies.

We may now move on to an examination of some of the differences among the traditional societies, both non-Western and
Western, out of which modern states have grown—the traditional
settings that have influenced modern systems of stratification.

THE MEDIEVAL WEST AND THE EMPIRE OF THE OTTOMANS
One important range of variation in traditional stratification
systems has been described by Machiavelli, with his usual matter-
of-fact clarity, in the fourth chapter of *The Prince:*

> . . . the principalities of which there is any historical record
> are managed in two different ways: in the first, one man is
> prince and all others are slaves, who act as ministers and aid in
> governing the country through his grace and permission; in the
> second type, there are a prince and barons, and the latter hold
> their positions not through the grace of their lord but through
> the antiquity of their blood. Such barons have states and sub-
> jects of their own, who recognize them as lords and have a
> natural attachment to them. The ruler has most authority in
> governments administered by a prince and his slaves, because in
> all the province nobody is recognized as superior except himself,
> and if the people obey any other they think of him as a minister
> and appointee, and do not feel any special love for him.
>
> The examples of these two kinds of government in our times
> are the Turk and the King of France.[10]

Max Weber has referred to this contrast to which Machiavelli
draws our attention as that between patrimonialism and feudalism,
adding his usual caveat to the effect that the concepts refer to ideal
types and that actual cases are always mixed. This of course was
true of the cases cited by Machiavelli. In medieval Europe there
existed, along with the hierarchies of hereditary, aristocratic fief
holders, appointed personal officials of kings and princes, like the
English sheriffs and the continental *ministeriales.* And in the Otto-

10. Niccolo Machiavelli, *The Prince and Other Works*, translated by A.
H. Gilbert, Chicago, Packard and Co., 1941, p. 104.

man Empire there were sometimes persons whose position approximated that of the feudal lord. The contrast, however, remains a real one and one that—since the empire of the sultans comprised the non-Western societies most familiar to Western thinkers—has played an important role in the development of thought concerning stratification, particularly in relation to the political order. It therefore provides an appropriate context in which to begin a discussion of some of the important differences to be found among traditional stratification systems. The Ottoman Empire does not, of course, represent the whole of the Islamic world, but as the last great premodern political focus of Islam it may appropriately serve as an example of Islamic society as a setting for modernization. Except where otherwise indicated, therefore, "Islamic society" will mean the realm of the Ottomans.

During the medieval period Islamic societies were at least as differentiated and sophisticated as were those of their Christian neighbors; during the earlier part of the period they were a good deal more so. Societies in both spheres rested upon peasant agriculture, skilled craftsmanship, and trade. Both were heirs to the culture of Graeco-Roman antiquity, which the learned of each combined with their respective monotheistic faiths (and of course with other cultural elements) to create new "high cultural" syntheses. In their patterns of stratification, however, the two systems differed greatly, thus providing an excellent illustration of the inadequacy of the view of such matters that limits itself to primary structural features.

Medieval Western societies tended to be divided into broad, culturally defined, almost hereditary strata—the estates. Western political theorists of that age were fond of organic analogies that compared the estates to parts of a human body, each having its fixed and necessary function.[11] No doubt there was a good deal more mobility between strata than these images suggest; also, they obscure the asymmetrical, but nevertheless very real, vertical ties of personal loyalty that often bound together peasant and lord. But such notions did, clearly, represent an elite ideal, an aristocratic class consciousness that in turn was in some degree emulated by humbler folk in relation to their own inferiors.[12] Along with this

11. Otto Gierke, *Political Theories of the Middle Ages*, translated by F. W. Maitland, Boston, Beacon Press, 1958, pp. 22–30.
12. Homans, *op. cit.*, p. 237.

ideology of aristocratic solidarity, and partly as an expression of it, there developed a marked cultural differentiation between the peasant, whose life and culture centered upon the annual cycle of agricultural tasks, and the noble knight, the bearer of a culture of chivalry that expressed his devotion to the protection of aristocratic honor and religion through military prowess.[13] Government was very largely in the hands of—indeed, essentially consisted of— the hierarchy of noble lords and vassals.

Islamic societies of the time also exhibited great inequalities of wealth and power, but the secondary culture and structure of stratification were strikingly different. Never, apparently, did there develop anything really comparable to the European estates, and in particular nothing at all closely resembling the closed feudal aristocracy. Rather, Islamic societies remained comparatively fluid and open to talent. As von Grunebaum's description of the social order of the Abbasids makes clear, this tendency toward social fluidity already existed in early medieval times:

> Money, though deprecated by the moralist, played its customary part. Education opened the doors of the great to the ambitious poor, and it was a prerequisite for public office, though princely whim did not always stop to scrutinize a favorite's qualifications. Political influence, military power, administrative rank, wealth, birth and schooling, in every possible combination, strengthened or counteracted one another in assigning a given individual his place in society.[14]

Under the later bureaucratic regime of the Ottomans, more relevant to our purposes, aristocracy of birth came to count for even less. The whole of what Gibb calls the "ruling institution"—the imperial administrative service—came to be staffed by men conscripted as young boys from among the non-Moslem subjects of the sultan, whose personal slaves they were considered to be.[15] It was this independence of recruitment to political office from considerations of ascribed status, and the resulting great personal power of the sultan and grand vizier over the appointment and

13. Sidney Painter, *French Chivalry*, Ithaca, N.Y., Cornell University Press, 1957.

14. Gustave von Grunebaum, *Medieval Islam*, Chicago, University of Chicago Press, 1946, pp. 211–212.

15. Sir H. Gibb and Harold Bowen, *Islamic Society and the West*, New York, Oxford University Press, Vol. I, Part 1, 1950, pp. 39, 199.

control of officials, that so attracted the attention of Machiavelli and other European thinkers familiar with the more decentralized and aristocratic polities of Europe. It was this that gave rise, in Western minds, to the image of "Oriental despotism." Nothing, indeed, is more indicative of the gulf that separates medieval European and Islamic secondary cultures of stratification than their different attitudes toward the legal status of slavery. In Europe, degrees of freedom correlated directly with social worth, and over the centuries the achievement of full personal freedom became a common goal of personal ambition and of social movements. In the Domain of Islam, however, legally unfree persons could so thoroughly monopolize the highest positions in the state that it became advantageous to free-born Moslems to assume slave status fictionally.

To be sure, this was not the whole story. In the countryside there were peasants who, while not formally unfree, labored under restrictions that sometimes led them to escape to the greater liberty of the city, much as their Christian contemporaries did. And here were "feudal" landholders, often members of the imperial cavalry, who held semihereditary "fiefs" and stood in something like the relationship of "lord" to those peasants. "Noble" blood was cherished by descendants of the Prophet. But a striking difference remained, nevertheless: the main lines of cleavage in society ran, not between hereditary, culturally differentiated estates, but rather between rulers and ruled, however these positions might in particular circumstances have been acquired.

How may we account historically for these differences between societies that otherwise were so closely related? This is of course too large a question to embark upon here. In any case, we are interested here more in the subsequent fate of the two systems under the impact of modernization than in their origins. We may, however, ask a more modest question and one more pertinent to our present concern: What part did Islam and Christianity, respectively, play in developing these differences?

A common answer has been given in the phrase "Islamic egalitarianism"; but so simply put, this seems inadequate, for Christianity also, in its primitive Gospel form, proclaims the religious equality of believers. In any case, religious doctrine seldom acts so directly upon social structure. Perhaps the difference lies, in part at least, in the greater concern of Islam to derive from its scriptures and traditions a concrete and detailed code of behavior covering every aspect of life. While, of course, law and government in medieval Christian Europe were also infused with religious influence, Islam, in a very real sense, simply *is* the *shari'a*, at least in relation to the external life. The Islamic ruler is thus not merely the defender of the faith; he is its direct administrator, and this in itself must have given added force to a universalistic code for behavior. It also meant that the holder of authority, whether religious or civil (to the limited extent to which such a distinction is possible in the Islamic polity) had to be educated in the law in a manner that was not required of the European lay feudal lord, although of course the clergy required education. Islamic "high culture" was thus embodied, to a greater extent than was the chivalric culture of the European nobility, in formal courses of study pursued in schools and universities, which thereby became channels for relatively universalistic recruitment into the political elite. The ultimate decay of the Ottoman state consisted in a retreat from this universalistic pattern into *de facto* hereditary recruitment and the purchase of office.[16] The decay of the Western feudal state, in contrast, involved greater political centralization and a strengthening of patrimonial universalism.

TRADITIONAL INDIA AND SUB-SAHARAN AFRICA

If the traditional Islamic social order was more fluid and open than that of the medieval West, that of traditional India, with its multiplicity of closed groups, was a good deal less so. Despite, therefore, the bewildering variety and seeming uniqueness of Indian patterns of stratification that, as Marriott has said, have tended to make them resistant to analytic treatment,[17] some discussion of these patterns would seem to be useful to our purpose. The obvious importance of India in any consideration of processes of

16. Gibb and Bowen, *op. cit.* In the attempted reforms of the last century of Ottoman rule, there was a reassertion of universalistic centralism. By this time, however, the regime was too fundamentally undermined by Western influence to succeed in this attempt. See Bernard Lewis, *The Emergence of Modern Turkey,* London, Oxford University Press for the Royal Institute of International Affairs, 1961, pp. 40–205.

17. Marriott, *op. cit.,* p. 1.

modernization in the non-Western world makes this doubly desirable.

Our discussion of stratification in feudal Europe and in the Ottoman Empire has been centered upon the state in a way that is less appropriate in the case of India, for two reasons: First, Hindu religion, which presumably has been the dominant influence in molding the culture of Indian stratification, appears to have been less directly concerned with the political order. There have, of course, been Hindu monarchies and, in connection with these, a tradition of thought concerning right government,[18] but Hinduism has on the whole directed its attention more to the perfection of the inner spiritual life and to the regulation of symbolic interpersonal behavior between persons presumed to be in different states of spiritual excellence than to the religious guidance of the polity as such. This tendency has been reinforced by a second factor: the Indian society upon which modernizing forces worked had been to a large extent politically "decapitated" by several centuries of Mogul and European domination. During the latest premodern period, therefore, indigenous patterns of stratification were reflected in village life and in a degree of India-wide Brahman cultural leadership but not, to the same degree, in the organization of a wider political order.

There are two principal aspects of traditional Indian society and culture that require some discussion because of the peculiar importance they may have had in creating a setting for the process of modernization of stratification: the "otherworldly" character of Indian religion as it enters into the "primary culture" of Indian stratification—the value system in terms of which roles are differentially evaluated; and, of course, the caste system. Both are exceedingly complex phenomena, and we can here do no more than outline some of their principal dimensions in relation to our present concerns.

Indian traditional religion was "otherworldly" in the sense that the application to everyday economic and political problems of a religiously informed body of thought was not for it a matter of major concern. The primary object of religiosity was rather the achievement, through contemplation, learning, and physical and emo-

18. D. Mackenzie Brown, *The White Umbrella: Indian Political Thought from Manu to Gandhi*, Berkeley, University of California Press, 1953.

tional self-discipline, of a state of inner spiritual perfection leading
to a union with the divine or to a favorable reincarnation. This
concern was reflected both in the classical scheme of the fourfold
division of society (*varna*) and, in large measure, in the reality of
traditional social life in the high position accorded the Brahman
as the most complete embodiment of this ideal. It was also conversely, reflected in the less worthy role assigned to the warrior-
ruler and the trader, in that order.

Here oversimplification is fatally easy. It is certainly not the case
that Brahmans and other Indians have lacked economic and political interests, as many village studies have shown and as Max
Weber has emphasized in his discussion of the general character of
Asian religions.[19] Indeed, Weber speaks of an "unrestricted lust for
gain in Asians large and small," which, he argues, is precisely the
result of a lack of religious guidance in the economic and political
fields—guidance of a sort that, we may add, was provided by St.
Augustine and the Moslem jurists.[20] For the problem of the distribution of wealth and power is present in any society; and in
addition in any peasant society, as we have noted, the political
and economic "pyramid" tends to be sharply "peaked," whatever
view the high culture may adopt with regard to it. Thus, it is impossible to exclude political and economic problems from social
life, but it is perfectly possible for religion to neglect or denigrate
them, and this is what traditional Indian religion seems to have
done. The principal creators and bearers of Hindu high culture,
and the persons allocated highest status in its view of society, were
not primarily exponents of religious law or moral virtue or wise
statecraft but rather persons who expressed most fully the ideal of
detachment from the world and the body in order to achieve the
fullest possible association with a transcendent divinity.

Furthermore, this role of principal bearer of the high culture
was allocated in a strictly ascribed way, and this brings us to the
second essential feature of traditional Indian stratification—the
castes. In traditional thought, the idea of caste was represented by
the scheme of the four *varnas*. In traditional social life it appeared

19. See especially F. G. Bailey's two books, *Caste and the Economic Fron-
tier*, Manchester, The University Press, 1957, and *Tribe, Caste and Nation*,
Manchester, The University Press, 1960; and Max Weber, *The Religion of
India*, New York, The Free Press of Glencoe, 1958.

20. Weber, *op. cit.*, p. 337.

in the form of the thousands of closed groups, ranging in scale from local clusters of a few families in a single village to very large bodies of persons stretching over wide regions of the subcontinent. The complexity of the caste hierarchy also varied widely, both in the numbers of distinguishable groups and in the numbers of ranks into which groups were classified.[21] Beneath all this variation, however, certain characteristic features stand out: Castes were hereditary and endogamous (or hypergamous), both features tending to maximize differentiation and exclusiveness; they were internally highly homogeneous with regard to rank, at any rate in terms of the wider stratification system; and they were ranked with respect to one another in terms of relative closeness to Brahman patterns of ritual behavior, commensality, and occupation. Within a local community, members of different castes tended to be bound to one another by obligations to supply mutual though often rather asymmetrical services, assigned in terms of a division of labor by caste.

The system (or systems!) was of course not so static nor so universally acepted as has sometimes been made out; if intercaste mobility was virtually excluded, there was certainly much competition for position among castes, both at regional and local levels, for the relationship of actual groups to the theoretical *varna* scheme could always be challenged. In the short run, however, and from the point of view of the life career of any individual, stratificatory position was probably more nearly fixed by ascription, and this ascription was probably more thoroughly legitimated by religion, than in any society of which we have knowledge.

This combination of thoroughgoing mysticism with rigidly ascribed status would seem to provide a singularly unpromising setting for modernization, for, whatever else the latter may consist in, it is generally agreed to involve a fundamental commitment to technological innovation and a degree of universalism in the allocation of occupational roles. That India nevertheless has thus far been in many respects one of the most successful modernizers among the new states indicates that the process of modernization is more complex than would at first appear. We shall have to return to this interesting problem subsequently.

There have, of course, been many other traditional societies and

21. Marriott, *op. cit.*

cultures upon the basis of which new states have arisen, and we cannot discuss them all. Before leaving the subject, however, it may be useful to draw attention to some of the peculiar features of Africa as a setting for the development of a number of the very newest among the new states. That part of Africa that stretches south from the Mediterranean to the southern borders of the Sudan belt and the Ethiopian highlands, and down the eastern coast as far as Sofala, was traditionally included within the world of Islam and Christianity. The remainder of the continent, however, differed from the other regions we have discussed in lacking the unifying influence of overarching literary high cultures. This is not, of course, to say that the many autonomous kingdoms and tribes lacked any sort of wider cultural community. Indeed, recent research on the linguistic and cultural history of Africa suggests that a very large part of the traditionally non-Islamic and non-Christian area was populated by peoples who were historically very closely related and shared much common culture.[22] But this is just the point: These wider unities were of the sort that are discovered by scholarly research. Not being embodied in a differentiated elite literary culture, they are less tangible—less easily made the objects of thought and action—than are such intellectualized literary complexes as Islam, Hinduism, and Christianity.

Traditional nonliterate Africa was not, however, entirely or even largely "tribal" in the sense discussed earlier in this essay. We have argued elsewhere that much of the continent was occupied by societies that might be called "protopeasant" societies—societies that, while they lacked literary culture, nevertheless exhibited patterns of structural differentiation not unlike those characteristic of the traditional peasant societies of the Near East, Asia, and Europe.[23] Along the Guinea Coast, in the region of the Great Lakes, and in the southeast there were great kingdoms, many of which counted their subjects in the hundreds of thousands, or even millions and in which village communities of agriculturalists were bound together by elites made up of rulers and their administrative staffs and religious specialists. The latter devoted themselves full time to politics and religion and were supported by the tribute and

22. Joseph H. Greenberg, "Studies in African Linguistic Classification III: The Position of Bantu," *Southwestern Journal of Anthropology* 5:309–317, 1949.

23. L. A. Fallers, "Are African Cultivators To Be Called 'Peasants'?" *Current Anthropology*, 2:108–110, 1961.

taxes of the village folk. Particularly in the west, there were substantial urban populations engaged in trade and skilled crafts.

Nevertheless, there remained in traditional Africa, even in the larger kingdoms with their elaborate political hierarchies, a kind of egalitarianism that seems to have had two principal roots. One of these was the pattern of kinship and family structure, which over much of the continent rested upon exogamous unilineal descent groups. Although in the structure of the state persons might stand to one another in highly asymmetrical dyadic relationships of economic and political superiority and subordination, every person tended also to belong to one or more extended, solidary descent groups that cut across such hierarchical structures. Exogamy produced, in addition, a set of affinal ties knitting descent groups together and inhibiting subcultural differentiation among them. At the village level, rights in land characteristically were heavily concentrated in the hands of kinship or local groups. Thus, tendencies toward crystallization of rigid horizontal strata were checked, in spite of the frequent concentration of power and wealth in elite hands.

The other factor that tended to inhibit the development of a more rigid stratification was, as we have noted, the absence of literary religious traditions, which might have provided the basis for more clearly differentiated elite subcultures. However much the traditional African king or chief might stand above his people in terms of power and wealth, he shared with them an essentially common set of notions concerning goodness and beauty and the nature of the world. To be sure, during the nineteenth century, as a result of the early work of missionaries, there began to develop for the first time in many areas a semihereditary, culturally differentiated elite characterized by Western education, adherence to Christianity, and a style of life based upon Victorian taste. These tendencies, however, appeared too late to come to fruition, for they were shortly overtaken by modernizing forces that prevented the solidification of a gentry class and tended to spread the new culture through all levels of society.

These few examples, of course, far from exhaust the variety of traditional systems of stratification. They may, however, serve to indicate the wide range of settings in which the processes of modernization have developed. We must now turn to an examination of these processes.

Structural modernization: differentiation of roles

IN referring on previous pages to the process of modernization, we have mentioned at a number of points that one of its
most characteristic features on the structural side has been the
emergence of specifically occupational structures and roles as dominant features of society and as foci of social stratification. We
must be clear about just what this means. Of course occupational
roles, in the sense of specialized tasks within a division of labor, are
nothing new in human history; these were common in all the
traditional societies we have discussed. What is specifically modern
is not specialization as such—although of course the development
of modern technologies has been accompanied by a much greater
degree of differentiation among occupational roles—but rather the
very widespread separation of occupational roles from domestic
life, and their location instead in specialized structures such as
business firms and governmental bureaucracies.

Few historical changes can have been as far-reaching as this in
their implications for social life. To Marx, more than anyone else,
we owe our understanding of what it has meant. Where once
nearly everyone did his daily work within his own or his patron's
household—that is to say, in a social context in which he stood to
his co-workers in a highly personal and total relationship of mutual
responsibility—now the great majority move daily between household and job, between two social worlds that not only are spatially
separated but, even more important, are in large measure normatively segregated and subject to different social rules. Even the
small businessman, the farmer and the private practitioner of a
profession—persons whose work may still be carried out most
nearly as an adjunct to the domestic group—are increasingly
viewed by the society at large—and by the income tax laws!—as
two persons: an employer and an employee. In this way the "self-
employed" are assimilated to the dominant structural pattern.

All this has had fundamental consequences for social stratification. When work remained essentially embedded within domestic
or wider kinship structures, it was but one among a total bundle of
features upon which the position of the group in the stratification
system depended. Even when occupational role was not legally or
normatively ascribed, as it often was, in practice for the vast majority of persons it could be learned and practiced only within the

domestic setting and hence was, *de facto*, hereditary. The development of distinct occupational structures—and also of extradomestic educational structures with the capacity to train persons for occupational roles—broke up this nexus—set occupational role free to become the principal focus and determinant of stratificatory position. Not completely, of course, for, as we have said before, so long as families persist as in some degree agents of socialization, they will influence the allocation of occupational roles; but now, to a very important degree, domestic units no longer *contain* the occupational structure, no longer determine the individual's place within it. Instead, the fate of the domestic unit itself, including its placement in the stratification system, depends upon the performance of one or more of its members within and according to the norms of, an external occupational system that cuts across kinship.

This, in turn, tends to have political consequences which we must discuss in a later section: in politics, as in economics, the individual comes to be influenced less by local, particularistic ties—comes to be a member of a wider, more impersonal polity. Nor does this process of structural differentiation take place in isolation from cultural developments. Indeed, there is a very important specifically cultural dimension to the modernization of stratification that we must discuss in the next section. For the moment, however, we may concentrate upon the process of occupational differentiation itself.

The widespread differentiation of occupational from other structures, along with further differentiation among occupational structures themselves, occurred first in the Western world and is now occurring with varying speeds in the new states as one element in the over-all process of modernization. It has not, however, occurred everywhere at the same rate and in the same way. We must ask ourselves how far the Western experience in this regard is being repeated, thus forming a reliable basis for prediction of the probable course of events in the new states, and how far the experience of the latter may be different in important respects. Again we are faced with a seemingly endless variety, out of which we can consider only some of the most important ranges of variation.

In the West, the differentiation of occupational from other structures came in the main as a result of the postmedieval rationalization and expansion of economies through the activities of private entrepreneurs. Its historical roots, of course, go back to the development in classical antiquity of the corporation—a structural unit having a legal "personality" distinct from those of its members. With increasing economic growth, this organizational form, which during the Middle Ages had persisted in the guilds, urban boroughs, and certain church bodies, was available for the creation of new kinds of economic enterprise: banks, trading companies and, ultimately, industrial concerns, drawing their leadership from existing merchants, gentry, and urban craftsmen and their workers from the latter and from the country villages.[24]

Throughout the early stages of this process, as Parsons has pointed out, persons at different levels within these business organizations stood in rather different structural positions with respect to them.[25] Participants in the new concerns were sharply divided between owner-entrepreneurs and employees, and it was the latter— the clerks and the new industrial proletariat—whose lives were now most clearly dichotomized between work and family, home and job. It was the worker who sold his labor to an external occupational structure in exchange for his family's basic subsistence. For the early capitalist—the owner-entrepreneur—the family-firm type of organization maintained the nexus between domestic and occupational structure. The firm was still the property of his domestic group. The full structural differentiation of the firm has only become complete during the late nineteenth and early twentieth centuries through the growth of the modern corporation, with its multiplicity of small stockholders and its hired management who, at least in formal structural terms, stand in the same relationship to it as do its industrial and white-collar employees.

Industry and commerce have not, of course, been the only fields for the differentiation of occupational structures in the West, though they clearly have in most cases provided the driving force in this process. The growth of government, an essential accompaniment of modern economic development despite the prominence of private entrepreneurship, has created large bodies of civil servants for whom the state is an occupational organization analogous to the firm. Practitioners of the learned professions, whose numbers have increased in response to the ever greater demand for

24. A. A. Berle, Jr., and Gardiner C. Means, "Corporation," *Encyclopedia of the Social Sciences*, Vol. 4, 1930, pp. 414–423.

25. Talcott Parsons, *Structure and Process in Modern Societies*, New York, The Free Press of Glencoe, 1960, pp. 98–131.

specialized knowledge and skills, have also been drawn into modern occupational structures. Many have become salaried employees of business or government, but even "private" practitioners are affected. As Parsons has pointed out, one of the functions of modern professional associations has been to separate professional practice from the private, domestic interests of the practitioner, much as the structural separation of home and job does in the case of the employee of business or government.[26] The professional becomes, in a sense, an employee of his profession.

And of course agriculture has also, in the main, been reorganized, either in the direction of the large-scale industrial farm, employing a hired labor force, or toward the mechanized and highly capitalized family farm in which, though dwelling and work-place may remain spatially contiguous, the enterprise is managed in a rigorously "economic" way, the entire product being sold for cash, out of which the family derives an income with which, in turn, everything consumed is purchased. Indeed, in the case of agriculture significant phases of modernization took place in western Europe and the United States well before the great growth of industry. Rural folk had in many areas ceased to be peasants in the sense of semisubsistence cultivators bound to the gentry by political and economic ties of subordinate dependence. Many had by then become small-scale agricultural entrepreneurs producing for a cash market, or else employees of large-scale estate farmers. Wage work and an impersonal market were therefore not novelties to many who moved to the towns to take up jobs in the new factories.

In the new states, the differentiation of occupational structures has not, of course, gone as far as it has in Western countries. As a very crude measure of the difference, we may note that in 1950 only about one-quarter of the "economically active" male population of Asia and Africa were engaged in nonagricultural pursuits, while in the West the proportion ranged from about two-thirds to more than four-fifths.[27] Even these figures underestimate the real structural difference, for agriculture has, as we have seen, become a more modern occupation in the West. In most of the new states,

26. Talcott Parsons, "The Professions and Social Structure," *Social Forces*, 17:457–467, 1938.
27. Kingsley Davis and Hilda Hertz Golden, "Urbanization and the Development of Pre-Industrial Areas," *Economic Development and Cultural Change*, 3:6–26, 1954, Table 2.

the great majority of the population are not yet involved in modern, differentiated occupational structures, and the occupational system remains little differentiated within itself; most persons remain semisubsistence peasant cultivators, often producing for a market but nevertheless carrying out their productive work within a village context in which occupation remains embedded in kinship and community structures—in which workmates are kith and kin. To put the matter in terms of the pyramid image, the stratification systems of the new states remain much more sharply "peaked" and more "broad-based" than those of Western societies.

It is not, however, crude differences in the degree of occupational modernization that mainly concern us here, for we cannot assume that the new states are merely less far along on a path identical with the one traveled earlier by the West. In important respects they are approaching modernization by different paths, and we must therefore examine qualitative differences in the *pattern* of occupational modernization, both among the new states and between them, taken together, and the West. In surveying some of these differences, we may look first at the elite and then at the "common man" level of society. We shall proceed topically, instead of area by area, in discussing this matter of structural modernization because differences in this regard do not correspond in any clear way with the sample areas we have chosen. When we turn to cultural modernization, we shall again proceed in terms of our three main examples.

BUREAUCRATS AND ENTEPRENEURS

First of all, as has often been pointed out, bureaucrats are more prominent, and entrepreneurs less prominent, in the elites of the new states than in those of the West—at any rate during comparable stages of modernization. There have been three main reasons for this: First, the early stages of economic modernization were mostly initiated, not by indigenous enterprise but rather by entrepreneurs from the West, where modernization was already well under way. We need not enter into a discussion of the famous problem, upon which Max Weber has shed so much light, of why this was so—why, that is, among all the traditional societies of the medieval period, it was in the West that modernization took place first. For our purposes we need only note that during the eighteenth and nineteenth centuries the West had vigorous entrepreneurs to spare for overseas enterprise, while in Asia and Africa such men were rare—though of course there was much variation in this respect.

(It is perhaps worth pointing out, however, that it is easy to overstress this contrast and to look, by way of explanation, for more profound cultural and structural differences between West and non-West than are in fact necessary to account for what happened. The advantage of initiative gained by Western peoples in being first may well have been of greater magnitude than the social and cultural peculiarities that made them first. There is doubtless something in the claim of non-Western nationalists who say that, while Western colonial enterprise may have contributed an initiative to over-all economic development, it also inhibited the development of indigenous entrepreneurship simply by getting "in the way," quite apart from colonial policies favoring nationals of the metropolitan powers. Rather ironically, contemporary East Africans feel themselves excluded from business by entrenched Indian enterprise in somewhat the same way as an earlier generation of Indians in India felt themselves blocked by Englishmen!)

A second factor, related to the first, is that, being industrial latecomers with the Western example constantly before their eyes, and lacking a strong indigenous private enterprise, the new states have since independence tended to push development at a pace and in a fashion that required that much of the initiative remain in the hands of the state. The pre-independence colonial governments, which tended to exercise a rather mercantilistic authority over the economies of the colonies, provided precedent for this way of doing things, which of course required expanded bureaucracies capable of the necessary planning and administration.

Finally, another result of the lateness of modernization in the new states is that modern commerce and industry themselves have come to them in later, more complex and large-scale forms in which the small individual entrepreneur is less prominent and the salaried executive more so than was the case in the West during comparable periods. This tendency is reinforced by the prominence in the economies of many new states of the large-scale production or extraction of raw materials for export. Even within "private business," therefore, many of the modern elite occupational roles are of the bureaucratic type, although of course as the economy expands, and in particular as the internal consumer market develops, there may arise new opportunities for individual enterprise in light industry and distributive trades.

All this is, of course, in the nature of a broad overview, and is subject to much local qualification and variation. India and Egypt, for example, have much more vigorous entrepreneurial groups than have, say, the African and most Southeast Asian countries, particularly if one excludes in the case of these latter countries such non-European immigrant merchant groups as Chinese, Indians, and Syrians. The former British dependencies in general, and India above all, are better supplied with trained civil servants than are other new states. Perhaps the most modern of all the states that have assumed sovereignty since World War II, in terms of the proportion of persons involved in modern occupational structures, is the Republic of the Philippines. On the other hand, some countries, like Indonesia and the Republic of the Congo (Leopoldville), came into nationhood with painful shortages of modern elites of all kinds. It is especially in this area of occupational modernization that differences in former colonial policies and practices make themselves felt. Britain's long, and relatively responsible (from the point of view of modernization), administration in India and the much briefer American administration in the Philippines left these countries with much more modernized occupational structures than did, for example, the long Dutch administration in Indonesia. It is in part for this reason that India, despite the apparently rigid nature of her traditional society, is today among the most modern of the new states.

Beyond such differences, however, a characteristic pattern remains: While there are developing in the new states the same broad types of modern elite occupations that appeared earlier in the West, the balance between the different groups—and in particular between bureaucrats and entrepreneurs—remains rather strikingly different.

WORKERS AND PEASANTS

When we turn to the new industrial and commercial wage-labor force, we again find occupational roles broadly familiar to Western experience, but with important differences. To begin, with, of course, this sector of the population remains small, by contemporary Western standards, in relation to the peasantry. But beyond this quantitative difference, the new wage workers, like the new elites, have come into existence under circumstances rather different from those in which their Western counterparts appeared. Like the new elites, they are mostly products of a more recent phase of modernization, in which the state has exercised greater initiative, or at any rate greater control, and in which technologically and organizationally more advanced—often larger-scale and more complex—forms have tended to be applied at the start. Although the governments of some new states—notably India—have for ideological reasons tried to encourage small-scale home industries, on the whole new states wishing to establish, say, a cotton textile industry, have equipped themselves with large factories and automatic machines rather than with spinning jennies. And governments, whether as state entrepreneurs or as custodians of the public welfare, have generally attempted, under the influence of modern welfare-state policies, to assure workers conditions of employment resembling as much as possible those of the modern West rather than those of the "dark, satanic mills" and Dickensian countinghouses of an earlier era.

Therefore, while the workers in the new states resemble their Western counterparts in becoming the occupants of full-time occupational roles played in differentiated occupational structures outside the family and local community, they have usually entered upon this condition under circumstances rather less productive of all those frustrations and anxieties that Marx subsumed under the term "alienation" than did the Western pioneers of industrial labor. There is an ample supply of alienated people in the new states; but industrial workers are not the most prominent among them, both because the industrial sector remains small and because workers tend to be relatively secure and prosperous in relation to their countrymen.[28]

Some of the political causes and consequences of these differences will be considered in the last section. Here we may usefully note one further area of variation: in the West, the early in-

28. See, for example, Morris D. Morris, "The Labor Market in India," in W. E. Moore and A. S. Feldman (eds.), *Labor Commitment and Social Change in Developing Areas*, New York, Social Science Research Council, 1960, pp. 173–200.

dustrial labor force was in the main recruited from among persons for whom independent agriculture was not an alternative pursuit. The new factories were largely staffed by persons who had already become putting-out craftsmen or wage workers, either in towns or on the land, where wage work had gradually replaced the various forms of servile employment as the medieval manor was transformed into a modern "capitalist" estate. The Western worker of the eighteenth and early nineteenth centuries was usually, therefore, committed by sheer economic necessity to some form of wage employment. In the new states today, there are extremely great differences in the degree to which this is so. In some Asian and Near Eastern countries, even where land is held in some form of peasant proprietorship, overpopulation produces an "industrial reserve army" on a scale beyond even Marx's fertile imagination. One consequence, as Morris has pointed out for India, may be a labor force deeply committed to employment and urban life.[29] In many of the African countries, however, wage work competes for labor with individual cash-crop agriculture—often quite lucrative in cotton, coffee, and cocoa areas. The result is a widespread pattern of oscillation between farm and job, village and town, sometimes on a cycle of months or years, sometimes through daily "commuting," combining wages and cash-crop agriculture in whatever way the particular local circumstances make most profitable.[30] In such circumstances, a differentiated, deeply committed labor force is slow to develop; its absence, in turn, influences the degrees and kinds of industrialization that are possible.

We have already, in speaking of other sectors of the occupational system, said a number of things about agriculture in the new states. It is not quite accurate to suggest, as we did earlier, that agriculture represents simply a residuum of occupational traditionalism in societies the other sectors of whose populations are modernizing, for agriculture has not, of course, remained unaffected by the changes at work elsewhere. To be sure, there remain in many countries large numbers of free or tenant peasants engaged in what is essentially subsistence cultivation.

In many areas the plantation production of cash crops under

29. *Ibid.*
30. Walter Elkan and Lloyd Fallers, "Competing Status Systems," in Moore and Feldman, *op. cit.*, pp. 238–257.

the direction of either European settlers or enterprising indigenous gentry was an important early form of articulation with the international economy, and in some this remains true. In such cases country folk may come to form a kind of rural proletariat, depending upon wages for a livelihood but still living in varying degrees something like a village life. In other areas, including some in which plantation development was prominent earlier but has since independence been eliminated by land-redistribution programs, the independent cash-crop cultivator is the characteristic figure. In only a relatively few cases, however, such as the rubber areas of Malaya and the cocoa areas of West Africa, are independent cultivators coming to resemble modern farmers, systematically seeking to extract the maximum productivity from the land. More commonly, particularly where overpopulation is a problem, there is a tendency for peasant agriculture to become more and more labor-intensive in order to absorb the additional people—a tendency that might be characterized as "antimodern."[31] In general, then, it seems true that the agricultural populations of the new states remain the least influenced by modern occupational structures.

SCHOOLS

Thus far we have considered the modernization of the primary structure of stratification through the differentiation of new occupational structures. It remains to say a word about the secondary structure through which persons are allocated among roles.

As we noted earlier, normatively ascribed status—the allocation of occupational and other status-relevant roles in terms of kinship —was not so universal a feature of traditional societies as is sometimes assumed. Nevertheless, even in such comparatively open traditional societies as the Ottoman Empire, the relatively undifferentiated nature of the occupational system, and the scarcity of educational institutions capable of providing occupational training outside the family, meant that, in practice, occupational roles were learned by most persons within a kinship group. The development of extrafamilial educational structures, and of course

31. Clifford Geertz, "The Development of a Javanese Economy: A Socio-Cultural Approach," Document c/56-1, Center for International Studies, Massachusetts Institute of Technology, Cambridge, Mass., 1956.

the proliferation of occupational roles themselves, are largely responsible for the great increase in opportunities for mobility that comes with modernization, whatever the traditional setting in which the process occurs.

A number of factors have, however, combined to give schools and universities an even more important role in the modernization of the new states than they played in the earlier experience of the West. First of all here, as in the primary structure of stratification, the relative lateness of modernization has made a difference. The earlier, more primitive industries of the West were able to make more use of traditional craft skills, learned in the family or through personal apprenticeship. Early entrepreneurs were clever and ambitious artisans, merchants, and gentry, drawing more upon traditional skills and inventiveness than upon formal education.[32] Formal education played a role, particularly in the spread of basic literacy and in creating in the elite a greater receptivity to technological and social innovation, but it did not become the major channel of recruitment into managerial and industrial roles until relatively late. Government service, of course, was more closely related to formal education, but remained a relatively small sector of the occupational structure.

In the new states the transplantation from the West of relatively advanced forms of commerce, industry, and civil service, requiring greater and more specialized training, has given formal education a greater prominence from the start. The lack of educated persons has been viewed by governments as a major obstacle to more rapid development, and this has led them to invest heavily in educational expansion. In consequence, it is probably true that formal education has played a substantially more prominent role in occupational mobility in the new states than it did at comparable periods in the West. Whether this means that over-all occupational mobility is greater in the new states—or at any rate in some of them—than it was in, say late eighteenth- and nineteenth-century Western Europe is difficult to say, for we lack adequate data, but it may well be so. The allocation of occupation on the basis of education does not, of itself, of course, mean equality of opportunity, for kinship groups may—

32. Sir Eric Ashby, "Education for an Age of Technology," in C. Singer, H. J. Holmyard, A. R. Hall, and T. I. Williams, *A History of Technology*, New York, Oxford University Press, 1958, Vol. V, pp. 776–797.

always do to some degree—influence access to education. But this influence may well be less marked in many of the new states than at earlier periods in the West, for education in the new states, despite its missionary beginnings in many areas, is today much more the creature and creation of government than it has been in most Western countries until quite recently. The same popular demands that lead governments to expand education as a means to national development and individual opportunity also push them toward provision for equal access to it.

A further factor that tended to give greater prominence to formal education in the new states was the colonial setting in which the earlier phases of modernization took place. Quite apart from the intellectual content of their curricula, schools were the places where one learned the language and customs of the Europeans who dominated the new occupational structures and with whom, consequently, it was necessary to communicate effectively in order to succeed occupationally. Even with political independence and an increasing cultural indigenization of the new occupational structures, there has remained in most cases between them and the rest of the society a cultural gap, greater than that usually found in the West, where modern institutions are indigenous and hence clothed in familiar idiom, that the school plays a crucial role in bridging.

In some areas, the expansion of educational facilities in response to popular demand has run ahead of the growth and differentiation of the occupational system, with the result that large numbers of persons enter the labor market with expectations of employment that the occupational system cannot fulfill. The point here is not, as is sometimes suggested, that the content of education makes persons unfit for the jobs available to them; a secondary-school education does not of itself make a man less fit to be a truck driver or even a peasant farmer. The sense of grievance felt by the underemployed secondary-school or university graduate results, rather, from the fact that governments in the new states are held directly responsible for the welfare and progress of their people in a way that was less true in the West during comparable phases of modernization. In facing these responsibilities, governments find it easier to expand educational facilities than employment opportunities, and this results in a constant decline in the market value of education. In consequence, the educated underemployed or unemployed are in many of the new states a more serious source of alienation and political disaffection than are industrial workers.

Cultural modernization: religion and science

THESE structural changes, centering upon the differentiation of occupational and educational systems, do not exhaust the processes of modernization that are at work in the social stratification systems of the new states. If we are more fully to comprehend these processes, we must also examine the changes that take place in culture—in the systems of belief and value by means of which persons relate participation in the new occupational structures to their aspirations for themselves and their countries. Indeed, there is an important sense in which the new occupational structures are not of significance to social stratification at all except in so far as this happens. The vertical dimension—the dimension of relative worth that we commonly regard as central to the very notion of social stratification—comes into being only insofar as persons interpret and evaluate roles in terms of some common culture.

This is not, of course, to say that the initiative for change lies wholly on the side of culture and that culture is the dominant force in shaping stratification systems. To say so would be to attribute to it an unwarranted degree of solidity and autonomy, and to ignore the pressure structural change can exert upon ideas. In actual societies there is rather a constant interplay between the structure of social relations, based upon proximate mutual understandings and expectations, and those more general common understandings concerning the larger meaning and worth of social relations that tend to develop in societies. Especially in societies of the complexity of those we are considering here, change may in varying degrees "originate" in either the sphere of ideological creativity or in the network of social relations. Compelling new ideas may call forth new kinds of social relations; new kinds of social relations, entered into by individuals with little thought concerning their larger meaning, may assume such magnitude that they challenge the existing consensus concerning the meaning and purpose of human endeavor. But seldom, if ever, can important changes be understood in either purely cultural or purely social terms.

In the modernization of stratification in the new states, however, structural changes have generally run ahead of cultural ones, for the new occupational structures we have been discussing were in large part introduced through the initiative of Western empire builders, entrepreneurs, and missionaries. New institutions were in many cases quite literally "transplanted," presenting members of non-Western societies with opportunities to participate in new roles in business firms, bureaucracies, plantations, mines and, perhaps most important of all, schools—structures whose affairs were managed in Western terms—before traditional cultures had had an opportunity to interpret and evaluate them. It is this element of abrupt confrontation, resulting from the relatively sudden expansion of Western power in the eighteenth and nineteenth centuries, that has led so many writers to use terms like "Western impact" and "Western challenge" in describing the modernization of the non-Western world.

There was, to be sure, an important element of this in the modernization of the West itself, for societies and cultures never change all of a piece, even when the impulse for change comes largely from within. Traditional Western culture, too, felt itself "confronted" in the course of modernization by new and disturbing forces; traditional elites felt themselves threatened by "new men." And, in the non-Western world, the abruptness of the "challenge" varied a good deal with the time and circumstances of contact. In India and Indonesia, for example, the relationship with the West developed much more gradually and over a longer time than it did in Africa, where a fully industrialized West quite suddenly, in the late nineteenth century, burst in upon the previously more or less isolated interior. In Egypt and the other lands of the old Ottoman Empire, which had always been in relatively close contact with the West and which in most cases never became fully colonial, cultural engagement came to a much greater extent contemporaneously with structural innovation, or even preceded it in some respects. But because modernization occurred first in the West and was everywhere, to one degree or another, imported from the West to non-Western countries, the traditional cultures of the latter have all faced the problem of coming to terms rather abruptly with kinds of activities and social relations that were not only different from those familiar to traditional societies but that also had developed out of an alien tradition and came backed by alien power.

It is against this background that we must try to compare the movements of thought and ideology that have been associated with the emergence of modern occupational structures in the West and in the new states.

THE WEST: INNOVATIVE UTILITARIANISM

In modern Western societies the new occupational structures have achieved a culturally dominant position in stratification systems in the sense that occupational performance has come to be generally accepted as the primary criterion of merit. This does not, of course, mean that there is anything like perfectly open recruitment to occupational roles or that nonoccupational criteria, such as patterns of behavior, speech, and style of life, often acquired through socialization in the family and hence of an ascribed nature, are not taken into account in persons' judgments of their own and others' status. These do indeed remain important features of the secondary structure and culture of stratification in the West, as we mentioned earlier. But at the heart of the modern Western culture of stratification there lies a commitment to the notion that the truly admirable man is the one who "does a job well," particularly an economically and socially useful job in one of the new occupational structures.

It is important to recognize that there are two distinct, though related, values involved in this commitment: equality of opportunity and productivity. While the first tends to be more prominent as a moral and political issue, the second is perhaps more fundamental as a characteristic of specifically *modern* Western culture, as Parsons and others have pointed out.[33] From the characteristically modern attitude that human life is subject to constant improvement through the application of intelligence and diligence,[34] the notion that talent should receive its opportunity to contribute to this process follows as a kind of corollary. But advance-

33. Talcott Parsons, *Structure and Process* . . . , *op. cit.*, pp. 98–131; J. K. Galbraith, *The Affluent Society*, Boston, Houghton Mifflin Co., 1958, pp. 334–356.
34. Reinhard Bendix, *Social Science and the Distrust of Reason*, University of California Publications in Sociology and Social Institutions, Vol. 1, No. 1, Berkeley, 1951.

ment according to merit can also be a feature of quite traditionalistic societies and can be applied in relation to quite traditionalistic ends, as we have seen in the case of the empire of the Ottoman sultans. Another well-known example is, of course, the traditional Chinese bureaucracy. It is the innovative utilitarianism of the modern West that is the most distinctive cultural counterpart and expression of its occupationally oriented stratification system and that underlies the high prestige within it of the entrepreneur and the engineer.

Much scholarship has been devoted to tracing the development of this element in modern Western culture. Max Weber has stressed the role of the Protestant Reformation in creating a spirit of "this-worldly asceticism" conducive to systematic, rationalistic devotion to a calling. An equally important and complementary development, clearly, was the deistic *modus vivendi* between Christianity and natural science that was arrived at during the seventeenth and eighteenth centuries. Although the notion that the truth is revealed not in God's word but in his work[35] did not by any means dispose of all the theological and philosophical problems posed by the existence within a single culture of these two bodies of thought, it did provide, and continues to provide, a tolerable personal solution for vast numbers of Western people.

In these terms it has been possible to believe not only that science and religion are compatible but also that the discovery of the laws of nature is actually a religiously sanctioned duty, a means of glorifying the Creator of the great ordered system of the universe. The application of science to practical technology could similarly be viewed as the fulfillment of the purposes of a rational and benevolent God. These ideas might even be extended beyond technology to society itself through the notion that the ultimate product of rationally ordered creation was rational man himself, destined by God's will to discover through reason the proper ordering of his society.[36] The Lutheran elimination of sacramental magic and the development of biblical criticism also contributed to the reconciliation of science and religion. Thus, a religious tradition continuous with the medieval past could take part in

35. Carl Becker, *The Heavenly City of the Eighteenth-Century Philosophers*, New Haven, Yale University Press, 1932, p. 62.

36. See, for example, Kant's "Idea for a Universal History with Cosmopolitan Intent," in *The Philosophy of Kant*, edited by Carl Friedrich, New York, Modern Library, 1949, pp. 116–131.

the formation of a new culture of stratification that admired and inspired the innovator.

Some such rapprochement between the religious ideas that move men most deeply and scientific technology is clearly required if modern occupational structures are to become fully "at home" in a society—if they are to become central to its stratification system in the sense of engaging the ambition and admiration of its members. Nowhere in the new states has such a reconciliation been completely achieved (nor, of course, has it in the West, though the process has doubtless gone further there), but everywhere the two sets of ideas seem to be at work upon each other. The attractions of modernity in terms of power and welfare appear to be too great to permit it to be rejected out of hand. But neither do traditional cultures and the traditional elites that sustain and are sustained by them simply melt away in the face of modern ideas and forms of organization. Nor are differences among traditions irrelevant to an understanding of the modernization of stratification. The triumph of modernity may indeed be in some sense inevitable in the long run, but the problems encountered along the way seem to differ rather markedly in different traditional settings, and these differences promise to influence the shapes that modernity will ultimately take in the various new states.

INDIA: SYNCRETISM

Perhaps the most interesting case is that of India, with its apparent paradox of, on the one hand, traditional mysticism bound up with a unique social rigidity and, on the other, one of the most modernized occupational structures of all the new states. Part of the explanation, no doubt, lies in the long duration and peculiar depth of British influence, but this can hardly account for a situation in which so many leaders of the drive toward modernity have found it possible to draw inspiration for their efforts from precisely that religious tradition which has seemed to so many observers to be so inimical to the modern spirit.

Whatever other factors may be involved, part of the answer undoubtedly lies in the extraordinary pluralism of the Indian religious tradition, encouraged by the fragmentation of Indian society into countless endogamous groups and by its loose association with the central organization of the polity during several centuries of

Mogul and British rule. The former provided an extremely rich
and diverse body of cultural resources for reinterpretation in
modern terms, while the latter freed higher culture from a too
intimate, rigidifying involvement with a particular political structure, at any rate above the local village level, where the caste
system was primarily rooted. Singer has pointed out that scholarly
Western interpretations of Indian religion, including that of
Weber, have commonly overemphasized the dominance, under
Brahman leadership, of the otherwordly renunciation aspect of
Hinduism, neglecting those religious traditions, more hospitable
to economic enterprise, that were associated with the merchant
castes.[37] In modern times, Gandhi has been able to draw from
the Bhagavad-Gita inspiration for a movement that, if not specifically technological and economic in its aims—indeed, in some respects quite the opposite—has nevertheless been strikingly successful in harnessing traditional asceticism to the very this-world task
of nation-building. Other modern intellectual and political leaders
have found in the same tradition support for a full-scale attack
on the problems of industrialization through Socialist planning,
leading Singer to propose, paraphrasing Weber, a study of "The
Hindu Ethic and the Spirit of Socialism."[38]

One cannot, of course, expect to find in any of the new states a
cult of the private entrepreneur of the sort that developed in the
nineteenth-century West. As we have seen, the structural situation
is all against it, as is nationalist ideology, which tends to associate
capitalism with Western domination. The modern elites of the
new states, like their economies, are inevitably "mixed"; entrepreneurs must yield much of the task of representing modernity
to bureaucrats and politicians.

All of which does not, of course, mean that there remains no
tension between Indian religion and cultural modernity. The magic
and mysticism of popular Hinduism are still real enough. And
within the body of modern Indian thought there are important
strains between the more secular, technocratic planners and the
Gandhians, for whom technological modernization can never be

37. Milton Singer, "Cultural Values in India's Economic Development,"
Annals of the American Academy of Political and Social Science, 305:81–91
May, 1956; review of Max Weber's *Religion of India, American Anthropologist*, 63:143–151, 1961.
38. Singer, *Annals, op. cit.*, 86.

an end in itself and must often take second place to other values.[39] One has the impression, however, that, in one way or another, most Indians who occupy modern elite occupational roles have found ways of relating these activities meaningfully to personal and national aspirations that they feel are informed by Hindu tradition. Perhaps the very luxuriant diversity of that tradition itself reduces the need for more complete cultural synthesis, making it easier for modern entrepreneurs and civil servants to share high prestige in the eyes of the same public with representatives of traditional saintliness. What many observers of the Indian scene feel is, from a political standpoint, a dangerous tendency toward disunity may also be a valuable source of cultural flexibility.

In all the new states, the interaction between traditional culture and the ideas associated with technological and occupational modernization is complicated by the historical association of the latter with Western imperialism, to the struggle against which the new states owe their very existence. A satisfactory synthesis therefore requires some form of ideological separation of modernity as a national goal from its specifically Western associations. Here again the Indian tradition of diversity and syncretism appears to have made this relatively easy, enabling Indian modernizers to innovate while retaining a deep sense of national identity and continuity—indeed, allowing them to develop a certain sense of mission to "save the West from itself" by demonstrating to Westerners the proper uses of modernity. This attitude is common in the writings of Tagore and Gandhi and in the pronouncements of contemporary Indian political leaders.

ISLAM: DOUBLE-MINDEDNESS

The Moslem peoples of the Near East, on the other hand, appear to have found both the reconciliation of modernity with traditional culture and its separation from the humiliating association with Western domination somewhat more difficult. At first sight this seems rather surprising. The Islamic world certainly shares with the West more of the classical background of modern thought, both religious and philosophical, than did Hindu India, and medieval Islam itself was a good deal more rationalistic, less magical in content, than Hinduism. Indeed, orthodox Islam, with

39. Singer, *ibid.*, 86–88.

its austere monotheism and legalistic rigor, was doubtless the most rationalistic of all the traditional world religions. But the very closeness of the Islamic association with the West over many centuries and the particularly humiliating nature of the later phases of this association, involving the decay of Ottoman power and a peculiarly rapacious and degrading pattern of Western domination, with few of the redeeming features of responsible colonialism, seems to have left modern Islam in a posture of defensiveness from which it has found it difficult to contribute a substantial religious element to Near Eastern modernist thought. Gibb has characterized "the attitude of the vast majority of the orthodox *'ulamâ'*," the body of the professionally learned, as

> . . . a strict and unbending refusal to countenance any kind of truckling to the new philosophies and sciences. For them, these are all nothing but *ahwâ'*—velleities, caprices, unsubstantial imaginings of the rebellious human mind, or satanic devices to ensnare the heedless and foolish. A thousand years ago their ancestors met the assault of Greek philosophy in the same spirit and stood their ground. If Islam is a divine revelation, as they believe, history will repeat itself: the forces of materialism, which the Divine Providence has permitted for a time to tempt and mislead the sick-hearted and the hypocrites, will surely be overcome. . . . It is not to be wondered at that to the generality of *'ulamâ'* the West stands for pure materialism.[40]

This is not to say, of course, that Islam has lacked modernist thinkers, merely that their success as synthesizers of the traditional and the modern has thus far not been so great as that of their counterparts in Hindu India. The case of the Egyptian Shaikh Mohammed Abdu, whom students of recent Islamic intellectual history speak of as the ablest and most influential of the modernists, is instructive in this regard. A student, and later a teacher, at the university mosque of al-Azhar who rose at the turn of the century to the office of Mufti of Egypt, Mohammed Abdu attempted in his own writings to reconcile Islamic theology with modern science, in a way rather reminiscent of eighteenth-century Western deism, and used his influence to press for the inclusion of scientific subjects in the curriculum at al-Azhar. He was, how-

---

40. H. A. R. Gibb, *Modern Trends in Islam*, Chicago, University of Chicago Press, 1945, pp. 47–48. See also J. M. Ahmed, *The Intellectual Origins of Egyptian Nationalism*, London, Oxford University Press, 1960.

ever, unable to carry the Egyptian 'ulamâ' with him on either score, despite his eminence, and Gibb remarks that his influence has largely been confined to the educated laity. This imperviousness of the 'ulamâ' to modern thought has been reinforced by their cohesiveness as the official exponents of the *shari'a*—the body of sacred law, drawn from the Koran and the traditions of the Prophet, which Islamic orthodoxy has regarded as a full and sufficient rule for life.

At the same time, there has grown up in Near Eastern countries a separate modern, secular educational system that inherits much of the prestige traditionally enjoyed by learning in Islamic lands and that educates members of the new political and technological elites. The result has been a rather sharp bifurcation between traditional and modern elites, and a marked tendency on the part of the latter toward what Gibb calls "double-mindedness." In Turkey, the heartland of the Ottoman Empire (and not, of course, a "new state" in the strict sense), this tendency toward disengagement of serious Islamic thought from the problems of modernity has been carried to an extreme by a thoroughgoing secularization.[41] Popular piety, of course, has continued to play an important role throughout the Near East in nationalist and pan-Arab enthusiasm, and even most members of the modern elites (at least outside Turkey) seem to remain attached to Islamic belief in some form. But, cut off as it is by the intransigence of the ulama from serious concern with modern problems, professional theology contributes little to this personal piety, which consequently tends either to express itself in mysticism, sometimes drawing upon the traditions of sufism, or else to become a kind of religious veneer for political nationalism.

Nowhere in the non-Western world do the traditional religious cultures easily find common ground with modern scientific and social thought, or traditional elites with modern ones—nor, we should remind ourselves, have they done so in the West. Everywhere in the modern world there exists among intellectuals in particular—but also among modern elites of other kinds—a strong affinity for secular ideologies that are more easily reconciled with modernity. Still, everywhere, East and West, the religious cultures

41. Bernard Lewis, *The Emergence of Modern Turkey*, London, Oxford University Press, 1961.

of the medieval past and the religious systems that informed them continue, even when specifically religious commitment has been lost and traditional elites swept aside, to play an important role in giving modern men a sense of identity and historical continuity —a sense of national and personal purpose and self-esteem that is of particular importance in a period of heightened national self-consciousness. When new elites take their places beside the old, or even displace them, the new men, so long as the rupture is not total, can draw upon the sentiments embodied in the traditional stratification systems in support of their own positions.

Looking at the new states of Asia and the Near East, and at the West itself, it is deceptively easy to become impressed by the alienation of modern elites from traditional culture or by the shallowness of their allegiance to it; to appreciate how important it still is in those areas, it is instructive to turn, by way of contrast, to the new states of Africa that lack such traditional cultures— lack, that is to say, traditional literary cultures based upon world religions.

AFRICA: THE SEARCH FOR CONTINUITY

Those African countries that lie to the south of the Sudan belt and the Ethiopian highlands—that is to say, beyond the reach of premodern Islamic and Christian influence—have great difficulty relating themselves to the traditional African past. Having acquired their boundaries through European diplomacy, they are often extremely heterogeneous ethnically and linguistically. Underlying cultural unity certainly exists over large areas of the continent: For example, the speakers of Bantu and related languages, who occupy a very large part of sub-Saharan Africa, are very closely related historically and share many elements of common culture. But, not being embodied in supertribal literature and religion, these common elements are difficult for elites to utilize in the creation of common cultures for the new states. Culturally and linguistically akin though they often are, the traditional states and tribes tended in the past, and tend today, to confront one another as sovereign entities. The positions of their traditional elites —the kings, chiefs, and religious practitioners—always rest upon loyalties that from the point of view of the new states tend to be divisive. It is therefore not surprising that in many African countries the system of stratification reveals a particularly sharp cleavage between traditional-tribal and national-modern elites and that "the tribal question" assumes great political prominence.

Rather paradoxically, the more the traditional elites succeed in modernizing themselves, the more divisive their influence becomes, for this merely serves to associate the desire for modernity with traditional state and tribal loyalties, thus sapping their peoples' loyalty to the wider society and polity. An excellent example is provided by the Kingdom of Buganda, which forms the geographical core and contains between one-quarter and one-third of the population of the soon-to-be independent British protectorate of Uganda. The Baganda are among the most modernized of Africa's peoples; they enjoy a high level of education, have a relatively advanced and prosperous agricultural economy, and a government that is relatively modern and efficient, being served by a corps of quite well-trained civil servants. Baganda physicians, lawyers, and teachers have taken their places alongside the chiefly hierarchy, itself now manned by educated persons, to form a single elite in the eyes of the people. But all this has merely served to make the kingdom more "indigestible" from the point of view of Uganda as a whole. Most Baganda, viewing the traditional kingdom as the natural vehicle for modernization, have stubbornly refused to give their loyalty to a wider national unit.[42] Similar tendencies have been exhibited by such West African peoples as the Ashanti, the Yoruba, and the Bakongo.

One consequence of this pattern has been to present modern African leaders with particularly difficult problems in "cultural management"—in the creation of bodies of ideas and beliefs that would persuasively express a sense of nationhood and legitimate their own leadership in the drive toward modernity. The new elites' common culture, and even their very language of communication with each other, are often acquired in mission schools and are taken directly from the West, as the Smythes have noted in their study of the Nigerian elite.[43] But this tends to be an ideologically unsatisfying situation, both because it provides no symbols in terms of which the elite may relate themselves to their people

42. L. A. Fallers, "Ideology and Culture in Uganda Nationalism," *American Anthropologist*, 63:677–686, 1961.
43. Hugh H. Smythe and Mabel M. Smythe, *The New Nigerian Elite*, Stanford, Calif., Stanford University Press, 1960.

and because it tends to perpetuate a sense of dependence upon the West, particularly galling to Africans who have experienced four hundred years of Western negrophobia. The new states of Africa and their modern elites must therefore perform a rather staggering feat of cultural creativity: They must, in addition to solving the problems of modernity, create a sense of national unity and self-respect without the resources of unifying tradition with which their Asian and Near Eastern counterparts have had to work. Such vague conceptions as "negritude," "African personality," and "African Socialism" represent early responses to this problem, as does President Nkrumah's attempt to create a synthetic Ghanaian culture by combining symbols drawn from various traditional tribal cultures.

It is perhaps worth pointing out, however, that this lack of traditional roots also has its positive side. If the Africans lack the cultural resources of tradition, they also are unencumbered by it. If they can solve the problems of continuity and cohesion, their very rootlessness may enable them to respond more flexibly to the problems of modernity and to maintain societies that are more open.

The politics of equality

WE may now return to the problem with which we began: the relationship between stratification and politics in the process of modernization. Politics—the distribution of the authority to make binding decisions—is not the same thing as stratification, as we noted earlier, but is related to stratification in important ways. As we have seen, political values and roles are part of the culture and structure of stratification, and political processes influence the distribution of persons through the stratification system. But the relationship is a reciprocal one; the pattern of politics is itself influenced by stratification, and it is this aspect of the matter that we will explore in this final section.

From the point of view of the uses and limitations of the Western experience of modernization as a guide to an understanding of contemporary events in the new states, this aspect is of particular interest, for what we may call the "politics of equality" have been a central feature of the modernization of the West in a way that has deeply influenced our thinking about what modernization in the generic sense means. Equality and inequality, in their various meanings, have been key concepts in our thought about recent Western political history, and we tend, almost without thinking, to cast them in a similar role when we consider the affairs of the new states. We may appropriately ask ourselves, however, how accurate the parallel really is—how far the circumstances that made stratification the kind of issue it has been in the modernization of Western politics are present in the new states today.

The politics characteristic of modern societies tend toward egalitarianism in three ways: First, they tend to be populistic. Political participation—membership in the civil society—is widely diffused. It is in principle a property of every adult person. The legitimacy of political acts rests upon the degree to which they may be represented as reflecting the "will of the people." There are, of course, societies that are modern in the sense of being highly industrialized and possessing modern occupational systems but in which effective power is held by a tiny political elite. But even these modern totalitarian regimes are populistic in ideology, claiming that their actions reflect the "real" or "objective" popular will unclouded by "subjective considerations," and are concerned to demonstrate this by securing the symbols of popular approval through manipulation and coercion. They differ from traditional authoritarianisms precisely in feeling the necessity to require their people to participate by actively consenting to political acts; traditional authoritarianisms required only that the people obey.

Second, modern politics, whether liberal-democratic or totalitarian, are egalitarian in the sense that one of the principal objects and justifications of politics is assumed to be a constant improvement in the social and material welfare of the common man. Material inequalities are justified on the ground that they provide incentives for extraordinary effort—effort that will be more productive of general material welfare than greater immediate material equality would be. The imposition of material hardships, as in the "forced-draft" industrialization programs of the Soviet Union and Communist China, are justified on the ground that they will result in greater future comfort and well-being for the masses. Traditional authorities, too, often assumed the burden of promoting the national wealth and power through military conquest and the manipulation of trade, but modern polities are expected to do more: whether through state planning or laissez faire (or, more commonly, of course, through some mixture of the two) they assume responsibility for promoting constant progress through technological and social innovation.

Finally, modern politics is egalitarian in that the state, again whether it is totalitarian or liberal-democratic, assumes responsibility for furthering equality of opportunity—responsibility for creating conditions, including most prominently widespread educational opportunities, which will allow talent to find its own place in the occupational system. There have, as we have seen, been traditional societies in which elites were relatively open to talent, but the undifferentiated nature of the occupational systems and the smallness of the elites in such societies made equality of opportunity highly theoretical for most of their members. Only in modern societies is it possible for the placement of most persons in the occupational system to be a matter for aspiration and choice, and only in such societies, consequently, can the state assume the burden of encouraging mobility for all.

All these features of modern politics follow more or less directly from the processes of structural differentiation and cultural modernization that we discussed in previous sections. All three aspects of egalitarianism just listed—populism, utilitarianism, and equality of opportunity—are logically related to the cultural commitment to progress through science and technology. The structural differentiation of occupational systems draws ordinary persons to some degree out of the matrix of local and kinship ties and makes them available for participation in a wider polity. Schools and the occupational structure itself provide vehicles for personal and group ambition and progress. All this seems generic to modernity everywhere.

Modern polities are thus characteristically populistic, progressive, and friendly to mobility, but they differ in the degree to which they are liberal-democratic or totalitarian. The new states aspire to modern egalitarianism in the senses discussed above, though they do not yet enjoy the conditions for its full achievement, and most of them also aspire—or at any rate began by aspiring—to liberal democracy. It is therefore of interest to recall some of the ways in which political egalitarianism, democratic liberalism, and totalitarianism have been related in the history of the West and to ask how far these relationships are or are not paralleled in the contemporary development of the new states. Again we must draw up an outline that greatly simplifies events but may have the virtue of serving as a model for comparative purposes.

THE WEST: THE DEMOCRATIZATION OF THE ESTATES

The traditional societies out of which the modern West grew were "highly stratified" in several senses. The elites were small and the common people were many. Wealth was highly concentrated in the hands of the feudal aristocracy, as also was political participation. The polity as a whole was highly decentralized, since sovereignty was distributed, along with rights in land, among a network of aristocratic lords and vassals, but, as between this landholding aristocracy and the peasants, authority was highly unilateral, the peasants often occupying a status of legal unfreedom and having recourse to no justice beyond that of the lord.

So far there is little here that is unusual in the general range of peasant societies. The legal details of European feudalism are not, of course, repeated elsewhere, but the pattern of a large, dependent peasantry supporting a small political and economic elite is common to peasant societies everywhere. Beyond this, however, there was in traditional Europe another kind of inequality that has not been so common elsewhere: Between the peasantry and the aristocracy there developed a cultural differentiation that became very marked. This was not merely a differentiation between "high culture" and "folk culture"; literary culture was pursued not so much by the lay aristocracy as by the church. Rather it was a differentiation between the culture of the peasantry, rooted in the cycle of agricultural life, and that of the mounted knight, the cavalier. The culture of chivalry, centering upon the glorification of military prowess and status honor, drew upon religion, as also did that of the peasant villagers. But the two sub-cultures drew from medieval Christianity different ideals, and integrated these into quite different styles of life and views of the world. Between the two there was a hereditary gulf; aristocratic and peasant status and culture were "in the blood," in principle immutable. What was an appropriate model of virtue for the noble was not an appropriate one for the peasant—in fact, was forbidden to him.

Of course this is an oversimplified picture. Besides the peasantry and aristocracy there were the clergy and the merchants and craftsmen of the towns, both in some degree open to mobility. And there were not just two great status groups, but several lesser ones as well. Both aristocracy and peasantry were subdivided in significant ways. Finally, the estates were, of course, crosscut by vertical ties of personal loyalty. But the fact of elaborate cultural differentiation, associated with self-conscious hereditary status, remains.

Next, we may ask: Through what processes have these traditional, highly stratified Western societies become the modern, relatively egalitarian ones of today? The modernization of the West was, first of all, preceded—perhaps it would be better to say "introduced"—by a period of political centralization and expansion of trade. The latter resulted in a growth in the numbers and wealth of the merchants and craftsmen in the towns, the former in the strengthening of the patrimonial element in the medieval state at the expense of the feudal. Both increased the opportunities for mobility. Then, in the eighteenth and nineteenth centuries, the modernization of agriculture and the growth of urban industries produced an increasingly large class of wage laborers, no longer tied to persons of higher status as personal dependents. These changes also further increased the numbers and wealth of the entrepreneurial class. All this was accompanied by increasing demands for wider political participation and state intervention on behalf of welfare and wider educational opportunity—in short, for those features of political egalitarianism that, we suggested earlier, are typically modern.

But what, in the course of all these changes, became of the cultural stratification so characteristic of the traditional West, and how does this relate to the growth of political egalitarianism? Certainly the cultural stratification did not disappear; its descendants are still with us in the form of the modern class cultures described by Richard Hoggart, Nancy Mitford, and William Lloyd Warner, and, of course, by countless novelists.[44] Particularly since the decline of differential political rights, and the rise in general affluence, these subtle differences of speech, behavior, and

44. W. L. Warner and P. S. Lunt, *The Social Life of a Modern Community*, New Haven, Yale University Press, 1941; Richard Hoggart, *The Uses of Literacy*, Fair Lawn, N.J., Essential Books, 1957; Nancy Mitford (ed.), *Noblesse Oblige*, New York, Harper, 1956.

style of life are in many ways the most tangible aspects of stratification, the sweetest fruits of personal success and the bitterest of failure.

It seems not unreasonable to suggest, as of course many others have suggested, that this cultural stratification has in important ways conditioned the modernization of politics in the West. What seems to have happened was something like this: As the hereditary estates of traditional Europe were gradually transformed into the much more fluid classes of today, the traditional cultural differentiations were carried over into modern life to form the basis for modern class cultures and modern class consciousness in politics—not, of course, without undergoing important transformations. Peasant culture must have contributed importantly to the new urban proletarian cultures that formed one of the bases for the working-class solidarity expressed in trade-union and Socialist movements.

This is not, of course, to suggest that economic and political grievances were not also important, along with the break in the personal tie between superior and subordinate and the separation of working life from domestic life, in producing a sense of alienation in the working classes. It does seem likely, however, that the sense of solidarity that directed working-class energies in part into labor and Socialist movements instead of into individual striving for mobility—a solidarity that also, of course, made individual mobility more difficult, since there was solidarity above as well as below—also owed something to this cultural differentiation. Richard Hoggart argues persuasively that the contemporary erosion of English working-class culture by the mass media, in addition, of course, to the achievements of the welfare state, tend to rob the working class of its leadership and sense of community.[45] It is also significant that the period of greatest class consciousness and of the greatest strength of Socialist ideology in the American labor movement coincided with the period of mass immigration from abroad into urban industries—the period when the American working class was most differentiated culturally from the other segments of society. Thus, for a certain period, ethnicity played a role in American stratification somewhat analogous to that of class culture in Europe.

45. Hoggart, *op. cit.*, especially Chapter VI.

The traditional aristocratic culture, too, had a further career, interacting with the burgeoning bourgeois culture of achievement in various ways to produce the cultures of modern Western elites. In general, as mobility came to be more and more a matter of wealth, the bourgeois culture of sober, competitive striving and the aristocratic culture of cultivation and *noblesse oblige* became successive steps in the careers of successful families, even in the United States where there was little direct continuity with the traditional system of estates.[46] Thus, in different ways both "lower" and "higher" class cultures and class consciousness conditioned the movement toward egalitarianism.

The political institutions within which the politics of equality developed in the West were also shaped by the stratification system of the medieval past. Indeed, the stratification system might be said to have provided the framework for the medieval state. In the medieval parliaments, representatives of the estates—nobility, clergy, and urban burgesses—held established rights and obligations vis-à-vis their kings. In particular the larger vassals, the barons, enjoyed as individuals substantial autonomy within their fiefs, and as members of corporate bodies exercised constitutional checks upon royal power.[47] During the period of centralization at the end of the Middle Ages, these institutions were threatened by the growing power of the kings and their patrimonial bureaucracies. In England they survived the attempted absolutism of the Stuarts and the upheavals of the Cromwellian period, and under the settlement of 1688 a constitutional pattern was arrived at that recognized the authority of parliament and established a framework for representative government.

Thus it was possible over the centuries, through the extension of the franchise, to absorb into what had begun as an aristocratic institution an ever widening circle of political participants. Medieval local government bodies, based upon the shires and boroughs, also survived to become modern representative local governments. These accommodations were both stimulated and facilitated by the increasing openness of the English aristocracy, which was thus able to maintain the tradition of responsible aristocratic political leadership while admitting to its privileges and responsibilities in-

46. Warner and Lunt, *op. cit.*, pp. 92–109.
47. C. H. McIlwain, *Constitutionalism, Ancient and Modern*, Ithaca, N.Y., Cornell University Press, 1940.

creasing numbers of recruits from below.[48] Thus was created the modern British "establishment"—diverse in its social origins but nevertheless a "status group" in the sense of being united by a feeling of common tradition and purpose, including, most importantly, a devotion to both equality and liberal democracy.[49] The occasional challenges to its modern legitimacy on the ground of insufficient devotion to equality would seem to be the price of a constitutional and social structural continuity that nourishes liberal democracy.

The difference in the manner in which these processes developed in England and France has been regarded by many of the most perceptive students of political modernity in the West as a kind of natural laboratory in which to observe the relationship between equality and political democracy. In France the continuity with traditional constitutional institutions based upon the estates was much more severely interrupted. By the end of the eighteenth century, as Toqueville shows, centralization had gone so far throughout most of the country that neither national nor provincial assemblies were capable of revival.[50] The independence of both the nobles and the burgesses had been destroyed, though the former retained their privileges and exclusiveness and hence attracted the envy and hatred of both the latter and the peasants. The alternative to autocratic centralism, therefore, was not the reestablishment of the traditional constitution, as Burke had urged[51] —this, Toqueville says, was no longer possible. The alternative was populistic centralism, and in the revolution France was the scene of the first experience of what Talmon calls "totalitarian democracy."[52] Large masses of people were politically activated by a millennial egalitarian ideology enunciated by dedicated leaders.

48. J. O. Lindsay, "The Social Classes and the Foundations of the States," *New Cambridge Modern History*, Cambridge, Cambridge University Press, 1957, Vol. VII, pp. 50–65.

49. Hugh Thomas (d.), *The Establishment*, New York, Clarkson N. Potter, 1959; E. A. Shils, *The Torment of Secrecy*, New York, The Free Press of Glencoe, 1956, pp. 47–57.

50. Alexis de Tocqueville, *The Old Regime and the French Revolution*, New York, Doubleday Anchor Books, 1955.

51. Edmund Burke, *Reflections on the Revolution in France*, New York, Gateway Editions, 1955.

52. J. L. Talmon, *The Origins of Totalitarian Democracy*, New York, Fredrick A. Praeger, 1960.

All mediating political structures, in terms of which constitutional adjustments in the direction of equality might have taken place, having been destroyed previously by royal encroachment, the leaders ruled by acclamation. "Nothing had been left that could obstruct the central government," says Tocqueville:

> . . . but by the same token nothing could shore it up. That is why the grandiose edifice built up by our kings was doomed to collapse like a house of cards once disturbances arose in the social order upon which it was based.[53]

The necessity for a radical break with the past in the pursuit of equality, instead of its gradual accommodation within continuing political institutions, left French society deeply divided into mutually hostile segments, a situation that ever since has tended to make stable democratic governments difficult.

Elsewhere in Europe and in the European settlements overseas there were other variations in the pattern of development of the politics of equality out of the highly stratified societies of the past, variations we need not trace further. Enough has been said to make the major point that concerns us; namely, that both the pattern of cultural stratification and the related political structure the West inherited from its peculiar medieval past deeply influenced the manner in which the politics of equality developed in the West.

To sum up rather crudely: The ascriptive and culturally differentiated stratification of the estates both stimulated and directed the rising egalitarian sentiments of individuals and groups. The different patterns of interaction between this drive toward equality and the political democratization of the medieval political framework seem to have produced in the West varying degrees of attachment to liberal democracy. We clearly should not expect that the politics of equality will develop in the same manner—that the same elements will play the same roles—in societies in which the traditional background is different in major respects.

THE POLITICS OF EQUALITY IN THE NEW STATES

The Ottoman Empire, which provided the immediate historical setting for the development of the politics of equality in the

53. Tocqueville, *op. cit.*, p. 137.

Near East, differed radically from traditional Europe, both in its political structure and in its pattern of stratification, as our earlier outline will have made clear. It was more egalitarian than traditional Europe in the sense that there was more mobility into the higher levels of the political structure. But the highly centralized and autocratic nature of the state, upon which this mobility depended, precluded the development of a constitutional balance of powers within the body politic. Occupational and ethnic corporations did, to be sure, enjoy substantial internal self-government, but these were not bound together in any framework of mutual responsibility for the polity as a whole. Neither was a group consciousness and sense of common responsibility for the whole lodged in a group of great families; the latter existed but they had no constitutional place. Even a solid social and cultural legitimacy seems to have been denied them. These qualities of a politically responsible status group were found rather in the two great arms of the Ottoman State—the imperial administrative service (including the janissary military forces) and the judicial-religious body, the ulama. Both were, in what Gibb calls the "Golden Age" of the empire— the sixteenth century—aristocracies of education and training rather than of birth, and their legitimacy as the adminstrators of Islamic universalism rested at least in part upon that fact.[54]

When, therefore, during the later period of the empire, the central authority weakened and tendencies toward hereditary oligarchy developed in the administrative service, these tendencies, instead of producing a responsible, legitimate hereditary aristocracy, appeared rather as a corruption of a previously more open society and an affront to religion. The association of this oligarchy with increasing European domination during the period of decay served to further discredit it. Attempts at reform and the reassertion of central authority by the sultans and their viceroys in Egypt during the nineteenth century served only, under the conditions then prevailing, to increase European influence. They also sometimes served, as for example did Mohammed Ali's oppressive program for forcing the commercial cultivation of cotton in Egypt, to stimulate populist and antiregime sentiments among the people.[55] Finally, the idea of nationality, perhaps spread from Europe where it was at the same time undermining the legitimacy of the Haps-

54. Gibb and Bowen, *op. cit.*, Vol. I, pp. 39–199; Vol. II, pp. 70–164.
55. David S. Landes, *Bankers and Pashas*, London, Heinemann, 1958, pp. 69–101.

burgs, gave focus to these resentments and anxieties.[56] The result was the dissolution of the Ottoman realm into a series of nation-states, often with an interlude of European administration.

In this setting, the politics of equality have tended to be expressed in ethnic nationalism, often backed by Islamic religious sentiments, and in antagonism to the remnants of Ottoman rule, to oppressive landlords, to the cosmopolitan foreign business interests that grew up during the last century of the empire and, of course, to European domination. With the defeat of these forces, however, the nationalist movements find difficultiy in organizing effective constitutional polities, for Near Eastern societies tend to lack internal differentiation along lines that might find expression in parliamentary party organization. (It is of some interest in this regard that perhaps the most successful constitutional regime in the area is that of Lebanon, where the diversity of religious groups has provided a political framework.) There is no tradition of a cohesive, responsible, legitimate aristocracy; proletarian movements, as so often in the new states, are led by intellectuals and are more expressive of nationalism and intellectual alienation than of independent class interests. The 'ulamâ' having thus far rejected the very idea of modernity, are in no position to provide a responsible lead in coping with its problems. In these circumstances, political energy tends in many cases to be directed outward into international affairs—into, for example, the pursuit of Pan-Arab unity—at the expense of attention to the problems of internal modernization.

The most successful mode of political organization in the area has been the military regime, backed by the civil bureaucracy. It is perhaps not far-fetched to see here an element of continuity with the past.[57] Like the administrative service of the empire, these are often open status groups: united by common education, outlook, and discipline, and open to mobility. They also contain the largest available body of persons with the technical knowledge relevant to the tasks of modernization.

India presents an entirely different picture. Where the Near Eastern polities are formlessly and sometimes somewhat aimlessly populistic, modern India, as we would expect from her traditional

56. Lewis, *op. cit.*, pp. 317–355.
57. *Ibid.*, pp. 284–287; Morroe Berger, *Bureaucracy and Society in Modern Egypt*, Princeton, N.J., Princeton University Press, 1957.

stratification system, is intricately crisscrossed by lines of differentiation along which political energies flow with vigor and purpose. Traditional Indian society was of course even more highly stratified than was the medieval West, in the sense that a greater number of closed groups were recognized and the structure of inequality was more fundamentally underwritten by religion. But the highly local nature of most of the castes, and their divorce, at least in recent centuries, from the central organization of the polity, prevented the development of a single national hierarchy of broad strata on the Western pattern. Their even more closed, corporate character made it difficult for modern egalitarian tendencies to express themselves in intercaste mobility, although of course the growth of a modern secularized group standing outside the caste structure has provided a field for individual movement. For the majority who remained within the caste framework, the politics of equality have been expressed instead through "caste associations"—regional groupings of related castes—which compete for political power within the parliamentary electoral framework and which promote the economic and social interests of their members.[58] Sometimes the associations operate independently of the national parties, sometimes within their state and local branches. By drawing upon the tradition of local caste struggles for position within the classical four-*varna* scheme, they are able to call forth traditional sentiment and solidarities in support of such modern goals as improved educational and occupational opportunities for their members.

Students of contemporary Indian society seem rather sharply divided concerning the meaning of these caste associations for the political future. The Rudolphs see in them a useful way of linking traditional and modern political processes and of articulating the aspirations of millions of village folk with an inevitably distant national politics.[59] Harrison, on the other hand, sees in their growth a threat to the cohesion of a country already deeply divided by linguistic and regional loyalties—loyalties the associations tend to express and to reinforce.[60] In comparative perspective, the caste associations would seem in any case to provide an element that is

58. Selig Harrison, *India: The Most Dangerous Decades*, Princeton, N.J., Princeton University Press, 1960, pp. 96–136.

59. Lloyd I. and Susanne Rudolph, "The Political Role of India's Caste Associations," *Pacific Affairs*, 33:5–22, 1960.

60. Harrison, *op. cit.*

relatively rare in the polities of the new states: a structure of political pluralism in terms of which large numbers of persons can pursue the politics of equality—can participate in the political process in ways that are effective and satisfying to them—but that at the same time tends to prevent the excessive concentration of power and public attention upon the center. It also makes possible the continued separation of the official agents of modernization—the civil service—from direct participation in political controversy. The fact that such pluralism also entails a certain loss of unity is perhaps merely the Indian version of one of the enduring dilemmas of democratic society, expressed by Abraham Lincoln in his message to the special session of Congress in 1861:

> Is there in all republics this inherent and fatal weakness? Must a government of necessity be too *strong* for the liberties of its own people or too *weak* to maintain its own existence?[61]

The problem for India, as it was for the United States a century ago (though, of course, the actual cultural and structural elements involved are different and, hence, so also must the solution be), is to find a political *modus vivendi* that protects the integrity of the central government without stifling pluralism.

When we turn to the new states of Africa, we find it extraordinarily difficult—even more so than in the case of the Asian states—to distinguish enduring features from transitory ones. The oldest of the African countries (Ethiopia and Liberia, of course, excepted) has been sovereign for less than a decade, the others for far shorter periods. We may, however, take note of some features that seem likely to condition the politics of equality in Africa for some time to come, whatever the fate of particular governments and sets of national boundaries.

First of all, the new African states are in most cases "nations" in only the most tentative sense. Lacking traditional bases for a sense of national unity, they tend to be congeries of traditional societies in varying stages of modernization, held together by the leadership of elites whose common culture is largely alien to the traditional cultures and discontinuous with them. The politics of equality, and indeed such political self-awareness of any kind as

---

61. Abraham Lincoln, "Message to Congress, July 4, 1861," in Richard Hofstadter (ed.), *Great Issues in American History*, Vol. I, 1765–1865, New York, Vintage Books, 1958, p. 402.

may be said to transcend the boundaries of the traditional societies, have thus far consisted in the main of the assertion of the dignity of things generically African, as against Western domination.

This sentiment is profound and widespread, for Western domination has, in Africa even more than elsewhere, often taken forms that were particularly damaging to indigenous peoples' sense of integrity and self-esteem. This has been particularly true for members of the elites who have experienced Western racism overseas or in local European colonial circles. During the period of nationalist agitation, all kinds of local (and sometimes incompatible) discontents and ambitions could be fused with these elite grievances. But such diffuse sentiments are more readily utilized in the organization of independence movements than in the continuing political life of sovereign states. With the achievement of independence, there emerges the problem of finding or creating structures within the social fabric of the various states in terms of which to channel the politics of equality.

At present there appears to be a tendency for the single strong party—the vehicle for the successful drive to independence—to dominate the politics of most of the new states through centralized governments. Such parties and governments, in the short run, draw strength both from their successful defiance of the colonial regimes and from their inheritance of the latters' institutional assets: relatively disciplined bureaucracies, armies, and police forces. In addition, large parts of the populations of many of the African states are as yet hardly politicized at all in the modern sense, having passed directly from the paternalistic rule of the European district officer, or *commandant du cercle*, to that of his equally paternalistic African successor. At present, therefore, the dominant parties can count upon the political quiescence of a large proportion of their countries' people as well as upon the enthusiastic support of most of the politically articulate. Over the longer run, however, the economic modernization of these countries, which is the common goal of all the new regimes, will tend to draw the peoples of the backward areas into political participation, and the unity derived from the period of agitation for independence will wane. The question of the legitimacy of the regimes, in terms of more diverse and deeply held values, will then tend to come to the surface.

It seems very likely that the future politics of most of the

African states will be dominated by the problem of the role to be played in their affairs by their constituent traditional societies—the "tribes." In the absence of national cultures that might be represented by, and help to legitimate, national elites (it is not, of course, out of the question that such may be created in time by gifted and responsible elites), the alternatives would seem to be two: on the one hand, a continued unity and centralization, increasingly maintained by authoritarian means; and, on the other, the evolution of constitutional arrangements, of a broadly federal sort, in which traditional solidarities might be represented and contained. In particular the possibility of something like stable, liberal democratic regimes in the African setting would seem to depend upon developments of the latter sort.[62]

Conclusions

IN this essay we have attempted a preliminary comparative sketch of the modernization of social stratification and politics in the West and in some of the new states. It is, of course, the merest outline of what a serious study of the subject would be, but it has enabled us to explore what appear to be some of the major ranges of variation and, perhaps, to reach a standpoint somewhat outside the peculiarities of the Western experience. It may be useful to summarize here some of our tentative conclusions:

1. There is a complex of features of social stratification and politics—what we have called the "politics of equality"—that may be said to be generically modern.

2. The particular form this complex will take in any given society is, however, influenced to an important degree by the traditional structure and culture of stratification within which it develops.

3. The form the politics of equality will take in the new states is also influenced, both structurally and culturally, by the circumstances of the encounter with the West.

4. The development of the politics of equality in a relatively liberal democratic direction depends both upon the existence of legitimate and responsible national elites and upon the channeling

62. An interesting discussion of this notion may be found in Colin Legum, *Congo Disaster*, London, Penguin Books, 1960.

of popular political energies through pluralistic structures. In various instances these later have included class, caste, associational and, perhaps, tribal structures. Perhaps the most interesting research task suggested by this preliminary survey is the further exploration of the variety of structures that may serve in this way.

Problems of law in the new nations of Africa

MAX RHEINSTEIN

THE COLLOCATION of sounds or signs L–A–W constitutes a word of many meanings. It occurs in such terms as the law of gravity, the law of supply and demand, the law of God, Canon Law, or the Law of Nigeria. In each of these terms the word "law" has a different meaning. Here, we are concerned with law only in the sense of the last term: the law of Nigeria, or the law of England, or of the United States of America, or some other politically organized community. Our concern is with law as a set of norms of social behavior as sanctioned by a government. We are concerned with such norms as that which prohibits stealing, under the sanction of imprisonment; or which requires the buyer of goods to pay the price, under the sanction of the sheriff's attaching the property of the defaulting buyer. We are also concerned with those norms by which the organization of the power structure "state" is determined, that is, constitutional law, and with those norms that indicate the kind of relationship in which a person must stand to the objects of wealth in order to be protected by the state, that is, the law of property. However, in this broad sense of government-sanctioned norm the term "law" embraces the entire field of regulation of human behavior by legislation, ordinance, decree, judicial precedent, and so on, irrespective of content. Here we shall not deal with those fields of legal regulation that are determined by considerations of economic, technological, or special social policy. We shall leave aside such laws as those dealing with matters of public health, customs duties, public education, social security, road traffic, or safety appliances in dangerous activities. We shall limit ourselves to what is occasionally referred to as lawyers' law, that is, those branches of the law in whose shaping and administration the specialists called "lawyers" have traditionally played a major role. Our concern will thus be with criminal law and procedure, private law in the sense of the law of contracts and torts, of persons and the family, and of property; we shall be concerned with commercial law, with the law of procedure in civil matters, also with the organization of the courts by which the law is administered, and with the personnel engaged in the administration of justice. The regulation of all these matters involves, of course, decisions of policy, to be made by legislatures, political leaders, or voters. Whether the nation's productive resources are to be owned collectively or individually, whether women shall or shall not have equal status with men, whether in the administration of criminal justice the state is to be all-powerful or whether it is to confront the accused on a level of equality, these are decisions of the highest political order, too important to be left to lawyers or any other specialists. But once these basic decisions are made, the lawyer is called in to implement them in those innumerable details that must be regulated competently if society is to function smoothly; and he is called in for the equally important task, which is, perhaps, his very own domain, to serve as society's troubleshooter, as the arbiter of disputes, the peacemaker, and the adjuster of frictions. How a nation arranges its system of law and courts, how it organizes its legal profession, and how it trains its lawyers is thus of the utmost importance.

If it is true that a society's law is the formalized outward expression of that society's life and values, it is obvious that the proper handling of the legal tasks is a matter of importance for a society that finds itself not in a state of rest, but in one of rapid transformation, such as the present-day nations of Africa, where profound transformations are taking place internally and in the relations with the world outside. In the following we shall try to list some of the major problems African nations will in the near future have to tackle within the domain of the law, meaning by African nations those of Africa south of the Sahara and north of the Limpopo River. The social and political structure, and consequently the law problems of North Africa and of the Union of South Africa, are different from those of the great bulk of the continent.

There are included, however, those regions in which British rule has yielded to local autonomy and that can be expected to be independent or fully self-governing within the near future. Of course, the vast region attempted to be covered comprises a large variety of territories of which each presents problems peculiarly its own. But there are, on the other hand, enough common features to justify the attempt of a generalizing survey. This survey will be one made by a legal comparatist who looks upon Africa from the outside and tries to view its problems, in so far as they are at all known to him, against a background of experiences of other cultures of the past or present. The reader should not expect to find answers to the problems, but merely suggestions in what ways experiences made in other cultures might be utilized in the attempts to solve the legal problems of Africa.

Legal problems of pluralism

COMMON to all regions of western, eastern and central Africa is, above all, the feature of social pluralism. In the midst of those Africans who live in accordance with the traditions of millennia of native civilization live the European settlers, traders, technicians, and so on, and those Africans who have adopted the ways of "modern" living, and between them dwells that steadily increasing mass of Africans who partake of both civilizations, trying, often uneasily, to know where they belong and which civilization's system of values is to be theirs. African traditions themselves are far from being uniform. They vary from tribe to tribe, and in places, especially in West Africa, they have been influenced and diversified by religious differences. There are, furthermore, in East Africa, Asian groups that have maintained their cultural identities.

To the variety of cultures there corresponds the variety of laws. In all the regions the law for Europeans is different from that for Africans; among Africans the law varies from tribe to tribe. Hindu and Islamic law apply in many respects to the legal affairs of Indians and Arabs, and, in different ways, Islamic law is of significance for Africans in many parts of West Africa, such as northern Nigeria or Senegal.

Legal pluralism is not unique of African nations and territories. It was common in the empires of antiquity, where peoples of different traditions lived together under a common rule. In Ptolemaic Egypt, Greeks lived under one law and Egyptians under another. In the Roman Empire a great variety of laws appears to have existed even after Roman citizenship had been extended to practically all free inhabitants in A.D. 212. In the Germanic kingdoms that were established upon the ruins of the Western part of the Roman Empire, each Germanic tribe lived under his own law, and the Roman or Romanized people continued to live under Roman law. In countries conquered by or converted to Islam, Christians, Jews, Hindu, and others have continued to live under their own religious laws into the present day.

As in Europe the new type of national state came to emerge, from the thirteenth century on, the system of "personal" laws had to give way to the new system of "territorial" law, uniform for all inhabitants. But this transformation was slow; the process extended over centuries. In France it culminated in the postulate of the Revolution of 1789 that the nation be *"une et indivisible,"* that all citizens be equal not only politically but also in their legal affairs, and that all primordial subdivisions be swept away or yield their demands of loyalty to that of the nation. In other countries of Western and Central Europe territorial uniformity of the law was not fully achieved until the revolutions of 1830 and 1848, and vestiges lingered on into the twentieth century. In Russia, marriage laws were different for Orthodox Christians, Catholics, Protestants, Jews, and Muslims, and tribal communities of the Eastern and Caucasian parts lived under their customary laws until all legal differences were swept away by the Bolshevik Revolution.

As state power came to establish itself besides or above the tribal, religious, or other personal communities, a body of territorially uniform state law grew up beside and above the personal laws, gradually displacing them and, in Europe, ultimately eliminating them altogether. But in the countries of the Near and Middle East, the dualism between territorially uniform state law and diversified personal laws still exists. The scope of the latter has almost everywhere come to be limited to the field of personal status, that is, the structure of the family covering the laws on marriage and divorce, the relations between husband and wife, and between parents and children. But personal laws also spill over into the field of property, as they determine to a considerable extent the succession to property upon death, the law of pious foundations, temples, or other religious bodies, and certain aspects of land tenure. In their efforts to strengthen the forces of national cohesion, governments of Islamic countries have been trying to reduce legal pluralism. But since in practical effect legal unification means secularization of the law, these tendencies have met resistance in that religious revival that is taking place in Islam itself, as well as in the non-Islamic religious bodies. Radical elimination of pluralism has taken place only in Turkey, where Kemal Atatürk had sufficient power in 1926 to substitute a uniform modern law of Swiss origin for the conglomerate of personal religious laws and territorially uniform acts that had made up the legal system of the Ottoman Empire. That conglomerate had been continued, however, in those parts that were severed from the Ottoman Empire before the Kemalist reforms. In Lebanon, Jordan, and Israel, that state of affairs still exists. Not only that personal laws are different for each religious community; they are also administered for each community by its own religious courts: shari'a courts for Moslems, rabbinical courts for Jews, and various kinds of ecclesiastical courts and consistories for the several Christian denominations and sects. In Lebanon there are no less than nineteen sets of personal laws and religious tribunals, all in addition to the state courts that administer those parts of the law that are uniform for all persons. Nationalist demands to do away with legal pluralism were strong enough in Lebanon in 1952 to rally the lawyers of the country to unite in a strike of protest, but not sufficiently strong to overthrow the system. In the United Arab Republic, Tunisia, Morocco, and Iraq efforts are under way to modernize the religious laws, especially Islamic law, and to entrust their administration to the regular courts of the state, but legal pluralism is still far from being eliminated, just as it still prevails, in matters of personal law, in India and Pakistan.

Law is not a body of rules that can be unified or modified at will by governmental fiat. It is the part of a society's set of norms of behavior that it regards as sufficiently important to be enforced through the power of the state, that is, through policemen, prison guards, sheriffs, or the public hangman. A dictator like Kemal Atatürk may be inclined and, to some extent, able to use the instruments of state power forcibly to bring about uniformity of the mores throughout his nation. The democratic way of life means that national integration be brought about by means other than force. Used with caution and wisdom, the law can be one of the tools to integrate a nation, along with such others as education, economic development, or cultural achievement, but law must not run so far ahead of realities as to induce discontent, separatism, and resistance. As long as a country harbors groups of widely differing mores, legal pluralism is inevitable. Under such circumstances its maintenance is a demand of political wisdom and a factor contributing to national integration rather than disruption.

In African countries, diversity of mores is marked, and is bound to exist for a long time to come. As long as it exists, legal pluralism will have to continue. It is simply not possible to apply the same set of family laws to the married couple that lives in accordance with modern conditions and to the polygamous family group living in the traditional ways of tribal custom.

We do not mean to say, however, that legal pluralism would have to continue unchanged in its present form. Quite the contrary. As in India or the Muslim countries, the legal situation in the African countries is characterized by the side-by-side existence of "modern" laws of nation-wide application and native customary laws of personally limited applicability. The line of demarcation between these two sets of law is not always perfectly clear, however. In India, Egypt, or Tunisia, it seems to be settled that the religious laws are limited to the matters of personal status. In many parts of Africa, the customary laws seem to have a wider range of application, namely, to apply to all civil disputes that are to be decided by native courts, which means practically to all disputes between "natives." They thus seem to apply not only to matters of marriage, family disputes, or problems of family property, but also to controversies arising out of contractual dealings or torts. The handling of cases by native courts applying customary law is unquestionably adequate where the controversy arises out of a deal of customary character such as, let us say, a sale of a piece of cattle, a small loan among villagers, or an arrangement about *lobola* (bride price). Decision by the native court under customary law also appears to be appropriate in the case of a bodily injury inflicted in

the course of a scuffle following beer drinking or of damage done
to crops by stray cattle. But what about an automobile accident
or a deal among fellow tribesmen to set up a partnership to carry
on a trucking business? I do not know whether such cases are in all
African countries handled by native courts and, if so, what law
they apply. I wonder whether the courts know it themselves. I
have heard that in at least some parts such cases do go before the
native court and that the judges simply apply some common-sense
rule, perhaps labeling it the rule of English law. That may be a
sensible approach, but can it be maintained as dealings among
Africans grow in number and importance and as foreseeability of
judicial decision becomes necessary in the planning of business?
Can matters potentially involving large values permanently be
handled by courts whose decisions are not collected in reports and
which are thus not known to the people engaged in business?
Informality, nearness, and inexpensiveness are great advantages for
a small-causes court, but is a court in which lawyers appear not
at all or only on rare occasions the appropriate forum for commercial disputes? Would it be wise, on the other hand, to require
all disputes of commercial significance to be handled exclusively
by the High Court, which may be remote from the scene, expensive and unfamiliar with local or tribal conditions?

The system of native courts was established at a time when
natives were "natives," that is, people living under primitive conditions in which disputes were all about matters on which more
or less clearly defined rules were given by tribal custom. Some regions are left in which such conditions still exist. In others, they are
a thing of the past, and the native courts have come to deal with
complex disputes arising out of conditions of modern life. Varying
efforts have been made so to reorganize the native courts that they
might deal with "modern" matters. How successful have such attempts been? Experiences should be gathered and compared from
different parts of the continent and be used in those efforts of court
reorganization that will become inevitable as modernization pro-
gresses.

Studies will also have to be made as to the proper demarcation
of the sphere of native jurisdiction and customary law from that
of the "national" modern law. As already mentioned, that line
does not always seem to be clear. Possibly, a measure of elasticity
constitutes an advantage in a time of rapid social change. Rigidity

of demarcation might well impede adjustment. But is the zone of uncertainty "right" for present needs, or too broad, or too small? Studies, again upon a comparative scale, would seem to be called for.

Clarification and, perhaps, reform, appear to be called for with respect to the law of intertribal contacts. In a dispute arising between two Kikuyu in Kikuyu territory the Kikuyu tribal court decides according to Kikuyu custom, and in a dispute arising in Luo territory between Luo, the Luo court decides according to Luo custom. But what happens in a litigation between a Kikuyu and a Luo who both live in a modern city like Nairobi? With the continuously increasing influx into the cities of Africans of different tribal origins, such disputes will become frequent. As a matter of fact, in the age of modern communications through the mails, the telegraph, and the telephone, contacts between people living in different parts of the same country are on the increase; people meet in political activities, through governmental action, and in commercial enterprise. People travel, by rail, car, or plane. But are there any clear-cut rules determining which law applies in disputes arising out of contacts of individuals of different tribal affiliations? I wonder.

As far as I can see, one or the other of two approaches appears to be taken as a way out: to apply the law of the court before which the case happens to come up; or to decide the dispute under "modern" law. Either approach appears to be adequate for some kinds of cases, but by no means for all. If a Hausa man sells his wares in the city of Ibadan and a buyer complains of the quality, no injustice were done if the Ibadan court would simply decide under Yoruba law. I am using the conditional tense because I do not know whether or not this really is the way in which such a case is handled. All I wish to say is that no great harm were done if it were so handled, and no great harm were done either if it were to be decided under English law. The matter is simple, and in all probability all the various laws concerned result in the same decision anyway. But the determination of the law applicable can be a matter of great significance when a thousand bags of groundnuts are sold by a seller in Kano to a buyer in Lagos, or if, in Lagos, a Yoruba man marries an Egba woman, or if a Muganda dies leaving an account in a bank in Kampala, a grocery store in Jinja, and, perhaps, other property in Kasese. What law applies when a man of one tribal affiliation goes into the trucking business with a partner from another tribe? Or if a young Yoruba, while driving his father's car in Lagos, runs down a Fulani. Which law determines whether the father is liable?

I suppose that some ways of handling such cases have been worked out. Are they satisfactory? Are they sufficiently certain to be predictable and thus to allow proper drafting? As far as I can see no systematic efforts have yet been made to establish clear and comprehensive systems of rules for such cases.

Situations of such kind are, of course, not unique to Africa. They have occurred and they continue to occur wherever people of different legal systems are in contact with each other. The problem thus had to be approached in the Roman Empire and in medieval Europe; it is of daily occurrence in the United States of America, where each of the fifty states has its own law but where people of all states continuously deal with one another. Above all, the problem is acute in the modern world at large, where laws are different from nation to nation but where people of all nations are in commercial and personal contact with each other. When, through a contract made over the telephone between Stockholm and Chicago, a German sells to an Italian Nigerian palm oil to be shipped in a Norwegian vessel from Dakar to Buenos Aires, which law is to be applied in a dispute that comes up for decision in a court in London?

Theoretically, three approaches are open. The first consists in simply applying to each case the law that is regularly applied by the court before which the case happens to come up. In our hypothetical case the court in London might simply apply English law, even though the transaction has no substantial contacts with England, and if the case should come up in a court in Paris, it would be decided under French law, and so on. The second approach consists in the application to the international or intertribal case of a law that is neither of the nations nor of the groups concerned but that applies, uniformly, to international or intertribal cases only. This approach, of course, presupposes that there exists, in addition to all the world's one hundred or so laws a law Number 101, peculiarly applicable to intergroup transactions. Finally, under the third approach one develops a set of rules that determine which one of the several different laws in question ought to be applied in cases of intergroup deals. Thus, one might say, for instance, that in all cases of contract disputes the law applicable is that of the place where the contract was made, or that claims arising out of an alleged tort are always to be determined under the law of the place where the accident or other allegedly wrongful act occurred, or that a marriage is valid only if it was permissible under the group laws of both groom and bride, and so on.

Of all three methods, history provides precedents, and their lessons ought to be considered in the solution of the problem that will have to be found by the African nations.

Method Number 1, that is, decision under each court's own law, the *lex fori*, has been the least satisfactory. Let me give as an illustration a case that came up some years ago in the United States. A Mexican living in Mexico had insured with a New York insurance company a ship plying in Mexican waters. The ship met with an accident, but the owner failed promptly to proceed against the insurer. When at long last he proferred his claim, the company pointed to a clause in the policy under which claims had to be brought forward within one year of the accident. Such a clause is valid under the laws of both Mexico and New York. The ship-owner, however, had an ingenious lawyer, who discovered that the State of Texas has on its statute book a law that says that any clause of an insurance policy providing for a period of less than two years shall be invalid. The insurance company happened to have an account with a Texas bank, which fact, under Texas law, sufficed to render the company amenable to the jurisdiction of the Texas courts. The shipowner availed himself of this opportunity; the Texas court applied its insurance statute, and held the insurance company liable under the policy. Fortunately, the case could be carried from the Texas courts to the United States Supreme Court, which held that the Texas decision was so unjust that it amounted to a deprivation of the insurer of his property without due process of law and thus to a violation of that clause of the Constitution of the United States that commands that no member state of the nation may "deprive a person of life, liberty or property without due process of law."[1]

Why was the decision of the Texas court unfair? Because it applied a law the application of which neither party could foresee when they made their contract. Insurance companies have to

1. *Home Insurance Co.* v. *Dick* (1930) 281 U.S. 397, 50 S. Ct. 338, 74 A.L.R. 701.

compute their premiums on the basis of the risk they are to assume. The duty to pay compensation for accidents occurring two years ago is more burdensome than that of paying for accidents that are only one year in the past. Had, at the time of the issuance of the policy, the insurer known that it might be held to pay for an accident more than one year old, it would have asked a somewhat higher premium. The Texas courts compelled the insurer to pay something for which he had received no return.

Applied without restriction, the system of simply deciding all cases under the *lex fori* inevitably results in surprises, namely, the surprise of having applied to a case a law with the application of which the parties neither did nor could reckon when they engaged upon their transaction. If the system of the *lex fori* is to be workable at all, it has to be supplemented by rules of jurisdiction that prevent a court ever coming at all to decide a case for which the *lex fori* would be an unexpected, and thus an unjust, law. Of such kind was, indeed, the English system of the seventeenth and early eighteenth centuries, which was, by and large, so designed that English courts would apply no law other than that of England, but, on the other hand, would not go into action in cases that had no substantial connection with England and English courts. Toward the end of the eighteenth century it became clear that that system was unworkable. Assume that two Englishmen had made a contract in France, and the seller failed to deliver. As, under the then prevailing notions, English law was regarded inappropriate for a contract made outside England, no English court would take jurisdiction. Whether or not a French court would deal with the case depended on French law. If the English seller had no property in France, no French court would go into action against him. There was thus no court at all in which the buyer could pursue his claim. The system resulted in frequent denials of justice and had to be abandoned.

The best known illustration of the second of the three possible approaches is represented by the Roman Empire. In its strict original sense, Roman law was the law of the city of Rome. When that city conquered, first Italy, then the countries around the Mediterranean and beyond, it did not extend to the conquered regions its own law. In Italy and in the highly civilized regions of Greece and the Hellenized Orient, each city-state, even though made subject to the rule of the city of Rome, was left with its own law. But commerce and personal contacts grew among citizens of the various parts of the empire, and so there grew between them disputes that came up for decision before Roman magistrates. When they were confronted with disputes between citizens of different parts of the empire, these magistrates developed a novel technique: they would apply neither the law of one nor of the other of the communities of the litigants, nor the law peculiar to the citizens of their own city of Rome. They rather fashioned for such cases a new law of their own, which they distilled from all the laws known to them and which they regarded as expressing the notions underlying, and so to speak, common to all, the nations known to them. This *ius gentium*, as it came to be called, was different from the Roman law proper, the so-called *ius civile*, as well as from the laws of all other communities comprised in the empire. In a litigation between citizens of the city of Rome, the magistrate would thus apply the *ius civile*, but in a dispute between a citizen of Rome and that of another community, or between citizens of two other communities, the magistrate would apply the *ius gentium*. In the course of time, the *ius gentium* came to swallow up the *ius civile* as well as, it seems, the laws of the other communities, and thus came, at least to some considerable extent, to be the one and only law for all parts and communities of the empire. As long, however, as the *ius civile* and the other community laws flourished alongside the *ius gentium*, the different group laws applied to disputes arising within the respective groups, while a different, empire-wide, uniform law was used for the decision of intergroup disputes. To a limited extent a similar situation existed in medieval Europe, where a universal Law Merchant applied to mercantile disputes, especially of an intergroup nature, while local laws applied in local disputes.

Under that system the legal pattern is similar to the linguistic pattern of Africa. Among themselves members of the same tribe speak their own language, but when people of different tribes meet, they use in East Africa Swahili or, in West Africa, English, or French, or Haussa.

Could not such a pattern also be used for intertribal disputes in Africa? In such parts of West Africa where Islam predominates in the religious field, Islamic law performs, to some extent at least, the function of a *lex communis*. Otherwise, no legal counterpart exists to the *lingua franca* of Swahili. The only existing laws that could conceivably be used in that function would be English law in regions of English, and French-Belgian law in the regions of French-Belgian colonization. Are they appropriate for the purpose? The question can be answered neither affirmatively nor negatively in a general way. The problem would require incisive study for every region and for every branch of the law. Of special importance would be the study of the experiences made in those parts where a Western law has already been established as the intertribal common law or where one has undertaken to substitute it for the tribal laws even in intratribal relations.

Such an example could, for instance, be provided by Kenya, where, by Ordinance of 1960, the English law of contract has been decreed as the common law of the land in substitution for all pre-existing tribal rules relating to problems of contract. How has this highly complex law fared in the hands of native judges? The English law of contract has been developed to suit the needs of one of the world's most highly developed systems of commerce, industry, and finance. Its norms are contained in hundreds of volumes of judicial precedent. In order to know and understand it one has to undergo a systematic study of several years. The judges of the native courts have not gone to law school; some of them may not have gone to any school at all. They have no libraries at their disposal, and if they had they would hardly find their way through the maze of precedent and technical language. It would, indeed, be interesting to know how Kenya native courts have applied the English law of contract. But will one ever know? Their decisions are not reported. Perhaps they have reduced the English law of contracts to a set of common-sense rules of rough-and-ready application. But is such a law still uniform? Is it predictable and certain as a law must be if it is to serve the needs of an economy in which credit has come to play an ever increasing role? On the question of the African *lex communis*, the last word has not yet been spoken. For some kinds of intertribal disputes a common law may well be the answer, but what disputes these should be, and what law, has not yet been finally determined.

Even if a *lex communis* should emerge as the legal order of some kinds of intergroup disputes, another approach will have to be used for the many intergroup cases that will remain. That approach will have to be along the lines of the third of the three systems that are theoretically possible in the handling of intergroup disputes. The third system has come to be known as that of the law of conflict of laws. It was invented by Italian lawyers of the twelfth and thirteenth centuries, when the cities of northern Italy had made themselves virtually independent and had begun to enact their own statutes. In cases involving dealings between citizens of different cities, the scholars and the courts came to regard as inappropriate both the system of always applying the *lex fori* and that of disregarding both statutes involved. They rather found it appropriate to apply to the case the statute of either one or the other city depending upon which of the two cities had the "closer" contact with the case. The essential question thus was that of determining for each type of dispute which of the statutes in question is more appropriate to be applied. On that question extensive controversies arose, and many divergent opinions have been advocated; but the system as such has been continued through the centuries and has come to be that which is now universally applied all the world over in disputes concerning parties belonging to different countries or legal systems. If, for instance, a dispute arises out of a sale concluded between a seller in Hamburg and a buyer in Chicago, the court before which the controversy comes up for decision will apply either the law of Germany or of Illinois. In choosing between the two, the court will apply some such rule as "Problems of the law of contract are to be decided in accordance with the law of that country in which the contract was made," or "Problems of the law of contract are to be decided under the law of the country that was agreed upon, or is to be regarded as having been agreed upon, by the parties," or "Problems of the law of contract are to be decided under the law of that country with which the contract in question has the closest connection."

Unfortunately, in the present state of world organization, or absence of it, courts of different countries may apply different rules. If the case comes up in Germany, the court will (probably) apply as to the obligation of each party the law of the country where that obligation was to be performed, while a court in Illinois is likely to hold that the case be decided under the law of that country in which the contract was concluded. The same dispute may thus be decided under different substantive laws, depending upon which country's court happens to be the forum.

The situation is simpler when the "conflict" is between the laws not of two sovereign nations, but of two different parts of the same nation in which there prevail different substantive laws but which are all coordinated by a law of conflict of laws uniform for the whole country. Such a situation exists, for instance, in the United Kingdom of Great Britain and Northern Ireland. The substantive private laws are in many respects different in its three constituent parts, England, Scotland, and Northern Ireland. But the law of conflict of laws is the same in all parts. Irrespective of whether a case comes up in London, in Edinburgh, or in Belfast, the court will determine the validity of an alleged contract by the law agreed upon by the parties or, in absence of such agreement, by the law of that region with which the contract in question has its most essential contacts. It will determine the validity of an alleged marriage, as far as formalities are concerned, by the law of the place of celebration and, as far as the parties' capacity to marry is concerned, for each party by the law of his domicile, and so on.

It is such a set of rules of conflict of laws that each African state will have to develop for intergroup disputes. That task will be anything but easy. It will require intensive study of existing patterns and needs as well as of experiences made in other pluralistic countries, for instance, Indonesia, Burma, or the Islamic countries of the Mediterranean. In developing such rules for the intrastate handling of intergroup disputes, attention should be paid to international disputes, and as far as possible the rules should be so formulated that they are capable of being applied to disputes between members of different groups within the same nation, for instance, a Hausa and a Yoruba within Nigeria, as well as to disputes between persons of different nations, for instance, a Yoruba in Nigeria and a Yoruba in Dahomey.

Rules of intergroup-conflicts law will, it ought to be reiterated, be needed only in so far as the matter in question is not regulated by a uniform law applicable to members of all groups, for instance, in Kenya, English law for all contracts of all Kenyans. The determination of that question of what shall and what shall not be regulated uniformly for all members of the nation irrespective of group membership is, of course, exactly the question of how far pluralism shall continue to exist. That question is one of the most delicate, but also one of the most important, the African nations will have to determine. It is of an eminently political character.

Political leaders will be likely to favor national uniformity over pluralism. But, as we have stated, political wisdom counsels caution and restraint. How speedily or how slowly pluralism ought to be overcome cannot be answered apodictically for all places and for all times. But one point is clear: in efforts to overcome pluralism as well as in those to smooth pluralism as long as it continues, through a set of workable rules of intergroup conflict of laws, the political leaders need the assistance of lawyers, and not just of any kind of lawyers but of lawyers who have specially studied the intricate field of legal regulation of intergroup relations.

Of the innumerable problems of this field, *one* must be specially mentioned because of its special importance in a society of such rapid change as that of present-day Africa. Clear-cut rules will be necessary in all parts to render it possible for an individual to change his subjection to the law of one group to that of another. The African who moves from the bush into the city and adopts the urban, modern way of life cannot for all times remain subject to the tribal customs of marriage, succession, or land tenure. In the regions of French and Belgian legal traditions such rules seem to exist. By being registered as an *évolué*, an African ceases generally to be dominated by tribal custom and comes to be regulated in his civil matters by the "modern" law. In the regions of English law tradition no such well-defined technique of full change of status seems to exist. Only to some extent is a change of status involved in the choice between customary marriage and registered marriage. Clearer definitions of the consequences of registered marriage upon both the parties directly involved and their issue may appear desirable, as well as the establishment of a method of change of status apart from and independent of marriage. Again, the warning must be sounded that no efforts of reform should be undertaken, in this respect as in any other, without previous study of the local situation and local needs, as well as of successes and disappointments experienced elsewhere.

Besides, another warning may be appropriate. Repeatedly we have expressed the belief that in one respect or another "clear-cut rules" might be desirable or even necessary. One ought not to overlook, however, that there also exist problems with respect to which clarity of regulation might do more harm than good. In other words, there are problems that one had better not try to regulate by clearly defined rules and norms. Intergroup relations may well hold many such problems. The very attempt at defining by clear rules a hitherto existing state of workable muddling through may unnecessarily engender heat; and even more heat may be engendered by an effort abruptly to change a situation that is on the way to adjusting itself. Political wisdom must decide what is preferable in the long-run interest of the nation: to hasten change by reform legislation, even at the expense of creating opposition, or of letting the change work itself out slowly and imperceptibly.

Law reform—customary law

TO keep pace with the rapid social change that is going on all over Africa, adjustments will have to be made in both the customary laws and the "modern" law.

In the field of customary law, two topics are of prominent significance: the status of women and land tenure. Africa is aiming at a society in which, as in Western society, women occupy a position of equality or near equality with men. Equal status of women is indeed one of the most peculiar features of modern civilization as contrasted with older ones, including the civilization of African tradition, in which full membership in the body social is the privilege of men, just as it was in the Teutonic and Hebrew worlds, among the early Romans and Greeks, or as it still is, or was until very recently, in all parts of the Islamic or Hindu world or the countries of East Asia. In African society the position of women has traditionally been one of inferiority. In most African societies a woman is subject to the power of a male adult that is not adequately described by the modern term of "guardianship," but which appears to be close to the "munt" of ancient Germanic society as well as to similar institutions of other ancient peoples, such as Babylonians, Hebrews, and Romans. African marriage is not a transaction between the groom and the bride, but between the groom, his father, or his group on the one side, and the father or the group of the bride on the other. To what extent, if any, attention is paid to her wishes and feelings is a question of fact. As far as the customary law is concerned, she is the object of the transaction, the essence of which consists in the purchase by the groom, or his group, of the procreative power of a female of another group and of the "munt" over her. Marriage is polygamous; the husband is the master, and the wives occupy positions of obedience and subordination. If the marriage becomes intolerable for a wife she may, as a general rule, not escape from it unless her father or brother repays to the husband the *lobola* (bride price) received from the husband. Unwillingness or inability to do so appears to be a not infrequent source of conflict. If the husband dies, his wives are inherited by his heirs, that is, his sons, brothers, or other relatives. Occupying a position of subordination, a female also has, as a rule, no standing in court. If any lawsuit is to be carried on, it must be done by her "munt-walt" on her behalf.

The situation just described does not apply to every community in every detail, but it states the average pattern of native tradition and thus of the customary law. Clearly the tradition cannot endure in a society in which women can obtain an education, may occupy positions ranging all the way from housemaid or waitress to head nurse, laboratory technician, teacher, librarian or, perhaps in a few years, physician, attorney, or entrepreneur, in which they can vote in political elections, can be elected to membership in a parliamentary body, and may even hold cabinet positions. In so far at least as it sanctions polygamy, the traditional pattern is incompatible also with Christianity. Monogamous marriage has thus been made available to Africans by legislative enactments introducing the possibility of "registered" or other forms of Christian marriage, legally monogamous and indissoluble except by judicial divorce. Patterned upon the English law of the Victorian era, divorce is generally available only on the ground of adultery. Whether Africans, even Christians, look upon marriage in the same way in which it was regarded by the middle classes of Victorian England is open to doubt. On the other hand, cruelty and desertion, established as grounds for divorce in England in the 1930's and 1940's, do not yet generally figure in the colonial ordinances. In some districts of strong missionary influence the number of registered marriages is considerable. To what extent the Christian ideal of marriage is actual in these marriages would be a fascinating question to investigate. Tensions between the alien ideal and the patterns of reality have resulted in situations of conflict and human tragedy. Simply rendering available a choice between customary and registered marriage has not solved the problem of the changing status of women. It has begun to make itself felt in the native courts, which have begun in varying degrees to allow the changes that have occurred in fact to find expression in the law. Sometimes women have been allowed to conduct their own lawsuits, and an occasional court has refused to coerce a wife into the "companionship" of an abusive husband or under the whim of a despotic father. In these respects and others, native courts have been groping their way, and they will continue to do so. The process may be slow and uneven, but in a field of such subtlety and such variety of local configuration, judicial adaptation of the law to varying modes of changing mores may well be preferable to, and more practicable than, the blunter tool of wholesale legislative reform. Much wisdom and knowledge will be needed on the part of the native courts. In part it will be provided by the men of wisdom, actual or presumptive, sitting as judges in the native courts. But in the operation of the native courts, lawyers will come to play an increasingly important role, as judges, attorneys, and administrative supervisors. For the proper exercise of their functions they need more than expertness in legal rules and procedures.

In the field of land tenure, the principal tool of reform will have to be legislation. Reform is needed because the traditional forms of African land tenure are not well suited to the needs of a market economy, however well they may have served the needs of the subsistence economy of tribal life. The traditional forms of African land tenure are different from those in which land is held in modern Europe or America. They have often been misunderstood by Western observers, administrators, and judges, although they greatly resemble institutions of early Germanic type. The concepts of ownership, fee, title, or lease, by which modes of individual or corporate landholding are expressed in the Western world, do not fit the African scene. It is doubtful whether one should speak there of land being "owned" at all. Land is used by families, lineages, tribes, or other groups that tend to exclude others from it, and whose claims are recognized by others as well as by the government. Within the group, allocations of certain, but not necessarily all, lots are recognized, in some cases for perpetual, in others for less firmly guaranteed use. The recognition may result simply from occupancy and cultivation, or from allotment by a chief, a council, or some other "authority." Rarely all the land "belonging" to a group is actually cultivated. It is indeed one of the characteristics of the agriculture of at least some regions that land is cultivated for a few seasons only and then allowed to return to its natural state of bush, rain forest, or savannah, so to remain for years until, in a more or less regular cycle, it is cut or burned over, and for another two or three years again used for crops. "Title" to the land not presently cultivated is sometimes far from being clear. In parts of Kenya, Nigeria, and other regions too, a family may regard itself as having a "right" to unused land, and may then be inclined to allow its temporary use to some outsider, who is expected to move out again as soon as he is requested to do so by the "owner," even though he may have been in possession for decades.

A good many agricultural experts regard the system of alternating short-term cultivation and long-term fallow as the one best suited to the soils and climates of the major part of tropical Africa. But there are regions where it seems to be possible to engage in more intensive methods of farming, and among Africans desiring to produce cash crops for a widening market a desire has grown up to develop new forms of land tenure that would give the cultivator the security of title he now lacks and without which he will hardly be inclined to make improvements requiring outlays of labor or capital, not to speak of mortgage credit for improvements. More intensive cultivation, especially with the use of machines, is in many parts also rendered difficult by the fact that a family "owns" its land not in one contiguous piece, but in a number of lots, often tiny and distributed all over the area of the major group.

Schemes for the reform of land tenure have thus cropped up in many parts and will appear to be increasingly urgent in the near future. In their implementation lawyers are indispensable. The legal skills required in a scheme of land-tenure reform are high, but they do not suffice. Land reform is likely to meet resistance; it will inevitably have adverse effects on quite a few members of the community concerned; and it may well uproot the whole community as such unless it is carried out with caution and understanding. The nature of the existing tenure system must be described in legal terms, and clearly defined new institutions of land ownership, use, and credit must be designed; security of title and acquisition must be guaranteed. The best way to achieve such security is through a system of registration of land titles. Such systems have already been established for limited areas, but one system does not fit all, and the establishment of land registration requires a machinery that is expensive and that, if it is to function, requires skilled personnel. Whether or not it can be set up and operated without a previous survey and platting of the land is doubtful. The successful establishment and operation of a scheme of land-tenure reform requires the cooperation of technicians in the legal skills with experts in other fields. The most important among them are the agronomists, the anthropologists, and the local administrators. The anthropologists have comprehensive understanding of native ways of life, and comparative knowledge of similar schemes successfully or unsuccessfully undertaken in other parts. The administrators are familiar with the peculiar traditions, needs, idiosyncrasies, troubles, natural conditions, and so on, of the locality. Besides, the lawyers, who have usually been, and are likely to remain, in the driver's seat, have to cooperate with the experts as well as with the political leaders in the government and the parliamentary bodies.

Status of women and land tenure are but two topics of customary law with respect to which changes will have to be made. Of the many others only one will be mentioned here: succession of property upon death. In the measure in which property comes to be individually owned, the problem of its orderly reallocation upon the owner's death becomes important, for the individual and for society. Institutions similar to the last will and testament have come to be recognized in many African groups. But if the economy of individual production for, and participation in, the market is to function smoothly, it is necessary to elaborate a set of clear-cut rules for succession both testate and intestate. The formalities and other requirements for the making of a testamentary disposition must be clearly defined, just as the rules on the distribution of property in the case of death intestate. Modern Western law will have to serve as a model in many respects, but there is no need for discarding all the customary rules on who is to be entitled to share in the distribution of an intestate estate, or on the limits that ought to be set to freedom of testation in the interest of the family or the community. But in many respects the customary rules of succession will have to be adapted to the conditions of modern society, including rules that, like those of Islam, constitute parts of a sacred tradition. Reforms recently undertaken in such strictly Islamic countries as Morocco, Tunisia, or Egypt, indicate that the shari'a is not incapable of adaptation to change.

As to the methods in which changes of the customary law are to be brought about, we have already seen that the task will be partly that of legislation and partly that of judicial adaptation. As African societies change, so changes, for instance, the status of women. In that respect, the law, in the sense of judicially sanctioned and governmentally enforced norms, becomes relevant only in situations of dispute. If courts fail to adapt their rules to the changes of society, tensions and tragedies will occur. But the function of lawyers and judges here is not to guide the development of the mores, but to follow it and to channel it into orderly ways. As to land tenure, the role of the law is different. Land tenure, that is, the system of rights in land, is in itself a set of legal institutions. The social and the legal institutions are identical. The former cannot change in any way other than through the change of the latter, and if the legal change is to occur at all, it must be brought about through legislation. With respect to both institutions of customary law, status of women and land tenure, changes of the law are needed, but in the former field the task will be primarily that of following social change, in the latter that of rendering the social change possible. The roles to be played by the lawyers will thus be different, but in both fields they will be delicate.

The job of adapting the customary law to modern conditions is delicate particularly because in that process the very nature of the customary law is likely to undergo a transformation. In a certain sense it may be said that the very term "customary law" is contradictory within itself. Law, in the sense of state-enforced rules of behavior, contains an element of rigidity, especially when it is administered by courts of which one expects consistency, that is, frequently at least, faithful adherence to precedent. Custom can be rigid, too, but, as such at least, it is not tied up with the formalistic machinery of a court. The word, indeed, has more than one meaning. In one sense "custom" simply means the existence of a continuous pattern of behavior, of actions predictably repeated in similar situations, or, more simply, a habit. The habit may be brought about simply by the force of habituation, maturing, in extreme cases, into a conditioned reflex. Why do many of us have tea in the morning? Because we have always done so, because others have done so before us, and because others are doing so around us. We hardly think that there is any necessity to have tea rather than coffee, or water, or nothing at all.

But there are other cases where we follow a certain pattern not only out of sheer habituation or imitation, but out of a feeling that we "ought" to do so, that the following of the pattern is required of us by some norm. That norm may be propriety or etiquette or some other feeling, vague or distinct, that we must act in the way in question, even if we should wish to act in a different way. In Western society, for instance, it is not only habit that men wear trousers rather than skirts; they feel that they ought to do so, that wearing trousers is "right" and wearing skirts "wrong."

The feeling of oughtness may have many different bases: fear of the spirits, the gods, or the Lord; expectation of pangs of conscience or contrition, or expectation of disapproval of one's fellow citizens, neighbors, colleagues, fellow tribesmen, and so on. In that sense, custom acquires a third meaning: the behavior expected of a member of a group by his fellow members, such expectation resulting in disapproval in the case of noncompliance. It is in that sense that we speak of the customs of a people, a profession, or a tribe. Custom in that sense consists of the pattern of behavior actually followed and expected to be followed, so that a group member's failure to follow the pattern will provoke frowning, ridicule, censure, shunning, boycott, or, perhaps, some pattern of retaliation, as, for instance, a beating, a feud, a duty to pay blood money, or expulsion or death. As long as the custom remains custom, the sanction follows either completely spontaneously or at least in a hardly formalized manner. The flouter of the sex custom may find himself ostracized without any formal proceedings. People simply shun him or make him feel their displeasure, but there may be some talk or even a deliberation in some council of tribesmen, elders, chiefs, and so on. Imperceptibly the custom shades into law where the sanction is imposed by the formalized body of a court, following prescribed rules of procedure. But the rule remains flexible, in the sense that it changes as the group's habits change and the group's ideas change about right patterns and wrong ones. And then, at a certain point, the norm begins to harden; it is applied by the court no longer because it corresponds to the group's convictions as to what is the right way of doing things, but simply because it had been applied by the court to a similar case in the past, or because it has been written down in some book enjoying authority. The rule is applied by the court no longer because it is the custom, but because it is law.

Customary law, in the full sense of the term, thus partakes of the nature of both custom and law; it dwells in the sphere where the two sets of norms meet and interpenetrate. It holds a delicate balance constantly being threatened with either dissolving into the vagueness of custom or being ossified as law through the process of following precedent or simple reduction to writing. Such has been the problematic of customary law, wherever it has occurred, in ancient Greece or Rome, in medieval Europe, or in nineteenth-century Germany. Such is also the problematic of customary law in Africa, and this problematic is bound to be made more acute as the courts of customary law have more and more to deal with problems for which certainty and predictability of judicial decision become important. Such predictability is essential as to all those topics that belong to the modern market and credit economy, that is, especially, the fields of contract and property. The interest in consistency of decision may outweigh that in accordance of judicial decision with tribal convictions and their changes. The need for consistency in turn requires the development of tools. So far hardly any decisions of native courts are reported and published. Thought will have to be given to the establishment of a system of reporting decisions of native courts. The task will not be easy; there are the problems of language and of cost, apart from that of developing the skills competent reporting requires.

Under the leadership of Dr. Allott of London, an effort is presently under way to reduce the customary laws of Africa to writing in the form of a "restatement." Such a stocktaking is probably indispensable at the present juncture. Efforts at development and reform require that we know what we have. But caution will also be necessary to guard against the danger of the Restatement being treated as a code. The letter of its sections must be treated as an attempt to articulate what is oftentimes incapable of clear articulation, and to reduce to memory what often constitutes but the fleeting momentary form of a phenomenon of constantly changing shape.

Law reform—modern law

SIDE by side with the customary laws, all African states and territories have their systems of modern law. Initially the modern law was a tribal law, too, the law of the white man's tribe, the tribe of the British, French, or Belgians. But its scope has expanded as the African tribes come to be more and more interwoven with the white man's tribe, and as the ways of life of the two groups have come ever closer to assimilation. Today the modern law thus occupies a double position, that of the tribal law of the white, and that of the common law of the land. In its former function it is a personal group law of a pluralist society, in the second the territorial law of a society that is approaching the form of the territorially unitary nation.

Even as the personal law of the white man's tribe, the modern law is not in all respects up to date. Introduced in each African territory by special ordinance or decree, it has not everywhere partaken of all the modernizations that have subsequently occurred in the home countries. One such case has already been mentioned. In the British regions the English law of marriage and divorce was introduced in its Victorian or Edwardian shape. The English reform laws of 1937 and 1950 have not touched the colonies and have not been received by them, or by all of them.

But the main problem of the modern law arises out of its gradual extension to the affairs of Africans. This process will continue. The question of the extent to, and the rate at, which such extension is to take place is a political one. But in so far as extension takes place, a technical question arises, namely, that of the form in which the extension is to be undertaken. In the regions of codified French and Belgian law, the task is perhaps easier than in those of the English Common Law. Of course, the codes and their innumerable amendment acts do not represent the actual law of France or Belgium. The codes must be read together with that vast gloss of case law that has accumulated around them. But the number of volumes of Dalloz, Sirey, or the Pasicrisie belge is not so large as that of the English Law Reports. For the needs of a native small-causes court, even a small library of leading French textbooks might suffice. Many more books are needed to constitute even a modest library of English law. Besides, the technique of handling the Common Law is more difficult to learn than that of handling the Civil Law of France or Belgium. A way out was tried when English law was introduced into India, there to be administered by Indian staffed courts. It was reduced to a set of codes, such as the Indian Contract Act of 1872, the Indian Easement Act, the Indian Penal Code, the Indian Evidence Act, and so on. Most of these Anglo-Indian codes were, in turn, introduced into the territories of British East Africa to be applied in the legal affairs of Europeans and Asians. But, quite recently, it was enacted in Kenya that the uncodified contract law of England was to replace both the Indian Contract Act as to Europeans and Asians, and the customary law as to Africans. I do not know why this step was taken. It will be important to learn how the case law of the English Law Reports fares in the native courts.

ADMINISTRATION OF JUSTICE—THE RULE OF LAW

What the law will be depends not only upon the content of its rules but, perhaps even more essentially, upon the personnel by which it is to be administered. Will the dualism be maintained of native courts and "modern" courts? How will the judicial business be distributed among the two sets of courts? If the native courts are to assume tasks of administering "modern" law, how will they be organized and staffed? How will appellate procedures be organized? Is each of the new countries to have its own court of ultimate resort? Such a decision would be unfortunate. Apart from the scarcity of personnel of supreme-court caliber, does national sovereignty require the destruction of that large measure of legal uniformity that has so far existed within each, the French and British group? In all the African states it will be crucial to find a way of organizing the legal profession so that it constitutes what it has been in England and in France: a pillar of a society in which men are free under the law. To find the right way will be no easy matter. Two cliffs are to be avoided: that of subservience of the legal profession to the government, and that of leaving free rein to the possible abuse of those vast powers that are concentrated in the legal profession. A lawyer must be sufficiently independent to stand up for the legal rights of the protagonist of an oppositionist cause. But he must not be free to fleece clients, and the lawyers' professional organization must not become a pressure group using its influence for the selfish purposes of its members. Some measure of control will be necessary. In old countries the control rests in traditions that cannot be duplicated. By whom shall the controls be exercised in the new countries: the government or the bench, or solely by public opinion, or through the bar's own *esprit de corps*? Probably all these factors have to be brought together. But how? Much discussion will be needed, and much exchange of experiences.

Discussion, exchange of experiences, and research are needed in all those innumerable tasks with which the makers and administrators of African law will have to cope. These tasks are too many, too formidable, and too complex singly to be attacked by each African country. The tasks call for cooperation. Many laws will have to be prepared. Legislative drafting is a delicate art. The number of truly skilled legislative draftsmen is limited. Even more difficult is the research work that has to be carried on before drafting. What are the social needs? What is the economic situation? How will an intended innovation affect the economy and the social structure? How will it be received by the people affected? How can it be explained to them? Lawyers must cooperate with experts in economics, anthropology, political science, and so on. The number of competent experts is limited. How can the existing skills be best utilized for all the African countries? How can the badly needed new experts best be trained? The answer seems to lie in the establishment of one central research institute or, perhaps, a couple of cooperating institutes, one for West Africa and one for East and Central Africa. Discussion and exchange of experience will finally be needed if there is to be maintained in Africa the "rule of law" in the sense of incorruptibility and impartiality of the administration of justice. The establishment of such an administration of justice has been a great achievement of colonial rule. It must not be allowed to decay in independent Africa.

Concerning the role of education in development

MARY JEAN BOWMAN
C. ARNOLD ANDERSON

IN THE CONTEMPORARY WORLD we are deluged with arguments and exhortations about problems of social, political, and economic development, and particularly about the dilemmas of the "developing" countries. Both new nations and old ones are putting more effort and faith in education than ever before—education not only of elites but also of the masses of the world's population. Education is widely valued for itself, and educational progress enhances national pride, any practical economic effects aside. But increasingly there seems to be a tendency to "justify" it in economic terms. That education is one of the few sure roads to economic progress has become a contemporary creed. Yet evidence remains slim and confused, and while human-resource development certainly should and must receive increasing attention, there are

The authors appreciate the permission granted by Brookings Institution releasing this material for publication in the present volume. It constituted part of an analysis prepared for a conference on research needs and priorities for development, and appeared in processed form in *Research Needs for Development Assistance Programs*, August, 1961.

dangers in too simple a faith. It can lead to misplaced efforts and destructive frustrations in countries that can ill afford either.

This paper utilizes international comparisons of income and educational levels to point up some of the more basic questions.[1] The data are admittedly crude; indeed, their defects could be expounded through every page that is here used to say something else. More important, measurement of association is not identification of causation, nor can material of this kind provide direct evidence concerning the vital questions of the *processes* by which educational and other factors interact to produce (or impede) development. Nevertheless, observed trait clusters are not wholly accidental, and they offer clues in the formulation of potentially fruitful hypotheses. Also, weak empirical associations can challenge preconceived beliefs and assumptions. The correlations computed and charted here are thus best viewed as a twofold challenge. First, they challenge too simple assumptions that have been gaining increasingly widespread acceptance. Second, they challenge educators and social scientists to go out and dig in some potentially fertile but as yet uncultivated fields of academic endeavor.[2]

Education and income in a multiple-factor matrix

THE timely appearance of the Ginsburg and Berry *Atlas of Economic Development* supplies a convenient starting point for exploring world patterns of education in relation to various demographic and development variables. These data, supplemented by UNESCO literacy and school attendance reports and by Woytinsky's income estimates for 1938, constitute our empirical base.[3] The *Atlas* and a longer paper by Berry include a factor analysis of

1. For previous treatments of some of the data analyzed here, see J. B. D. Derksen, "Illiteracy and National Income," and Hilda H. Golden, "Illiteracy and Urban Industrialization," Chapters 9 and 10, respectively, in UNESCO, *World Illiteracy at Mid-Century*, Monographs on Fundamental Education, No. 11, 1957. See also the introductory chapter of UNESCO, *World Survey of Education*, Volume II.

2. For a more extensive discussion of research needs and priorities, see our "The Role of Education in Development: Research Needs and Priorities," forthcoming in a Brookings Institution publication. This analysis is included also, under the title "Concerning the Role of Education in Development," in the processed conference report of August, 1961, *Research Needs for Development Assistance Programs*.

3. Brian J. L. Berry, "An Inductive Approach to the Regionalization of

trait clusters for nearly a hundred countries; explicit educational variables are included together with closely related variables such as newspaper circulation.

In their first basic pattern (called the technological scale) all of the forty-three variables used have very high values, with infant mortality and birthrates the lowest. Newspaper circulation and national product per capita matched or exceeded the basic pattern values of all variables except those associated with per capita energy consumption and fiber use. A close relationship between any educational index and either per capita income or, especially, energy consumption would imply a strong position for education in this scale. We can therefore infer that the ensuing analyses measure sufficiently well for our purposes the place of education in a whole cluster of technological traits.[4]

Two variables were selected for special attention, however. The first was energy potentials per capita (not energy consumed), chosen on the assumption that energy potentials might constitute permissive or limiting factors that conceivably concealed effects of education on national income. More precisely, it was assumed that education might actually have contributed tangibly to the income of countries with poor basic resources; their incomes might be high relative to what could have been attained otherwise even though they had not climbed very high on the international income scale. Energy potential was thus viewed as a proxy variable for productive potentials other than those due to past capital accumulation, and independent of socioeconomic organization or the quality of the labor force. It is used here only to classify countries into three categories within each of which educational indexes are related to incomes. Various measures of education were related also to energy consumption per capita, but this exploration was not

Economic Development," in Norton Ginsburg (ed.), *Essays on Geography and Economic Development* (University of Chicago Press, 1960), pp. 78–107; W. S. and E. S. Woytinsky, *World Population and Production* (New York, Twentieth Century Fund, 1953), p. 389.

4. However, this tells us little about countries deviating markedly from the prevalent pattern in a scattergram relating education to income or energy use. Supplementation of the factor analysis by elaborate multiple correlation using many independent variables was considered, but we decided that it would have dubious additional explanatory value. Most of the variables are too closely intercorrelated; they serve better as measures of technological development than as clues to what brings this about. In fact there are no available indexes for most of the presumptively important causal or constraining factors in growth that are not at the same time measures of levels attained.

promising; the zero-order correlation between energy potentials and income is virtually zero.

One might expect that along with energy potential the basic agricultural resources (relative to population) would condition income potentials, especially through the lower- and middle-income ranges. However, no good index of agricultural potential is available. The closest approximation was cultivated hectares per capita. This ratio is in fact positively associated with national product per capita. However, the relations are diminished by the effects of industrialization upon the growth of urban population. Looking only at countries with more than the median proportion of population engaged in agriculture, a closer relationship might be expected; but examination of the data indicated that this was not the case. Taking the world as a whole and each energy potential group separately, a low ratio of cultivated land to population contributed little to explaining low incomes relative to educational attainments or vice versa through most of the land population range. This may be an important factor for extreme cases such as Japan and possibly elsewhere in the Far East.[5]

Literacy

TO what extent is literacy, spread through what proportion or segment of the population, an essential ingredient of economic advance? To what extent, on the other hand, may literacy be superfluous or inoperative in early stages of development? Dogmatic assertions on this topic are common enough, but firm evidence is scarce.

Lacking the necessary case studies of how literacy operates, the chief evidence is of two kinds: longitudinal, looking back to the earlier histories of presently developed nations, and cross-sectional comparisons of countries at particular dates. Both approaches suffer from the fact that literacy, like other elements in education, is both a means of production and a consumer good, expenditure on which rises with income. Moreover, literacy is part of a "package" borrowed from the West, and it may be the other items

5. On this and other questions concerning Japan, see below. In the Caribbean there are ratios of cultivated land to population as low as most in Asia, but income is not low relative to education.

in the package that are most significant for growth. Nevertheless, the available evidence is suggestive.

Archival research on literacy in European countries at early stages of development has scarcely begun, but a few clues are already at hand. Perhaps two-fifths of the young males in Czarist Russia prior to 1914 were literate. Similar and higher rates are inferred from signatures on marriage licenses in England and France prior to their industrial revolutions. These levels of education may not have been essential for the ensuring economic changes, but the presumption that they were cannot be ignored. These literacy rates, higher than in most underdeveloped countries today, emerged gradually and in a quite different environment. There was at that time not so clear an image of a high-income society to stimulate national aspirations and create the pressure for speedy development that goads "new nations" today. There was no comparable problem of dealing with a frustrated pseudointelligentsia with unrealistic occupational and status aspirations.[6] For the most part, Europe moved into the industrial era almost unwittingly; the problems of coordinating economic-opportunity distributions with expected returns to schooling were slight. Moreover, for both agricultural and industrial revolutions, education moved on many fronts, not merely or even mainly within schools. The economic growth of Europe proceeded by a gradual, unplanned process in which jobs and skills fed into each other, facilitating adaptations of a qualified labor force as much in response to as in anticipation of economic change.

Bearing these facts in mind, the patterns revealed by Figures 1, 2, and 3 and summarized in Table 1 should not be surprising. (Ranks in newspaper circulation are used to identify countries on the charts and incidentally provide additional information.)

In none of the thirty-two countries with adult literacy below 40 per cent was 1955 per capita income as high as $300, and the

6. This does not mean there was no concern about this problem; there have always been members of elites who feared an oversupply of educated men, as is still true in Western countries today. It is also too easy to overlook the fact that Czarist Russia was far ahead of most underdeveloped countries today in both its economic and educational attainment. To get to the Czarist level would mean a major advance for many of today's developing countries. For an illuminating discussion of the questions concerning various sorts of elites, see Edward Shils, "Political Developments in New States," *Comparative Studies in Society and History*, Vol. 2 (April and July, 1960), pp. 265–292, 379–411.

TABLE 1

Distribution of Countries by 1955 Gross National Product per
Capita and Percentage of Adult Population Who Were Literate
in 1950–54

Per Cent of Adults Literate 1950–54	Gross National Product per Capita, 1955 (in U.S. Dollars)						
	UNDER $100	$100– 199	$200– 299	$300– 499	$500 AND OVER	TOTAL	PER CENT
90–99	–	–	1	2	21	24	27
80–89	–	–	1	2	1	4	4
70–79	–	1	3	5	1	10	11
60–69	–	2	2	2	–	6	7
50–59	1	1	3	1	1	7	8
40–49	1	2	3	1	–	7	8
30–39	2	1	4	–	–	7	8
20–29	–	4	–	–	–	4	4
10–19	5	6	1	–	–	12	13
Under 10	7	2	–	–	–	9	10
Total	16	19	18	13	24	90	
Per cent	18	21	20	14	27		100

only country with literacy below 30 per cent and an income over
$200 was oil-rich British North Borneo. It is tempting to conclude
that a literacy rate of 30 to 40 per cent is a prerequisite to incomes
exceeding $200 in most cases and $300 in all. This may well be the
situation, though the charts cannot prove it.

Through the range from 30 to 70 per cent literacy (twenty-seven
countries) there is remarkably little increase in income with rising
literacy rates. In fact only five of the twenty-three countries with
literacy between 40 and 70 per cent had income over $300. That
other factors were especially favorable in one or another way is
evident when we look at what countries these were: Venezuela,
South Africa, Colombia, Panama, Cyprus. In all five cases income
distributions were highly unequal, and mean incomes exaggerate
the situation of the populace. European participation is of course
exceptionally important in South Africa and Cyprus. Venezuela is

Figure 1.

Gross national product per capita, 1955 (in U.S. dollars) and percentage of adults who were literate, 1950. Top third of countries in energy potential.

(SOURCE: Norton Ginsburg and Brian Berry, *Atlas of Economic Development*, 1961.)

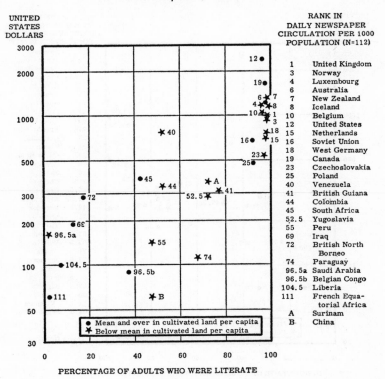

PERCENTAGE OF ADULTS WHO WERE LITERATE

exceptionally rich in oil, South Africa in minerals.[7] Taking into account the special characteristics of countries with literacy rates under 70 per cent that managed nevertheless to attain incomes above $300, the data strongly suggest that rising literacy alone contributes very little to development over the range from 30 to 70 per cent literate. Two-thirds of the fourteen countries with literacy rates between 70 and 90 per cent do manage to exceed average in-

7. The advantages of oil resources to Venezuela (as to British North Borneo) are particularly evident, as is also the tragedy if this income flow is wasted.

Figure 2.

Gross national product per capita, 1955 (in U.S. dollars) and percentage of adults who were literate, 1950. Middle third of countries in energy potential.

(SOURCE: Norton Ginsburg and Brian Berry, *Atlas of Economic Development*, 1961.)

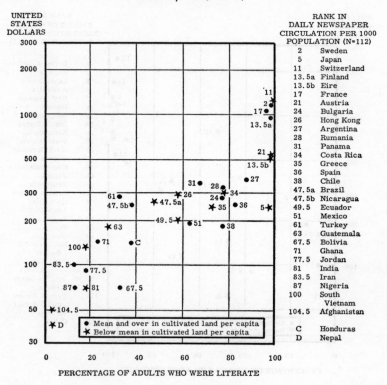

comes of $300 though not above $500. Moreover, the others, still under the $300 level, underline the fact that extending literacy to a majority of the population is no guarantee of even moderately high income; it may be necessary, but it is clearly not a sufficient condition.

Among the twenty-four countries with per capita income exceeding $500, only three had 1950 literacy rates under 90 per cent; these three exceptions were Puerto Rico, Uruguay, and Venezuela, and only the latter was under 80 per cent. It could of course be argued that wherever incomes reach $500 or better the demand for

Figure 3.

Gross national product per capita, 1955 (in U.S. dollars) and percentage of adults who were literate, 1950. Lowest third of countries in energy potential.

(SOURCE: Norton Ginsburg and Brian Berry, *Atlas of Economic Development*, 1961.)

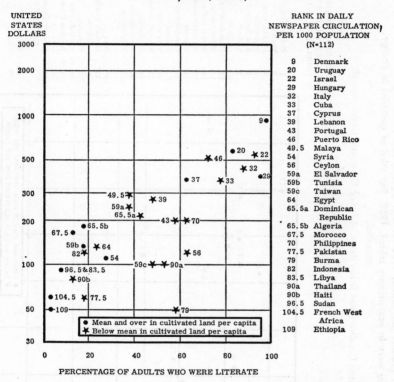

UNITED
STATES
DOLLARS

RANK IN DAILY
NEWSPAPER CIRCULATION,
PER 1000 POPULATION
(N=112)

Rank	Country
9	Denmark
20	Uruguay
22	Israel
29	Hungary
32	Italy
33	Cuba
37	Cyprus
39	Lebanon
43	Portugal
46	Puerto Rico
49.5	Malaya
54	Syria
56	Ceylon
59a	El Salvador
59b	Tunisia
59c	Taiwan
64	Egypt
65.5a	Dominican Republic
65.5b	Algeria
67.5	Morocco
70	Philippines
77.5	Pakistan
79	Burma
82	Indonesia
83.5	Libya
90a	Thailand
90b	Haiti
96.5	Sudan
104.5	French West Africa
109	Ethiopia

● Mean and over in cultivated land per capita
✴ Below mean in cultivated land per capita

PERCENTAGE OF ADULTS WHO WERE LITERATE

education as a consumer good establishes the high literacy. However, additional considerations support the conclusion that whatever the consumption component may be, literacy of something like 90 to 95 per cent is necessary to realize incomes over $500, barring exceptional circumstances. A complex industrial society depends upon many kinds of mass-communication media, and without near universal literacy these channels can function only imperfectly, requirements for higher levels of education aside. But to distinguish among countries in the higher ranges of education and income a more sensitive educational index is needed.

Figure 4.

Gross national product per capita, 1955 (in U.S. dollars) and percentage of total population who were in post-primary school, 1950. Top third of countries in energy potential.

(SOURCE: Norton Ginsburg and Brian Berry, *Atlas of Economic Development,* 1961.)

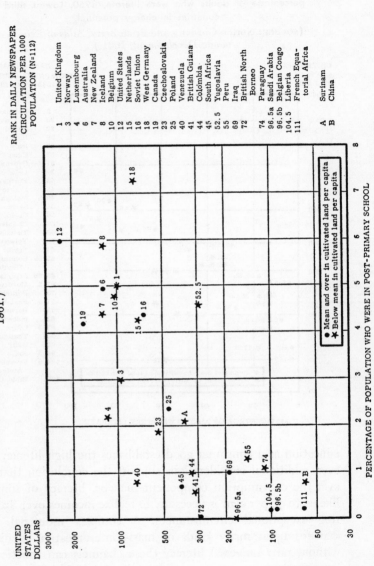

RANK IN DAILY NEWSPAPER CIRCULATION PER 1000 POPULATION (N=112)

1	United Kingdom
3	Norway
4	Luxembourg
6	Australia
7	New Zealand
8	Iceland
10	Belgium
12	United States
15	Netherlands
16	Soviet Union
18	West Germany
19	Canada
23	Czechoslovakia
25	Poland
40	Venezuela
41	British Guiana
44	Colombia
45	South Africa
52.5	Yugoslavia
55	Peru
69	Iraq
72	British North Borneo
74	Paraguay
96.5a	Saudi Arabia
96.5b	Belgian Congo
104.5	Liberia
111	French Equatorial Africa
A	Surinam
B	China

Percentage of population in postprimary school

THE level of adult literacy indicates the minimum educational equipment of the contemporary labor force. Postprimary enrollments measure adult educational levels, however, only to the extent that they are correlated with similar enrollments of an earlier generation. Among countries that have recently extended secondary education on a large scale it is too soon to expect any marked effect on national output; Yugoslavia (Figures 4 to 6) is an example. This index is a crude one in any case, mainly because of the wide range of quality in secondary and higher education. For countries like Eire or Luxembourg, there is a downward bias due to attendance abroad. Yet with all these qualifications, the looseness of the relation between extent of postprimary schooling and economic level is more impressive than the existence of a slight positive association.

Literacy rates and postprimary enrollments are of course positively correlated, but there are interesting deviations from the predominant pattern. Particularly striking are the high postprimary rates relative to literacy in Egypt, Jordan, and India (low literacy), in Lebanon and Taiwan (40–50 per cent literacy), and in Puerto Rico, Yugoslavia, the Philippines, and Cyprus (literacy 65–80 per cent).[8] In some cases this is clearly a recent development, and adult literacy rates are rising rapidly as today's youth grow up. In other countries there is a long-established elite with distinct educational privileges. Some of these elites appear to have made little contribution toward raising incomes in their homelands.

Correlations were computed relating literacy and postprimary education to per capita incomes for countries with literacy under 90 percent, and for all countries (Table 2). The variables were:

X_1 = logarithm of per capita gross national product, 1955
X_2 = literacy rates, 1950–1955
X_5 = postprimary enrollments relative to population, 1950.

In view of the wide income range among countries with literacy exceeding 90 per cent combined with the fact that almost all these countries had incomes above $500 and vice versa, the correlations involving literacy were limited to countries in which rates were

8. The postprimary rates for Puerto Rico and West Germany seem too high.

Figure 5.

Gross national product per capita, 1955 (in U.S. dollars) and percentage of total population who were in post-primary school, 1950. Middle third of countries in energy potential.

(SOURCE: Norton Ginsburg and Brian Berry, *Atlas of Economic Development,* 1961.)

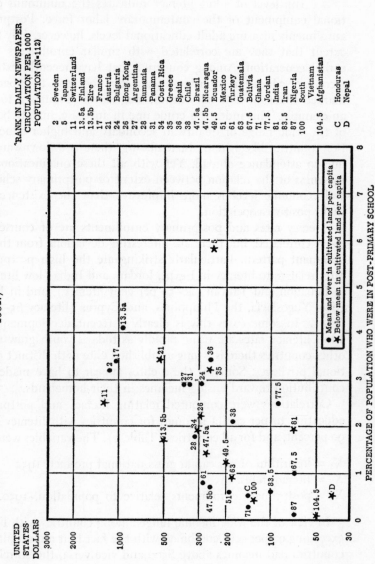

RANK IN DAILY NEWSPAPER CIRCULATION PER 1000 POPULATION (N=112)

2	Sweden
5	Japan
11	Switzerland
13.5a	Finland
13.5b	Eire
17	France
21	Austria
24	Bulgaria
26	Hong Kong
27	Argentina
28	Rumania
31	Panama
34	Costa Rica
35	Greece
36	Spain
38	Chile
47.5a	Brazil
47.5b	Nicaragua
49.5	Ecuador
51	Mexico
61	Turkey
63	Guatemala
67.5	Bolivia
71	Ghana
77.5	Jordan
81	India
83.5	Iran
87	Nigeria
100	South Vietnam
104.5	Afghanistan
C	Honduras
D	Nepal

TABLE 2

Countries with Under 90% Adult Literacy	Total	All Countries Energy Potential Level		
		HIGH	MIDDLE	LOW
$r_{12}{}^2$	0.432	–	–	–	–
$r_{15}{}^2$	0.283	0.485	0.531	0.355	0.443
$r_{1.25}{}^2$	0.443	–	–	–	–
Number of countries	55	77	26	25	26

under 90 per cent. This focuses on literacy-income relations at low and intermediate stages of economic development only, automatically excluding the most highly industrialized.

The correlation between postprimary enrollments and incomes are low, but especially when the countries most advanced in literacy are excluded. Literacy alone is a considerably better predictor within this range (as well as for all countries). Adding postprimary education in a multiple-correlation analysis improves the prediction slightly, but not significantly.

Obviously, it would be absurd to conclude from these data that a well-trained elite is unimportant for development. These charts and other information about the history of secondary and higher education point to two facts. First, high-income levels (over $1,000) have been attained in countries with only moderate (but not low) postprimary enrollments among present-day youth and, by inference, among present-day adults. Second, poor countries with sizable educated elites relative to their literacy position do not necessarily have much economic advantage over countries otherwise comparable but with low postprimary enrollments. Looking at this in another way, of the nine countries with the lowest incomes relative to their (moderate) literacy rates, only the Belgian Congo and Ceylon had low postprimary enrollments relative to literacy. The facts suggest that the distribution of investments in secondary as against primary education may be "out of line" in certain cases, though the scope for substitution between one and another emphasis within education would appear to be a wide one. But much more important, the data impel us to raise questions about the nature of elite education and about the rela-

Figure 6.

Gross national product per capita, 1955 (in U.S. dollars) and percentage of total population who were in post-primary school, 1950. Lowest third of countries in energy potential.

(SOURCE: Norton Ginsburg and Brian Berry, *Atlas of Economic Development*, 1961.)

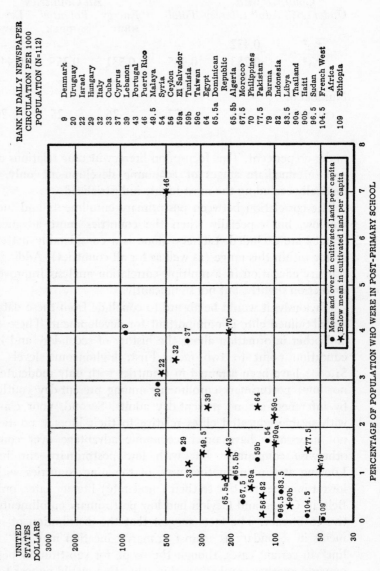

lations between elite and populace—not only within the educational system but throughout the social structure. They point also to questions concerning the quality and content of primary education, and suggest that there are wide cultural differences in subsequent self-education. One clue to the latter behavior is newspaper circulation, which is exceptionally high relative to postprimary enrollments in Britain, Scandinavia, and Switzerland, exceptionally low in Mediterranean countries, Puerto Rico, and the Philippines.

Primary enrollments and income-education relations over a generation

INTERMEDIATE between literacy rates and postprimary enrollments as an index of educational levels is primary enrollment.[9] The scatter of 1930–1934 primary enrollments against 1955 incomes is shown in Figure 7. For all countries, regardless of location or energy potential, the correlation is slightly closer and more consistently linear (using logs of income) than is that with literacy rates, and it is much higher than the correlation with postprimary enrollments. The more consistent linearity here than on the literacy charts is attributable partly to the fact that primary enrollments differentiate among countries at the top whereas literacy rates do not. The income plateau observed on the literacy charts over the middle range of educational performance (30–70 per cent literacy) is not repeated in the intermediate ranges of primary enrollments to quite the same degree. However, examination of the countries at the income extremes within the middle-education range indicates that there is a plateau here also.

As shown in Figures 1 to 6, British North Borneo and Venezuela have markedly high incomes relative to education, for sufficiently obvious reasons. At the other extreme, Japan, Eire, Paraguay,

9. UNESCO has published the percentages of 5–14-year-olds in primary school for 1930–1934 and 1950–1954. In some countries numerous children have moved into secondary school at ages of 12 to 14 and are not counted in this index; in half the countries with high primary enrollments in 1930–1934 this rate declined during the next twenty years. Nevertheless, outside Europe the 1950–1954 rates are quite good indexes, and the 1930–1934 rates are useful even for European countries. Differences in school starting age also distort the picture. Where pupils begin at seven, the share of 5–14-year-olds in primary school will be smaller than where entry is at five or six. Yet the total schooling in the first case (as in Sweden) may be greater.

Figure 7.

Gross national product per capita, 1955* (in U.S. dollars) and percentage of population, age 5–14, who were in primary school, 1930.**

(SOURCE: *Norton Ginsburg and Brian Berry, *Atlas of Economic Development*, 1961, and **UNESCO, *World Survey of Education, Volume II, Primary Education*, 1958.)

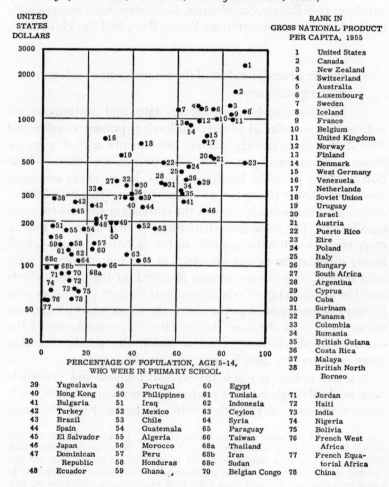

UNITED
STATES
DOLLARS

RANK IN
GROSS NATIONAL PRODUCT
PER CAPITA, 1955

PERCENTAGE OF POPULATION, AGE 5–14,
WHO WERE IN PRIMARY SCHOOL

1	United States
2	Canada
3	New Zealand
4	Switzerland
5	Australia
6	Luxembourg
7	Sweden
8	Iceland
9	France
10	Belgium
11	United Kingdom
12	Norway
13	Finland
14	Denmark
15	West Germany
16	Venezuela
17	Netherlands
18	Soviet Union
19	Uruguay
20	Israel
21	Austria
22	Puerto Rico
23	Eire
24	Poland
25	Italy
26	Hungary
27	South Africa
28	Argentina
29	Cyprus
30	Cuba
31	Surinam
32	Panama
33	Colombia
34	Rumania
35	British Guiana
36	Costa Rica
37	Malaya
38	British North Borneo

39	Yugoslavia	49	Portugal	60	Egypt		
40	Hong Kong	50	Philippines	61	Tunisia	71	Jordan
41	Bulgaria	51	Iraq	62	Indonesia	72	Haiti
42	Turkey	52	Mexico	63	Ceylon	73	India
43	Brazil	53	Chile	64	Syria	74	Nigeria
44	Spain	54	Guatemala	65	Paraguay	75	Bolivia
45	El Salvador	55	Algeria	66	Taiwan	76	French West Africa
46	Japan	56	Morocco	68a	Thailand		
47	Dominican Republic	57	Peru	68b	Iran	77	French Equatorial Africa
48	Ecuador	58	Honduras	68c	Sudan		
		59	Ghana	70	Belgian Congo	78	China

Chile, and Ceylon have very low incomes relative to what their 1930–1934 primary enrollments would predict. These deviations have have shown up in other comparisons also, especially for Japan. Yet only Ceylon is in the lowest third in energy potential; in in fact, Paraguay is high. Four of the five are below the median in cultivated land per capita, but only Japan and in a lesser degree Ceylon are extreme in this respect. The median hectares per capita for 129 countries is 0.48; the values for the individual countries were: Chile 0.78, Eire 0.42, Paraguay 0.33, Ceylon 0.17, and Japan 0.06. The low incomes relative to primary attendance and literacy in Chile and Paraguay are at least in part misleading; estimates of income in Chile have been recently revised upward substantially, and the education data for Paraguay are probably grossly over-stated.[10]

On the assumption that education is a causal factor in economic productivity, the logical comparison would of course be the one just presented, using the earlier index that best indicated the education of the contemporary labor force. However, education is also an effect of income; hence we related both 1930–1934 and 1950–1954 primary enrollments to both 1938 and 1955 incomes[11] (Table 3). The variables are:

X_1 = logarithm of gross national product per capita in 1955

X_3 = percentage of population age 5–14 in primary school in 1950–1954

X_4 = percentage of population age 5–14 in primary school in 1930–1934

X_6 = logarithm of gross national product per capita in 1938.

Whether the earlier or later incomes are used, the correlations with 1950 education tended to be higher than those with 1930 education, taking all countries together. Even though this over-all pattern is consistent and appreciable only within the low-energy group, the presumption that education is predominantly a causal variable in the development sequence is not upheld. In fact, 1938 incomes predict 1950 education of children remarkably well for all

10. The Japanese case and some of the puzzles presented by the entire Asian and Latin American pictures will be discussed further when we look at the situation by world regions.
11. Since 1938 income data were available for fewer countries, correlations were computed first including only countries for which a full set of estimates were available—mainly Europe and the Americas.

TABLE 3

Countries for which 1938 income data are available	All Countries: Energy Potential Categories			Excluding countries with 1950–54 literacy 90% or over
	TOTAL	HIGH	MIDDLE	LOW	
r_{63}^2	0.712	0.411	0.622	0.771	0.568
r_{64}^2	0.583	0.632	0.673	0.397	0.338
r_{13}^2	0.663	0.741	0.543	0.675	0.290
r_{14}^2	0.591	0.627	0.632	0.365	0205
Number of countries	51	20	19	12	29
Including countries for which 1938 income data are lacking					
r_{13}^2	0.686	0.681	0.628	0.662	0.422
r_{14}^2	0.586	0.562	0.689	0.447	0.317
Number of countries	77	26	25	26	55

countries and for all energy levels except the highest.[12] The wide income spread among countries with intermediate literacy levels is reflected in the low correlations when those having 90 per cent or more literate in 1950–1954 are excluded (the last column of the above tabulation). Also, for the countries with less than 90 per cent literacy in 1950–1954, the superiority of the correlation of 1938 income with 1950 primary enrollment over all other correlations is very marked; r_{63}^2 came out at 0.568 whereas for the corresponding countries r_{14}^2 was only 0.205.[13]

There is of course a strong serial-income correlation. This raises the question: How well did 1938 income predict that of 1955 and

12. The latter are dominated by the countries in which the 1950 primary enrollment rates were most distorted by entry of children into secondary school. In many of these countries primary enrollment rates as here measured actually declined. For the high-energy group especially, better education measures might have strengthened the prediction of 1950 educational indexes based on 1938 incomes, bringing them in line with the other energy potential groups.

13. In view of the low zero-order correlations between 1955 income and 1930–1934 primary enrollments among countries with less than 90 per cent adult literacy in 1950–1954, it is hardly surprising that inclusion of 1930 en-

how much is this prediction improved by adding education variables? The data in Table 4 are directed to this point, using the 1930–1934 primary enrollment data as the only ones that provide a time-lead measure.

TABLE 4
Energy Potential Category

	TOTAL	HIGH	MIDDLE	LOW
r_{16}^2	0.746	0.783	0.728	0.700
$r_{1.64}^2$	0.773	0.804	0.751	0.710

It is evident that, taken alone, 1938 income predicts 1955 income better than any of the education indexes do and much better than 1930 primary enrollments in particular; adding the latter raises the coefficients only a little—certainly not significantly. But this does not answer the question as to relations between changes in education and subsequent changes in income. Earlier literacy rates are available for only twenty-eight countries (even including cases in which the data are of extremely doubtful validity), and most of these were in the 90 per cent and over literacy category by 1950. Scattergrams comparing 1930 to 1950 changes in primary enrollments with 1938 to 1955 changes in per capita incomes showed very low correlations. While this is partially attributable to the crudities of the measures, especially primary enrollment rates in 1950–1954, it certainly gives no support to the assumption that increasing schooling is uniformly followed by rising incomes.

Finally, tests were made substituting 1950 per capita energy consumption (X_7) for 1955 per capita gross national product. It might be expected that relations between education and per capita energy consumption would be closer than those between education and income, since energy consumption is more closely associated with technological change and hence with alterations in the job

rollments did not improve predictions based on 1950–1954 literacy alone or on 1950–1954 literacy and postprimary enrollments in combination. In fact, for all countries with less than 90 per cent literate in 1950–1954, the values of $r_{1.245}^2$, were so little above those of r_{12}^2 and $r_{1.25}^2$ respectively, as to make no difference when rounded to two places. Replacing the 1930 by 1950 primary enrollments improved these correlations slightly, from $r_{12}^2 = 0.432$ to $r_{1.23}^2 = 0.456$, and from $r_{1.25}^2 = 0.443$ to $r_{1.235}^2 = 0.628$. Note that for these countries r_{12}^2 is 0.432 and r_{13} is 0.422; the correlation of concurrent adult literacy with income is slightly, but only slightly, higher than that between 1955 income and 1950–1954 rates of primary enrollment.

structure and its educational demands. However, these correlations in fact turned out to be lower; the following findings are illustrative. For countries with less than 90 per cent literate in 1950, the correlation between energy consumption and literacy was only $r_{72}^2 = 0.253$ as against $r_{12}^2 = 0.432$. For the same countries r_{75}^2 was 0.062, and for all countries it was 0.390 as against r_{15}^2 values of 0.283 and 0.485, respectively. For all countries r_{73}^3 was 0.493, while r_{13}^2 was 0.663. (The zero-order correlation between X_1 and X_7 was 0.582.)

These various findings point up the importance of interactions between education and economic conditions through time, and also, comparing the energy categories, the diversities in time sequences. We might surmise that a long-term interaction between educational and economic development operates regardless of whether immediate motivations that lead people to school are of a consumer or an investment nature. Alternatively, one might argue that the skill demands of an expanding economy stimulate more education, thereby creating an income-to-education sequence at the same time that the reverse is also operating. Both processes may in fact be involved, along with other factors that impede or foster them. The data suggest also, though they cannot prove, the occurrence of important, distinct stages in educational lead and lag: an early stage of education-economic breakthrough; a plateau in which diffusing education is still not sufficient to support a high-level economy; and a third stage in which another economic breakthrough is possible, built on a well-educated population. In addition, evidence of other kinds strongly underlines the problem of culturally and institutionally conditioned disjunctions between schooling and economic roles of the graduates of the schools in many of the less developed countries. The observed relationships are open to many interpretations that suggest the importance of giving serious thought to Akerman's thesis concerning structural changes in the development process.[14] Educational-income relationships may be quite different in one time and place from another. Many tasks for both the economic and

14. See, for example, Johan Akerman, *Theory of Industrialism* (Lund, Gleerup, 1960). For a brief statement concerning this approach and its relation to theories of "balanced" versus "unbalanced" growth, see the first section of our "The Role of Education in Development: Research Needs and Priorities," *op. cit.*

educational historians and other social scientists are hidden in this puzzle, which illustrates the fallacy of posing questions about the role of education in unidimensional and one-direction terms.

Geographic perspectives

THAT major geographic areas of the world are at quite different levels of educational attainment and economic development is common knowledge. Here we are interested, however, less in identifying regional levels than in contrasting regional patterns of relationship between education and income. A sorting of countries by world areas spotlights questions that arise when adjacent countries that have many things in common manifest quite different economic-educational attributes. A geographic focus facilitates the search for multiplier and diffusion processes relating to education and development. For example, external economies associated with access to markets and energy resources are often poorly identified by data for single countries—as the contrast between Japan and Denmark clearly attests. Possible effects of broad cultural traits some of which are common to large regions and of diversity within regions (for example, North versus South America) are more readily suggested when relations between education and other traits are examined for the world areas separately.[15]

Figures 8 to 15 present education-income relations for these clusters of countries. The best educational predictor of 1955 incomes differs. For Europe taken alone, literacy is a poor discriminator, and there was virtually no association between 1955 incomes and 1950–1954 postprimary enrollments. Even adding the high-income and well-educated countries of Australia, New Zealand, Canada, and the United States left the correlation very low. Hence, only 1930–1934 primary enrollments are shown on Figure 8. The positive association between the two variables is unmistakable; however, in the range from 60 to 70 per cent enrollment there is a wide variation in income.

Deviations from the dominant pattern are as interesting as the general relationship. Distinctly below the income level that would normally be associated with its educational position is Eire, which

15. Berry (in Ginsburg, *Essays, op. cit.,* pp. 96f.) also identifies regional clusters in development.

Figure 8.
Countries of Europe, the United States, Canada, Australia, and New Zealand. Gross national product per capita, 1955* (in U.S. dollars) and percentage of population, age 5–14, who were in primary school, 1930.**

(SOURCE: *Norton Ginsburg and Brian Berry, *Atlas of Economic Development*, 1961, and **UNESCO, *World Survey of Education, Volume II, Primary Education*, 1958.)

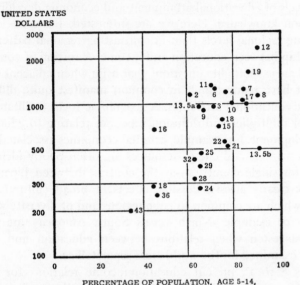

PERCENTAGE OF POPULATION, AGE 5-14,
WHO WERE IN PRIMARY SCHOOL

RANK IN DAILY NEWSPAPER CIRCULATION PER 1000 POPULATION (N=112)

1	United Kingdom	11	Switzerland	21	Austria
2	Sweden	12	United States	22	Israel
3	Norway	13.5a	Finland	24	Bulgaria
4	Luxembourg	13.5b	Eire	25	Poland
6	Australia	15	Netherlands	28	Rumania
7	New Zealand	16	Soviet Union	29	Hungary
8	Iceland	17	France	32	Italy
9	Denmark	18	West Germany	36	Spain
10	Belgium	19	Canada	43	Portugal

poses problems resembling those of retarded areas within advanced countries. By contrast, a cluster of countries, chiefly Scandinavian, have incomes above what their primary enrollments would predict —in part because of downward bias in the education index. Soviet incomes are much higher than 1930 primary enrollments predict; here both the pace of change on many fronts and intensive devel-

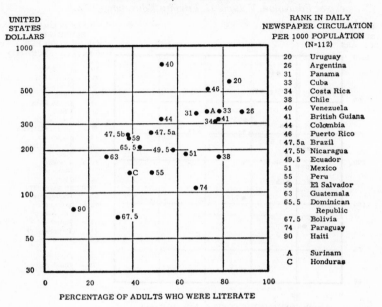

Figure 9.

Countries of South and Central America. Gross national product
per capita, 1955 (in U.S. dollars) and education. Percentage of
adults who were literate, 1950.

(SOURCE: Norton Ginsburg and Brian Berry, *Atlas of Economic Development*, 1961.)

UNITED
STATES
DOLLARS

RANK IN DAILY
NEWSPAPER CIRCULATION
PER 1000 POPULATION
(N=112)

20	Uruguay
26	Argentina
31	Panama
33	Cuba
34	Costa Rica
38	Chile
40	Venezuela
41	British Guiana
44	Colombia
46	Puerto Rico
47.5a	Brazil
47.5b	Nicaragua
49.5	Ecuador
51	Mexico
55	Peru
59	El Salvador
63	Guatemala
65.5	Dominican Republic
67.5	Bolivia
74	Paraguay
90	Haiti
A	Surinam
C	Honduras

PERCENTAGE OF ADULTS WHO WERE LITERATE

opment of schools invalidate the crude comparison implied by the
chart. Thus, much of the unexplained variance would have been
eliminated with a more adequate measure of mass schooling.

The countries of Latin America present quite a different set of
education-income relations (Figures 9 to 11). Here the 1930
primary enrollments are the poorest predictors of income, while
literacy rates predict much better.[16]

The Latin American charts raise basic questions, many of which
are relevant to other parts of the world also. Why have so many of
these countries developed so slowly—both educationally and in
economic level relative to what had been accomplished in spread-

16. Venezuela is out of line on all charts, owing to oil incomes. The
anomalous position of Chile and Paraguay may well be due to the errors
in income estimates for the former and in education data for the latter noted
earlier. The contrast with Brazil and Colombia is striking.

Figure 10.

Countries of South and Central America. Gross national product per capita, 1955* (in U.S. dollars) and education. Percentage of population, age 5–14, who were in primary school, 1930.**

(SOURCE: *Norton Ginsburg and Brian Berry, *Atlas of Economic Development*, 1961, and **UNESCO, *World Survey of Education, Volume II, Primary Education*, 1958.)

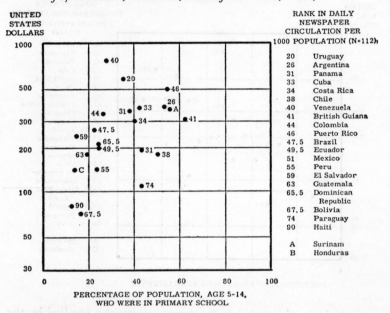

UNITED
STATES
DOLLARS

PERCENTAGE OF POPULATION, AGE 5-14,
WHO WERE IN PRIMARY SCHOOL

RANK IN DAILY
NEWSPAPER
CIRCULATION PER
1000 POPULATION (N=112)

Rank	Country
20	Uruguay
26	Argentina
31	Panama
33	Cuba
34	Costa Rica
38	Chile
40	Venezuela
41	British Guiana
44	Colombia
46	Puerto Rico
47.5	Brazil
49.5	Ecuador
51	Mexico
55	Peru
59	El Salvador
63	Guatemala
65.5	Dominican Republic
67.5	Bolivia
74	Paraguay
90	Haiti
A	Surinam
B	Honduras

ing education? How have incentive and opportunity patterns varied among these societies? How are graduates of various schools channeled into economic life? To what extent are members of the elite protected and eased into bureaucratic sinecures? Are the educational system and the infrastructure of roads and communications mutually supportive of diffusion processes that could both spread education and contribute to economic initiative and informed economic calculation? Could planned concentration on particular sectors of the economy (planned imbalance) break through the stagnation of these countries? If so, what are the strategic points at which schools and the content of schooling come into play, and at what points might development assistance from abroad contribute most? Though broad and rather general answers can be given to these questions for several countries, it is

Figure 11.

Countries of South and Central America. Gross national product per capita, 1955 (in U.S. dollars) and education. Percentage of population who were in post-primary school, 1950.

(SOURCE: Norton Ginsburg and Brian Berry, *Atlas of Economic Development*, 1961.)

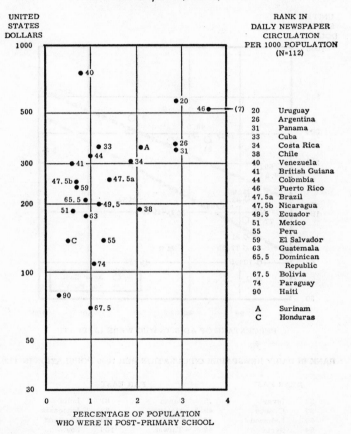

UNITED
STATES
DOLLARS

RANK IN
DAILY NEWSPAPER
CIRCULATION
PER 1000 POPULATION
(N=112)

20	Uruguay
26	Argentina
31	Panama
33	Cuba
34	Costa Rica
38	Chile
40	Venezuela
41	British Guiana
44	Colombia
46	Puerto Rico
47.5a	Brazil
47.5b	Nicaragua
49.5	Ecuador
51	Mexico
55	Peru
59	El Salvador
63	Guatemala
65.5	Dominican Republic
67.5	Bolivia
74	Paraguay
90	Haiti
A	Surinam
C	Honduras

PERCENTAGE OF POPULATION
WHO WERE IN POST-PRIMARY SCHOOL

essential to locate the critical points in educational-economic strategy and assess reaction thresholds and multiplier potentials.

Boundaries between Asia, Europe, and Africa are arbitrary, and those between Near and Far East even more so. With certain exceptions, the countries of the Near and Far East are at quite different income levels relative to their education, and the Near Eastern countries that have been culturally most closely linked

272   MARY JEAN BOWMAN and C. ARNOLD ANDERSON

Figure 12.

Asian countries. Gross national product per capita, 1955 (in U.S. dollars) and education. Percentage of adults who were literate, 1950.

(SOURCE: Norton Ginsburg and Brian Berry, *Atlas of Economic Development*, 1961.)

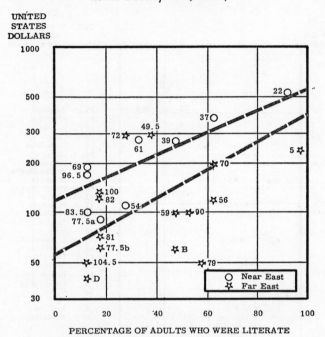

PERCENTAGE OF ADULTS WHO WERE LITERATE

RANK IN DAILY NEWSPAPER CIRCULATION PER 1000 POPULATION (N=112)

NEAR EAST		FAR EAST			
22	Israel	5	Japan	81	India
37	Cyprus	49.5	Malaya	82	Indonesia
39	Lebanon	56	Ceylon	90	Thailand
54	Syria	59	Taiwan	100	South
61	Turkey	70	Philippines		Vietnam
69	Iraq	72	British North	104.5	Afghanistan
77.5a	Jordan		Borneo		
83.5	Iran	77.5b	Pakistan	B	China
96.5	Saudi Arabia	79	Burma	D	Nepal

to Europe have the highest incomes relative to schooling (Figures 12 to 14). This shows up particularly clearly with respect to primary enrollment, but it appears also when incomes are related to literacy rates. Malaya and British North Borneo in the Far East

Figure 13.

Asian countries. Gross national product per capita, 1955* (in U.S. dollars) and education. Percentage of population, age 5–14, who were in primary school, 1930.**

(SOURCE: *Norton Ginsburg and Brian Berry, *Atlas of Economic Development*, 1961, and **UNESCO, *World Survey of Education, Volume II, Primary Education,* 1958.)

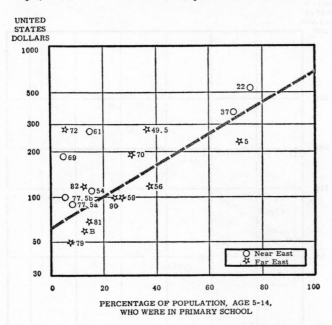

RANK IN DAILY NEWSPAPER CIRCULATION PER 1000 POPULATION (N=112)

NEAR EAST		FAR EAST			
22	Israel	5	Japan	77.5b	Pakistan
37	Cyprus	49.5	Malaya	79	Burma
54	Syria	56	Ceylon	81	India
61	Turkey	59	Taiwan	82	Indonesia
69	Iraq	70	Philippines	90	Thailand
77.5a	Jordan	72	British North Borneo	B	China

fall into the Near East pattern. Only part of the income advantage of the Near Eastern countries rests on oil. Both cultural diffusion (including education in the broadest sense) and external economies associated with linkage into European markets are involved.

Japan was decidedly out of line in all the charts previously presented, its income being too low relative to education. However,

Figure 14.

Asian countries. Gross national product per capita, 1955 (in U.S. dollars) and education. Percentage of population who were in post-primary school, 1950.

(SOURCE: Norton Ginsburg and Brian Berry, *Atlas of Economic Development*, 1961.)

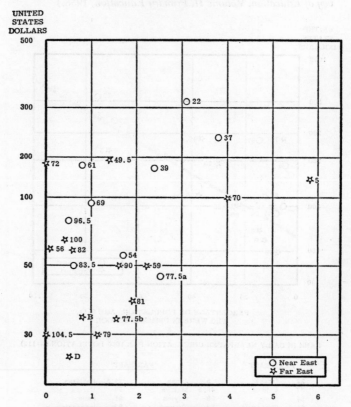

PERCENTAGE OF POPULATION WHO WERE IN POST-PRIMARY SCHOOL

RANK IN DAILY NEWSPAPER CIRCULATION PER 1000 POPULATION (N=112)

NEAR EAST		FAR EAST	
22	Israel	5	Japan	81	India
37	Cyprus	49.5	Malaya	82	Indonesia
39	Lebanon	56	Ceylon	90	Thailand
54	Syria	59	Taiwan	100	South
61	Turkey	70	Philippines		Vietnam
69	Iraq	72	British North	104.5	Afghanistan
77.5a	Jordan		Borneo		
83.5	Iran	77.5b	Pakistan	B	China
96.5	Saudi Arabia	79	Burma	D	Nepal

Figure 15.

Gross national product per capita, 1955 (in U.S. dollars) and African countries. education.

(SOURCE: Norton Ginsburg and Brian Berry, *Atlas of Economic Development*, 1961 and UNESCO, *World Survey of Education, Volume II, Primary Education*, 1958.)

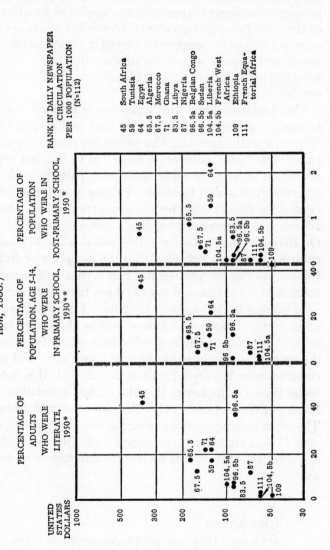

Rank in Daily Newspaper Circulation per 1000 Population (N=112)	
45	South Africa
59	Tunisia
64	Egypt
65.5	Algeria
67.5	Morocco
71	Ghana
83.5	Libya
87	Nigeria
96.5a	Belgian Congo
96.5b	Sudan
104.5a	Liberia
104.5b	French West Africa
109	Ethiopia
111	French Equatorial Africa

seen in relation to other Far Eastern countries, Japan looks very prosperous; its income falls into line with the literacy-income and primary enrollment-income relations displayed by other countries of the area. Japanese educational accomplishments are impressive even in a European perspective; viewed in the Asian context its economic performance appears equally so. But to say this is also to stress the magnitude of the task of economic development throughout Asia.

The "population problem" is commonly invoked in discussion of economic development in the Far East and certain other areas, often in a sense of despair. The writers are among the worriers, but growth rates aside, population density as such is not wholly a disadvantage. Given favorable settlement patterns and conditions otherwise reasonably favorable, a dense population favors more rapid diffusion of education and practices conducive to economic advance at lower costs for building a communication infrastructure. On the other hand, sheer numbers makes a breakthrough in agriculture exceedingly difficult. With the exception of British North Borneo, no Far Eastern country had even a half-hectare of cultivated land per capita, and most had less than a quarter-hectare.

In turning to the countries of Africa (Figure 15), we are examining education-income relations within the lower segments of both distributions. Only in South Africa, where European incomes distort the average, was 1955 income above $200, and only in two countries were literacy rates above 20 per cent. It is not surprising under these circumstances that the neatest associations are in the literacy-income relations rather than for other education measures. The most striking deviants from the dominant pattern—the Belgian Congo on literacy and Egypt and Tunisia on postprimary enrollments—have already been noted and require no further comment.

Conclusions

ALTHOUGH there are positive correlations between the level or spread of education and economic levels, these connections are loose ones. Indicators of the spread of primary education are better economic predictors than the extent of postprimary schooling. But the latter is a poor measure of the current highly trained labor

Figure 15.

African countries. Gross national product per capita, 1955 (in U.S. dollars) and education.

(SOURCE: Norton Ginsburg and Brian Berry, *Atlas of Economic Development,* 1961 and UNESCO, *World Survey of Education, Volume II, Primary Education,* 1958.)

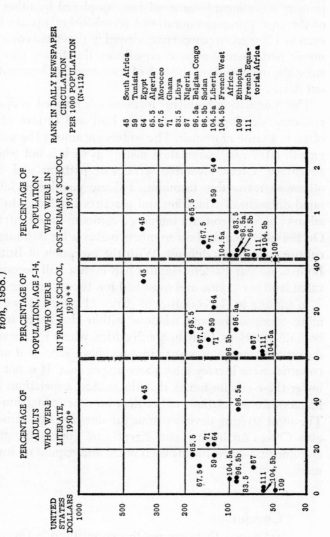

45	South Africa
59	Tunisia
64	Egypt
65.5	Algeria
67.5	Morocco
71	Ghana
83.5	Libya
87	Nigeria
96.5a	Belgian Congo
96.5b	Sudan
104.5a	Liberia
104.5b	French West Africa
109	Ethiopia
111	French Equatorial Africa

seen in relation to other Far Eastern countries, Japan looks very prosperous; its income falls into line with the literacy-income and primary enrollment-income relations displayed by other countries of the area. Japanese educational accomplishments are impressive even in a European perspective; viewed in the Asian context its economic performance appears equally so. But to say this is also to stress the magnitude of the task of economic development throughout Asia.

The "population problem" is commonly invoked in discussion of economic development in the Far East and certain other areas, often in a sense of despair. The writers are among the worriers, but growth rates aside, population density as such is not wholly a disadvantage. Given favorable settlement patterns and conditions otherwise reasonably favorable, a dense population favors more rapid diffusion of education and practices conducive to economic advance at lower costs for building a communication infrastructure. On the other hand, sheer numbers makes a breakthrough in agriculture exceedingly difficult. With the exception of British North Borneo, no Far Eastern country had even a half-hectare of cultivated land per capita, and most had less than a quarter-hectare.

In turning to the countries of Africa (Figure 15), we are examining education-income relations within the lower segments of both distributions. Only in South Africa, where European incomes distort the average, was 1955 income above $200, and only in two countries were literacy rates above 20 per cent. It is not surprising under these circumstances that the neatest associations are in the literacy-income relations rather than for other education measures. The most striking deviants from the dominant pattern—the Belgian Congo on literacy and Egypt and Tunisia on postprimary enrollments—have already been noted and require no further comment.

Conclusions

ALTHOUGH there are positive correlations between the level or spread of education and economic levels, these connections are loose ones. Indicators of the spread of primary education are better economic predictors than the extent of postprimary schooling. But the latter is a poor measure of the current highly trained labor

force. Especially important, this index gives no clues to the nature
of secondary and higher education. More precise indexes of education and of productivity would improve the correlations; however,
there can be no doubt that a large unexplained 1955 income variance, and variance in rates of economic advance, would remain.
And part of any observed association is attributable to effects of
income on education.

More broadly, the empirical data analyzed here, taken together
with other types of evidence, suggest several basic hypotheses that
may illuminate search for understanding of the roles of education
in economic development (or stagnation):

1] Economic gains associated with growth of a literate minority
may level off quickly, the economy remaining on a low plateau,
until education has built up to a point at which widespread transformation is possible. There is perhaps an educational threshold
in the extension of primary schooling that must be reached before
further extension of such schooling can be brought into economic
play. This may be linked with, and clearly parallels, problems of
breakthrough into societal "external economics of scale." However,
there have been some exceptions. To understand what is involved
we need careful longitudinal studies for particular countries as
well as cross-sectional data of the type used here. And the variant
situational conditions that characterize countries that have been
most extreme in manifesting stagnation plateaus *versus* those that
have most clearly deviated from this pattern need special attention.
2] While an educated elite is a necessary condition of sustained
economic development, it is not a sufficient one. In fact some educated elites may even impede developments relative to what could
occur without them; they may have this effect if they reinforce
status values and/or special privileges that are incompatible with
economic advance. There can be wasteful and even dysfunctional
investments in education. This is closely related to (though not
identical with) Hypothesis 3.
3] A polarization of society and absence of a communication continuum among the subpopulations may inhibit effective economic
utilization of any given level of schooling even when it has not
checked the spread of such schooling. The loose but positive correlations between "competitive" political systems and economic

development noted by Coleman,[17] Hagen[18] and others may well relate mainly to the existence of a middle class. Some of the exceptions might cease to be exceptions if this redefinition were adopted. However, to say this is also to point to the fallacy of considering status structures as unidimensional. This third hypothesis then has two variants (and could of course be elaborated into more). One of these, in line with the way in which it was initially stated, focuses on the "communication" factor; the other emphasizes the emergence and growth of a mundanely active "middle class," whether or not in its origin "deviant."

At least two types of lead and lag have been implied in these hypotheses, and these two types can have quite different implications with respect to the use of economic criteria in decisions concerning public support of education. Distortions of elite education such as are involved in Hypothesis 2 lie back of and strengthen arguments against public subsidy of classical elite education in some developing countries.[19] This position has received less attention than it deserves. On the other hand, there may be a strong long-run case in economics for public subsidy of elementary education that may seem in the shorter run (even over two or three decades) to be almost purely "consumption" with little if any productivity effect. And such subsidy might best be overtly "justified" on the basis of noneconomic values. Such an approach might minimize politically critical and economically obstructive frustrations of expectations while laying the foundations for a breakthrough into a new socioeconomic structure.

That economic development involves a process of structural transformation of a very fundamental and sweeping kind is evi-

17. See James S. Coleman, "Conclusion: The Political System of the Developing Areas," in C. A. Almond and J. S. Coleman, et al., The Politics of the Developing Areas, Princeton, N.J., Princeton University Press, 1960.

18. See Everett E. Hagen, "A General Framework for Analyzing Economic and Political Change," in Research Needs for Development Assistance Programs, Brookings Institution, processed, August, 1961.

19. Arthur Lewis, among others, has argued the case for distinguishing between "consumption" and "investment" outlays on secondary and higher education, identifying the former as outlays on types of education that are in surplus as evidenced by the incidence of unemployment among intellectuals. He makes this distinction a criterion with respect to priorities in public subsidy of education. See, for example, his discussion of this problem in The Theory of Economic Growth, Richard D. Irwin, Homewood, Ill., 1955, passim.

dent, even though this fact is rarely given the full recognition it should have. This transformation, or series of transformations, entails conflict and requires major adaptations and adjustments by the individuals and groups who make up a society. It both contributes to and depends upon human resource development of many kinds, including "education" outside schools. This means that a framework adequate for analysis of the role of education in economic development must define education broadly, distinguish among its components and their interrelations, and encompass consideration of multidirectional processes in the interplay between educational and other economic factors. However, there are signposts that can help guide such study. These center on three kinds of questions or problems: (*a*) problems of scale and structural breakthrough, such as have already been noted, (*b*) conditions and processes that determine the pace and persistence of intrasector diffusion, and (*c*) the operation of intersector multipliers.

Under (*b*) come questions concerning what factors make for, what impede, the diffusion of elementary, intermediate, higher education, and of scientific and technological versus classical training. Under (*c*) come questions concerning what fosters, what impedes, mutually supportive educational and economic development. One of the vital problems here—incidentally, also linking (*c*) with (*a*)—is that of transfer of know-how as distinct from transfer of knowledge or of educational systems. In this context the interplay between schooling and on-the-job training becomes especially important. Also, back of both (*b*)and (*c*) and as part of them, it is necessary to view attitudes, actual opportunities, and opportunity perceptions as dynamic variables on a par with the more conventional kinds of economic data, to be observed and studied as an integral part of the overall development process. Neither the static bias of traditional anthropology nor the "other things equal" approach and formal growth models of the economist can provide the needed framework. Both are too lacking in a genuine time dimension and treatment of structural shifts. Neither attacks the most essential points: the "how" and the "process" questions of socioeconomic change.

Political socialization and culture change

ROBERT LEVINE

WITH THE GROWING RECOGNITION that political behavior is an aspect of culture and as such is regularly transmitted from generation to generation, social psychologists and political scientists have been paying increasing attention to *political socialization*, that is, the means by which individuals acquire motives, habits, and values relevant to participation in a political system. The concept of political socialization covers topics as diverse as the effect of parent-child relationships on images of authority and the role of the army in building national loyalties in youth.[1] Although systematic re-

An earlier version of this article was presented at the meeting of the Society for Applied Anthropology, Pittsburgh, May, 1960.

1. Socialization in its most general sense is the acquisition of dispositions toward behavior that is positively valued by a group, and the elimination of dispositions toward behavior that is disvalued by the group. It is assumed that the valued behavior has some relevance to the maintenance of group functioning, as in the case of behavior required for performance in a social role. Within this general process, political socialization is the acquisition by an individual of behavioral dispositions relevant to political groups, political systems, political processes. Examples of the kinds of behavioral dispositions included are: attitudes concerning the allocation of authority, the legitimacy of a regime, and political participation; patterns of decision-making and deference; images of leaders and foreign nations; group loyalties, antagonisms, and

search on such topics is just beginning and for the most part has not been cross-cultural in scope, its implications for the comparative analysis of new nations are many and varied. In this chapter, the concept of political socialization and research pertaining to it will be explored from a comparative point of view in the context of the new and changing nations of Asia and Africa.

The role of socialization in political stability and change in new nations

IN his book on political socialization, Hyman[2] attempts to explain why, in surveys of American youth and adults, party affiliation seems established earlier in life than political ideology and why parent-child correlations in party preferences are higher than such preferences in political attitudes. His explanation, in brief, is that political issues change over the years while parties endure. An American parent who attempts to give his child an ideological orientation cannot anticipate the issues that will be meaningful by the time he reaches adulthood; whereas socializing the child with respect to party preference gives him not only a loyalty to a stable organization but also an organizing principle for coping with new issues as they emerge.[3] The hypothesis behind this interpretation

stereotypes. The last kind is of obvious importance in multiethnic nations, particularly ones whose national boundaries have recently been enlarged or otherwise changed. It is assumed that the degree of relevance of a kind of behavior to politics varies with the nature of the political systems under study and the theoretical framework used. For example, if embezzlement of public funds is a pronounced pattern in one or more of a set of political systems being studied comparatively, and if the analyst has a theory in which its frequency is a variable significantly related to the functioning of the political system, then it would be of interest to relate it to cultural values, concerning theft, self-control, prerogatives of authority, and so forth, and to examine the means by which these values were learned. If political violence among civilians is a variable of interest in a particular comparative study, then variations in culturally patterned means of inciting and expressing aggression and in the aggression training of children become relevant. Thus the concept of "political socialization" is as broad in its empirical referents as those aspects of social behavior that can be meaningfully related to the political system; it is the task of the investigator to focus his lens on some particular aspect in the course of political inquiry. It is obvious that authority patterns and intergroup hostility are likely to be significant in any comparative study of political socialization in the new nations of Asia and Africa, but the relevance of other variables must be determined for each research project.

2. Herbert Hyman, *Political Socialization*, New York, The Free Press of Glencoe, 1959.

3. *Ibid.*, pp. 46–47, 74–75.

has some interesting comparative implications that Hyman does not discuss. It would predict, for example, that in those Western European nations where ideological issues concerning church and state and class conflict are more enduring than political parties, attitudes concerning these issues should be formed earlier in life than party affiliation, and parent-child correlations on these attitudes should be higher than on party preference.

It is interesting to speculate on the application of this hypothesis to other areas. If any general characterization is possible, how do parents in the new nations of Asia and Africa socialize their children with respect to politics? What enduring aspect of the political system do they prepare their children to respond to? While there are few detailed empirical studies, it seems likely that the majority of such parents socialize their children for participation in the local authority systems of the rural areas rather than for roles in the national citizenry. The local system, compounded of traditional political patterns, forms introduced during colonial administration, and changes wrought under the pressure of contemporary economic conditions, is not only more enduring but also more familiar to the rural parent in a country where mass communication and mass education are not highly developed. The national government is not only more fluctuating and unstable, if only by virtue of the transition from colonial to independent status, but is also in many cases an urban phenomenon, isolated from the rural population by a huge cultural gap. The national government was created by the colonial power and greatly affected by independence; the local authority systems antedate colonization, were less affected by it, and have been less affected by self-government at the national level. In this situation it is reasonable to assume that the socialization process typical of the rural majority in new nations is functionally integrated to a greater degree with local authority systems than it is with the national political system. Such a picture may be overdrawn for a few of the older postcolonial nations of Asia, but it is not for most of Africa—where only a small fraction of the population live in cities and where many rural people are unaware of the nation in which they reside—and it is a fair working approximation of the general situation in new nations of both continents.

It must be recognized that local authority systems in the nations under discussion, while they may be generally referred to as "traditional" and "particularistic," often vary greatly from one ethnic group to another along many important dimensions: concentration of authority in decision-making units, institutionalization of leadership roles at various structural levels, the use of supernatural sanctions, the importance of social stratification in community decision-making, deferential behavior, and so forth. There are, for example, numerous African nations that contain, side by side, groups that were large independent monarchies eighty years ago and groups that had no political units larger than the village of several hundred persons. There is even considerable diversity in values concerning authority among the traditionally stateless ethnic groups which might seem at first glance to have had roughly the same political orientations; some tend in an authoritarian direction, while others are clearly egalitarian in their local decision-making patterns.[4] In terms of the theoretical framework on which this chapter is based, the variation in authority systems among the ethnic groups of the new nations means that there should be concomitant variations in the socialization patterns of the groups. In so far as such concomitant variations are revealed by empirical research, this theoretical framework will have received confirmation.

A possible key to the ontogenesis of authority values among the peoples of new nations is the domestic group (such as the extended family) and the wider kin groupings of which it is part, which serve to introduce the child into the political system by acting as models of authority roles as well as by more direct training. In America we often pay little attention to the family as a source of our ideologies concerning authority because neolocality and the emotional and economic independence of adult children from their parents tend to relegate parental influence to childhood memories. In those Asian and African societies that have extended family units, however, an adult male often lives with and is dependent emotionally and economically on his father or on another elder kinsman who legitimately exercises some degree of control over him. Norman M. Bradburn (personal communication) has noted that in Turkish cities the patrilocal extended family is maintained as a residential unit in apartment houses, with married sons occupying separate apartments in the same building as their parents; this is also found in India and elsewhere, and indicates that modern

---

4. Cf. the comparison of the Nuer of Sudan and the Gusii of Kenya in Robert A. LeVine, "The Internalization of Political Values in Stateless Societies," *Human Organization*, Vol. 19, pp. 51–58.

housing does not necessarily terminate traditional family relationships. In such situations parental influences on attitudes toward authority are not left behind in childhood but are reinforced many times over in adult life. The use of extended family (that is, father-son and elder brother–younger brother) relations as models for emperor-subject relations was explicitly encouraged in the Confucian doctrine of traditional China, but such modeling appears to be widespread even where it is not overtly recognized. Bradburn also finds that factory organization in Turkey is patterned after the extended family in considerable detail, with employer-employee relations conforming to norms derived from the traditional father-son relationship.[5] This kind of evidence suggests a correlation between domestic group authority patterns and local community authority patterns that should be carefully investigated in comparative research.[6]

The return to the picture of political socialization in the majority of families as being geared primarily to local political systems rather than national ones in new nations, this appears likely to persist for a long time. This assertion is based on the following considerations:

1] The population explosion means that, in countries with relatively undeveloped industrial economies, families of basically traditional orientation are multiplying and transmitting their own cultural orientations more rapidly than the rate at which the nation has the capacity to "modernize" them through industrialization and mass education.

2] The disparity in Western education and acculturation between the sexes in many (though not all) new nations presents obstacles to the development of a self-perpetuating, endogamous, "modernized" elite. Where Westernized males must marry traditionally oriented females, the children are likely to acquire traditional orientations from their mothers.

3] The assumption that urbanization per se leads to dissolution

5. Norman M. Bradburn, "Interpersonal Relations within Formal Organizations in Turkey," paper presented at meeting of Society for Social Research, University of Chicago, May, 1961.

6. For a more extensive theoretical discussion of this hypothesized correlation, see Robert A. LeVine, "The Role of the Family in Authority Systems: A Cross-Cultural Application of Stimulus-Generalization Theory," *Behavioral Science*, Vol. 5, 1960, pp. 291–296.

of traditional cultures is an untenable one. In a symposium on urbanization at the 1959 American Anthropological Association meetings, reports from Nigeria, Indonesia, India, and Mexico[7] all seemed to point to the conclusion that traditional values can persist in an urban setting, in one case because the cities are themselves traditional, in another because of the formation of ghetto communities, and in yet another because of traditional relations between village and city. This may be a short-range phenomenon but it is a striking one. Urbanization combined with the political competition of new nationhood sometimes intensifies interethnic rivalries and hostilities that had been dormant in the rural setting.

This emphasis on factors making for persistence of local, village, or traditional orientations may represent an anthropological bias. It should be noted, however, that there are indications apart from anthropological perspectives that support this point of view. For example, no new nation population is undergoing more intensive cultural homogenization than immigrant groups did in the United States, yet American ethnic groups, including their second- and third-generation members, show significant differences in patterns of family interaction, achievement motivation, religious values, social mobility, political behavior, forms of psychoses, rates of alcoholism, and so on. If it takes something like a century to wipe out these effects of transmission of traditional orientations in the United States, it will take considerably longer in the new nations of Asia and Africa unless they adopt the coercive measures involved in China's direct assault on traditional family life. Where such drastic measures are not used, the dual problems of heterogeneity and traditionalism in political life will probably remain for many years.

The persistence over generations of behavioral dispositions acquired in the milieu of the family or ethnic enclave, even when they are no longer reinforced by the broader cultural environment, can be understood in terms of individual development. Bruner, on the basis of American Indian studies, proposed the general hypothesis that culture patterns learned early in life are more re-

---

7. The papers were by William R. Bascom, Edward M. Bruner, Stanley Freed, and Oscar Lewis, respectively.

sistant to change in contact situations.[8] Values and kinship behavior comprised the kinds of patterns he found to be learned early. The same general assumption has been made independently by linguists working in the field of lexicostatistics, who distinguish between basic vocabulary, which changes at a slow and constant rate, and "cultural" vocabulary, which is highly susceptible to borrowings from other languages. Hymes states that some linguists have made the assumption that basic vocabulary consists of the names of things "which are likely to be learned early by a child, and, because of frequency, over-learned."[9] He cites studies that support this assumption,[10] although he concludes that further research into the matter is needed.[11] If linguistic research proves that vocabulary items learned earliest by the child are more persistent over generations, then the hypothesis that Bruner formulated for culture generally may be more reasonably expected to hold for another aspect of culture, such as political behavior. Other general support for this notion comes from experimental work by social psychologists that indicates that attitude preferences learned earlier have a long-range advantage over those learned more recently, despite temporary reversals.[12]

The only research applying the early-learning hypothesis to political behavior has been done on American children, but it has important theoretical implications for the comparative study of political orientations acquired in childhood and their functional significance for the American political system. Hess and Easton in a study of children in a Chicago suburb[13] and Greenstein in a study of New Haven school children,[14] found that affective and evaluative orientations toward political authority roles precede the ac-

8. Edward M. Bruner, "Cultural Transmission and Cultural Change," *Southwestern Journal of Anthropology*, Vol. 12, 1956, pp. 191–199.

9. D. H. Hymes, "Lexicostatistics So Far," *Current Anthropology*, Vol. 1, 1960, p. 5.

10. *Ibid.*, p. 7.

11. *Ibid.*, p. 32.

12. Cf. Carl I. Hovland, *et al.*, *The Order of Presentation in Persuasion*, New Haven, Yale University Press, 1957, and Norman Miller and Donald T. Campbell, "Recency and Primacy in Persuasion as a Function of the Timing of Speeches and Measurements," *Journal of Abnormal and Social Psychology*, Vol. 59, 1959, pp. 1–9.

13. Robert D. Hess and David Easton, "The Child's Changing Image of the President," *Public Opinion Quarterly*, Vol. 24, 1960, pp. 632–644.

14. Fred I. Greenstein, "The Benevolent Leader: Children's Images of Political Authority," *American Political Science Review*, Vol. 54, 1960, pp. 934–943.

quisition of factual knowledge about the behavior involved in role performance. Greenstein found that children as young as seven years old, who were practically devoid of information about what political leaders do, nevertheless evaluated fairly accurately the relative importance of various political positions and socially prestigeful occupational roles. In both studies evidence is produced to support the assertion that the earliest affective-evaluative images of political authority are derived from parents and familial relations; for example, Greenstein notes that the New Haven children described themselves as Republicans or Democrats, apparently following the party preferences of their parents, "long before they were able to make any meaningful statements about the parties, or even to link the party labels with the names of conspicuous party leaders such as the President and Mayor.[15] Hess and Easton found that the youngest children in their sample characterized their fathers as similar in many respects to the President of the United States.[16] Thus, political preferences and emotional tendencies reflecting parental influence are established in the individual before he acquires objective information about the political system.

Are these early affective and evaluative tendencies toward political objects relevant to the operation of the political system? The authors of these studies suggest that they serve important functions. The younger children in the Chicago suburb and New Haven had strongly positive images of the President of the United States. Hess and Easton comment:

> Our conclusions suggest the possibility that if the Presidency is a major link between the child and the structure of the regime, an attachment may be generated that is of a peculiarly potent sort. A consequence for the political system of a child's acquiring his attitude toward the President in this way is that one of the strongest bonds between human beings—that between parents and child—may mediate between maturing individuals and the political structure. If this is so it would contribute in a significant way to the stability of a regime by establishing strong emotional ties at a very early age of a sort that are known to be hard to dislodge.
>
> Furthermore, from the point of view of the stability of the American political structure, some such attachment early in life

15. *Ibid.*, p. 936.
16. Hess and Easton, *op. cit.*, pp. 640–642.

has positive consequences. As the child grows to adulthood, he is exposed to considerable debate and conflicts over the merits of various alternative incumbents of the Presidency and of other roles in the political structure. There is constant danger that criticism of the occupant will spill over to the role itself. Were this to occur under certain circumstances, respect for the Presidency could be seriously impaired or destroyed. But the data here suggest that one of the factors that prevents this from occurring is a strong parental-like tie with respect to the President's role itself, developed before the child can become familiar with the contention surrounding the incumbent of the office.[17]

Greenstein contrasts the children's affection for and trust of political authority figures with the widespread finding that adult Americans distrust politics and politicians:

The cynical imagery of Americans seems to be less functionally relevant to their political behavior than the positive side of their responses—their respect for high political leaders and their frequent willingness to hold individual leaders in great esteem. This is evident not merely from such relatively narrow mechanisms as the *fait accompli* effect[18] and the general willingness to accept the verdict of elections. The oft-proclaimed stability of the American political system—in spite of a remarkably heterogeneous population—suggests more broadly that powerful psychological mechanisms encouraging political obedience are present in the citizenry. These mechanisms may be as important as many of the more familiar historical, political, economic, and social factors which are drawn on to explain the complex phenomenon of political stability.[19]

If these authors have indeed found, as they claim, a psychological antecedent for political stability, then the comparative study of the images of children in new nations should reveal striking and enlightening variations as well as providing a test of their hypothesis. One prediction would be that in many of the new nations local figures and roles would have greater salience for children than national ones, and the emergence of national figures

17. *Ibid.*, p. 644.
18. This refers to the increased popularity of a presidential candidate just after he has been elected.
19. Greenstein, *op. cit.*, p. 942. Greenstein also proposes a regression hypothesis, that is, that, although later learning intervenes, conflict or crisis results in the individual falling back on the earlier attitudes.

into the early awareness of individuals might be of crucial significance for future political developments.

The view that certain fundamental political orientations will persist after they cease being appropriate does not necessarily imply that peoples in the newly independent countries of Africa and Asia will be consciously conservative or overtly reject political innovation. Even when innovations in political institutions are greatly desired and eagerly accepted, traditional patterns may intrude themselves into the new forms—a phenomenon that is not unknown to students of European and American political history. It is a matter of political syncretism, of old wine in new bottles. Informal organizational behavior, images of authority, modes of orientation toward leaders, opportunities for intergroup rivalry—these serve as the media through which traditional political patterns have an impact on the present. This kind of persistence can be seen in African separatist religious movements, which not only appear to be promoted in their development by frustrations in the political sphere but which also strikingly reflect traditional authority patterns in a novel institutional setting.[20] Bradburn's analysis of Turkish factory behavior in terms of interpersonal values derived from the traditional family is another example of this.[21] It may be that the novel institutional means of mobilizing people for action is of greater significance for certain kinds of political analysis, but the impact of traditional modes of political behavior should not be overlooked. One would expect, for example, that the influence of traditional patterns on *national* government would be greater in ethnically homogeneous countries such as Somalia and Basutoland, or in countries in which national government is dominated by a single ethnic group, than it would be where several ethnic groups of differing political traditions share the reins of power.

Socialization and Authoritarianism

IF one accepts as probable that political orientations derived from ethnic group traditions will have a continuing impact in the new states, then the content of these traditions and the

20. Cf. Bengt Sundkler, *Bantu Prophets in South Africa*, London, Oxford University Press, 1948, and Walter H. Sangree, "The Dynamics of African Separatist Churches," unpublished MS, 1960.
21. Bradburn, *op. cit.*

psychological mechanisms involved in their transmission become pertinent objects of comparative study. This discussion is limited to patterns of authority, and is conceptually derived from social-psychological analyses of "authoritarianism" and "authoritarian personality" in Western societies.[22] From the viewpoint of contemporary American values, the political and social patterns of most peoples of Asia, Africa, Latin America, and even Europe seem "authoritarian" since they involve more pronounced status distinctions and deferential attitudes than our own. A closer and more informed look, however, reveals vast differences in authority behavior among peoples of the world, suggesting that the concept of authoritarian personality may prove more applicable and useful cross-culturally than it has at the level of individual differences in our own society. Any such application, however, must be preceded by a careful analysis of social decision-making patterns and the amount of command and sanction power vested in leadership roles, a kind of analysis that has been rare in anthropological studies of political organization.

To illustrate the psychological mechanisms involved in the learning of authority patterns, it is useful to examine groups with contrasting authority systems for differences in political socialization. The first comparison presented is one of extremes: the East African kingdom of Buganda (in its nineteenth-century form)[23] and a utopian communist *kibbutz* in Israel (as described by Spiro).[24]

Buganda, with a population of approximately one million, was one of the most centralized monarchies in Africa. The king was a supreme ruler possessing arbitrary powers;[25] he appointed his

22. Cf. T. W. Adorno, E. Frenkel-Brunswik, D. J. Levinson, and R. N. Sanford, *The Authoritarian Personality*, New York, Harper, 1950, and E. Fromm, *Escape from Freedom*, New York, Farrar and Rinehart, 1941.

23. This comparison was suggested by S. J. L. Zake, "Child Rearing and Political Organization," seminar paper, Department of Anthropology, Northwestern University, 1959. Most of the material on Ganda child rearing comes from this paper, the author of which grew up in Buganda.

24. Melford E. Spiro, *Kibbutz: Venture in Utopia*, Cambridge, Mass., Harvard University Press, 1955, and *Children of the Kibbutz*, Cambridge, Mass., Harvard University Press, 1958.

25. This description of the nineteenth-century political system of Buganda is based on L. A. Fallers, "Despotism, Status Culture, and Social Mobility in an African Kingdom," *Comparative Studies in Society and History*, Vol. 2, 1959, pp. 11–32, and A. I. Richards, *East African Chiefs*, London, Faber and Faber, 1960, Chap. II.

favorites as governors of the districts without regard to hereditary qualification; he commanded a standing army, collected taxes from the whole country, and lived in a capital with a population in the tens of thousands. He was the top judicial authority and used extremely severe physical punishments like burning alive, mutilation, and destruction of property at will and frequently. All official positions in the Buganda political system, at national, regional, and local levels, were hierarchically ranked in a chain of command, so that each incumbent oriented himself to those above and below him, showing loyalty to the former and demanding it from the latter. There were, as Fallers points out, great differences in power, honor, and wealth that followed the distribution of authority, but no status groups such as social classes, since the king was able to facilitate social mobility through appointments and the distribution of benefices. The hierarchy was an ordering of individuals rather than groups.

> The Baganda simply do not think of people as being arranged in social layers; they think of social differences instead in terms of dyadic relations of inferiority and superiority. There is great sensitivity to distinctions of honor, wealth, importance, and authority as between particular persons, but no conception of broad groups of persons who are essentially equal with respect to these qualities.
> . . . The Baganda were . . . ideologically "non-egalitarian." There were clearly-defined roles for superior and subordinates and an elaborate body of terminology and gesture for talking out these roles.[26]

The top official serving the king had traditional titles that were ranked in a well-known order; according to Richards, these titles "formed the basis of a precedence scale and were used by anyone in authority such as a governor, sub-governor or holder of a benefice to grade those working under him."[27] In other words, the ranked status system operative at the highest level of the political system was explicitly imitated at lower levels. The despotism of the monarch was thus replicated, although in weaker form, throughout the political system.

Kiryat Yedidim, the *kibbutz* studied by Spiro, is a community

26. Fallers, *op. cit.*, p. 23.
27. Richards, *op. cit.*, p. 48.

of five hundred in Israel, and thus is not comparable in size and scale to Buganda. Neverthless, as a largely self-governing unit with a coherent political ideology, it may be contrasted with Buganda for the limited purposes of this discussion. The community was founded as an agricultural settlement based on collectivistic principles thirty years prior to the field study. The internal authority system of Kiryat Yedidim is summed up as follows:

> The distribution of goods is determined by the principle of "from each according to his ability, to each according to his needs," the latter being determined to a great extent by the entire group assembled in Town Meeting. This biweekly Meeting is the ultimate authority on all other matters which affect the kibbutz or any of its individual members. Authority is delegated by the Meeting to democratically elected officials who carry out policy determined by the Meeting, and who administer the various economic and social institutions of the kibbutz. Tenure of office is brief—never more than three years—which, it is believed, prevents the rise of a leadership caste or an entrenched bureaucracy.[28]

Social control in Kiryat Yedidim is achieved through expressions of public opinion and the ultimate threat of expulsion. Cooperation and voluntarism are stressed in the operation of the kibbutz; "labor is performed in work crews under the leadership of a foreman who, perceived as a primus inter pares, serves his tenure of office at the pleasure of his peers."[29] Thus, the authority structure of the community is egalitarian in the sense that leadership roles are rotated among various group members and are vested with little decision-making authority, command power, or special social status. Leaders occupy their positions at the sufferance of the assembled community and must orient themselves to the approval of those whom they lead, while the average member of the kibbutz need not pay deference to the leader as a person but only to the expressed will of the group. Like Buganda, Kiryat Yedidim has no social strata differentiated with respect to status and status culture, but, unlike Buganda, its authority system represents a conscious attempt to minimize hierarchy and superior-subordinate relations and to emphasize the consensus and cooperation of a group of peers.

28. Spiro, op. cit., 1958, pp. 4–5.
29. Ibid., p. 4.

Both Buganda and Kiryat Yedidim have socialization patterns designed to produce adults who have values and behavior patterns appropriate to the functioning of their respective political systems. They will be compared in regard to three aspects of socialization:

1. The conscious shaping of the child's interpersonal behavior by adults, in conformity with an ideal authority pattern.

2. The disciplinary techniques used to enforce conformity in childhood.

3. The authority structure of the primary interpersonal environment of the child.

In Buganda the learning of obedience and deference to superiors is a primary objective of child training. Children are trained to respond immediately to orders from an adult. They also learn to be quiet and inconspicuous in the presence of elders, to sit respectfully, that is, with the feet concealed underneath the body, and to walk past elders in a special manner commensurate with the respect in which they must be held. Questioning of parents is regarded as gross impertinence. Children are taught to call their fathers *mwami*, a term that means chief or person of power and wealth in the adult political system. In the nineteenth century, this training as applied to boys was consciously regarded by parents as preparation for the possibility of being sent as a page to the court of a chief or the king, where the qualities of obedience, loyalty, and deference to a superior were favored and could lead to political success. It is notable that Margaret Read in describing childhood among the traditional Ngoni political elite, in a less despotic but nevertheless monarchical state in Central Africa, indicates their similar emphasis on inculcating obedience, deference, and decorousness in young children.[30] One point of contrast, however, consistent with political differences between the two groups, is that the Ngoni encourage their children to share food and other valued objects equally among themselves, while the Baganda allow and expect the eldest to take the largest share and apportion the rest as he sees fit among the others. Thus, Ganda parents emphasize obedience and deference to superiors but not sharing among relative equals, in shaping the behavior of their children.

Disobedient or disorderly children in Buganda are severely

30. Margaret Read, *Children of Their Fathers: Growing Up Among the Ngoni of Nyasaland*, New Haven, Yale University Press, 1960.

punished with beatings and dire threats. The hard stem of a banana leaf is often used in beating children for infractions of parental rules, and they grow particularly to fear their fathers as strict disciplinarians.

The Ganda family environment to which the young child is exposed is characteristically hierarchical, with very pronounced dominance-submission relationships. Wives must be extremely submissive to their husband; traditionally, they might not rise in his presence. In a polygynous homestead, the wives are ranked among themselves. Siblings of the same sex are also graded in order of age, and the eldest, in addition to taking the lion's share, is held responsible for the conduct of the others. In children's groups the traditional titles of the kings' officials are used as a precedence scale to create a hierarchical order among playmates. All these ranking patterns in family relationships appear to have been more pronounced among chiefly families than among ordinary peasants, which means that those individuals more likely to occupy important political offices by virtue of opportunity were also more likely to be raised in a strongly hierarchical family environment.

In Kiryat Yedidim, learning to participate in the community on an equal and cooperative basis may be said to be the primary objective of child training. On a questionnaire concerning values they hoped to inculcate in their children, *kibbutz* parents put "work" and "love of humanity" first and second, and "good manners" and "respect for parents" last (that is, twelfth and thirteenth in a list of thirteen); "responsibility to kibbutz" was third.[31] They also responded overwhelmingly with "Definitely no," to the question of whether children should blindly obey their parents.[32] In the system of collective education that is employed, children do not live with their parents, are not under their legal control, and are not economically dependent on them. All this is deliberately designed to "emancipate" the child from parental authority and to establish an egalitarian relationship in which fathers and children are peers. Younger children are under the supervision of nurses who direct their activities and discipline them. Obedience is not an emphasis in the training given by the

31. Spiro, *op. cit.*, 1958, pp. 20–21.
32. *Ibid.*, p. 12.

nurses, and a great deal of childhood activity is voluntary and spontaneous. Even concerning the highly valued activity of agricultural work, Spiro states:

> Though these chores are now expected of them, no inducement, other than intrinsic satisfaction, is required for their performance. As in the case of other responsibilities, however, the nurses reinforce successful performances with praise.[33]

In regard to sharing, Spiro makes the following comments:

> One of the primary values that the nurse attempts to transmit, beginning with the very young children, is sharing. . . .
> In the Kindergarten the teacher perceives her most important goals to consist in helping her charges to be "human beings"— to help each other, and to have no feeling of "mine and thine" —and to become an "organized" group.[34]
> Although there are very few instances in which the nurse reinforces an act of sharing, many situations arise in the context of the daily routine which enable the nurse to stress the value of sharing or the subordination of personal desire to the desire of others.[35]

Thus, by contrast with Buganda, the socializing agents of Kiryat Yedidim lay little stress on obedience and emphasize sharing to a very great extent. The contrast with respect to physical punishment as a disciplinary technique is equally clear. Spiro states:

> The philosophy of collective education is opposed to punishment in general and to physical punishment in particular. . . .
> In the course of their training nurses are taught to eschew physical punishment, and no nurse in the kibbutz was ever observed to spank, hit, or slap a child.[36]

The most severe punishments administered in Kiryat Yedidim are threats of physical punishment, withdrawal of privilege, and shaming; nonpunitive disciplinary techniques are also used. The children's groups themselves exert powerful pressure toward conformity.

Finally, there is the question of the primary interpersonal environment to which the child is exposed in his early years. In Kiryat Yedidim, this environment for any growing individual con-

33. *Ibid.*, p. 211.
34. *Ibid.*, p. 43.
35. *Ibid.*, p. 188.
36. *Ibid.*, p. 185.

sists largely of his age peers. Children live apart from their parents
from a few days after birth onward, and they live in a series of
age-graded nurseries and dormitories, whose egalitarian character
has already been indicated in general terms. They also spend a
good deal of time with their parents; thus the husband-wife relationship is relevant. Since the wives are not economically dependent on their husbands, do not even cook for them, work full
time and are treated equally in the *kibbutz*, the husband-wife
relationship cannot be thought of as a model for authority behavior
that is at all at variance with the egalitarianism of the *kibbutz*
as a whole. In fact, collective education in the *kibbutz* is pred-
icated on the egalitarian character of every institution within
the community so that the child will have no role models for
authoritarianism.

This comparison suggests that extremely divergent authority systems have extremely divergent socialization patterns, if one takes
adult aims in shaping children's behavior, disciplinary techniques,
and the authority structure of the child's primary interpersonal
environment as the points of comparison. Emphasis on obedience
training, the use of severe physical punishment, and a hierarchically arranged interpersonal environment seem to be correlated
with an authoritarian political system, while emphasis on training
in sharing and cooperative effort, the use of nonphysical discipline,
and a peer-group environment with no pronounced status distinctions, seem to be correlated with an egalitarian political system.

What kind of impact can differences of this kind have on
contemporary political behavior in new nations? This can be
illustrated by a second comparison, made previously by the present
writer,[37] of authoritarianism among the Nuer of the southern
Sudan and the Gusii of southwestern Kenya. Since these two
East African ethnic groups are located only about one thousand
miles apart, in what many anthropologists would consider the
same culture area, and since they are also similar in social structure, the comparison involves a narrower range on the authoritarian dimension, one more likely to be found among the ethnic
groups of a single nation. Both are traditionally uncentralized
tribes of more than a quarter of a million (and less than half
a million) population, with segmentary patrilineages as the major

37. Cf. LeVine, "The Internationalization of Political Values in Stateless
Societies," *op. cit.*, pp. 51–58.

form of sociopolitical grouping, and a combination of agriculture and animal husbandry as a subsistence base. Both were characterized by blood feuds among territorial segments before being "pacified" by a British administration that introduced chieftainship and a court system. Despite the broad similarities, available data indicate that traditional decision-making, deference, and aggression patterns were quite different in the two groups. The Nuer were democratic in local affairs, rarely behaved in a deferential way to occupants of such local leadership positions as existed, and were prepared to engage in combat on slight provocation. The Gusii, on the other hand, had wealthy "men of power" who dominated local affairs in many communities, displayed elaborate deference and obedience to the most prominent of such men, and granted them a major role in the settlement of disputes.

Patterns of political socialization in the two groups were consistent with their differing patterns of authority and aggression. In the father-son relationship, for example, the Nuer father tended to be affectionate and nonpunitive, while the Gusii father was emotionally aloof and used severe physical punishment in discipline. The husband-wife relationship the Nuer child observed in his early years was one in which the husband was dominant but respectful, so that he considered striking his wife contemptible; the Gusii child grow up in a home in which beating and other displays of temper against the wives by the *paterfamilias* were expected and in which wives had to pay deference to their husband in a number of conspicuous ways. Concerning aggression, Nuer adults encouraged children to fight when attacked by other children, while Gusii parents rewarded their children for reporting attack to adults rather than settling it themselves in combat.

Under colonial administration, when courts were introduced for the peaceful settlement of disputes, the Nuer and Gusii reacted quite differently. Some Nuer were recruited to be judges but they were reluctant to give definite verdicts and sentence their fellow men to legal punishment. Also, despite an overwhelming show of British military force at the onset of colonial rule, the Nuer continued to engage in the prohibited blood feuds, requiring extensive police intervention years after their initial pacification and the establishment of courts. With the Gusii there was never any difficulty about finding elders who were willing to operate decisively in judicial office and inflict severe punishments when necessary. The people as a whole were quite ready to give up blood feuds for court litigation, and from the very beginning the courts were overloaded with cases, as they are today despite valiant efforts to expand judicial facilities. Thus, traditional ethnic variations in authoritarianism, transmitted to new generations in the socialization process after their structural forms have been superseded by a national governmental structure, cause consistent variations in political behavior under new conditions.

The validation of such analyses awaits comparative study by more objective methods. Although no adequate research instrument exists for the measurement of authoritarianism, some suggestive data are available to indicate that cross-cultural variations of this type have significant psychological correlates. In a large-scale quantitative study of young adults in Egypt and the United States, Melikian, using the controversial F scale and a questionnaire measure of adjustment, concludes:

> The relationships between positive attributes of personality and authoritarianism tend to be opposite in Egypt and the United States. They suggest that in Egypt the authoritarian Moslem may be more healthy psychologically, this perhaps because he is conforming to the general culture pattern. On the other hand the Egyptian Christian who is authoritarian, whose subculture is more fluid, presents a less healthy picture. Similarly in the United States, the more authoritarian Catholic may be somewhat better adjusted than the Protestant authoritarian whose subculture tends to be more liberal. Thus it appears that when the personality picture of the authoritarian is taken into account, the general culture as well as the religious context must be defined.[38]

Enough cross-cultural regularities emerge from studies of this kind to warrant attempts to operationalize the authoritarian syndrome in cultural terms and to test in comparative research hypothesized covariations between degree of authoritarianism and patterns of socialization.[39]

38. Levon H. Melikian, "Authoritarianism and Its Correlates in the Egyptian Culture and in the United States," *The Journal of Social Issues*, Vol. 15, 1959, p. 68.

39. Cf. Robert E. Lane, "Fathers and Sons: Foundations of Political Belief," *American Sociological Review*, Vol. 24, 1959, pp. 502–511, for suggested covariations among Western political systems.

Learning processes and political socialization

BROADLY speaking, three mechanisms[40] seem to be involved in the acquisition of political orientations in childhood:

1] *Imitation.* The child learns adult roles in large measure through imitating adult behavior; thus, the authority structure of the family or domestic group can be viewed as a set of role models. This is also true of the authority structures of the school classroom, the children's group, and other organized interpersonal situations that are part of the immediate social environment of the child.

2] *Instruction.* Political ideologies or politically relevant moral values are sometimes taught to children; or they become exposed to adult knowledge concerning political leaders, parties, ethnic groups, and so on. In other words, adults may give children a cognitive map of the political world and also explicitly tell them to which parts of that map they are supposed to attach positive and negative values. The process that Hess and Easton term "role specification" is relevant here; this is the increasing differentiation of the images of authority figures as the child grows older. In their own study they describe the prespecification phase as follows:

Attitudes toward figures such as the President are initially attitudes that have been held toward other authority figures. These attitudes are transferred to political persons who, to the child, are defined as standing in a position with respect to his family and community in something of the fashion that the father, and perhaps the mother, stand with respect to the children in the family. We propose, then, that the first step of political socialization is initially completed with essentially no information about the political figure himself except that he is an authority figure whose status exceeds that of the authorities with whom the child has been familiar. Obviously, an essential

40. The three mechanisms presented are outgrowths of the trichotomy of *role practice, tuition,* and *trial and error* set forth by Robert Sears, E. E. Maccoby, and H. Levin, *Patterns of Child Rearing,* Evanston, Ill., Row, Peterson, 1957. I am indebted to Edward T. Hall for his suggestion that his distinction of *formal, informal,* and *technical* learning bears a resemblance to the distinction discussed here; cf. Edward T. Hall, *The Silent Language,* Greenwich, Conn., Premier Books, 1961, pp. 69–73.

part of this first step is the definition of political authority which the adult world first presents to a child. However, this definition is probably an evaluative one, presented in terms of positive or negatively emotional tone.[41]

They show that the children in their sample are increasingly able to differentiate the role performance of the American President and another (foreign) chief executive political official from that of their fathers with increasing age (from second to eighth grades). This indicates the effect of political information in producing a progressively differentiated political cognitive map, and suggests that a mechanism akin to discrimination learning (as discussed by learning theorists) is involved. The degree of differentiation of political from familial authority figures as the child grows older may turn out to be a major dimension of cross-cultural variability.

3] *Motivation.* Through trial and error, children learn appropriate behavior. When they do the "wrong" thing, they are punished or otherwise corrected, and when they do the "right" thing, there may be some consequent reward. Some of the habits thus acquired have a "drive" character; that is, they come to have reward and punishment value on their own. The strongest anxieties and positive social motivations appear to be of this nature. Motives concerning achievement, aggression, and dependence may be relevant to political systems, in that the individual may respond to aspects of it not only in terms of which he has learned through imitation and instruction but also in terms of his emotional needs. For example, in Buganda, overt submission to a higher authority is not only a learned response sequence; it also serves to reduce anxiety concerning possible disapproval by a superior and to gratify the drive toward upward mobility that can be achieved only with the help of important persons. The motivational element adds intensity to political behavior. In relating adult political behavior patterns to motives originating in childhood, dependency and affiliative motives are probably most relevant to authority patterns, aggressive motives to intergroup behavior, and achievement and power motives to the competition for political position. Empirical

41. Hess and Easton, *op. cit.*, p. 643.

cases, however, should be expected to reveal numerous motives underlying each culturally patterned aspect of political behavior.

CHANGING POLITICAL BEHAVIOR

The preceding discussion has centered about the transmission of traditional political patterns to developing children, but the concept of socialization is limited neither to childhood nor to stable intergenerational transmission. What about the learning processes involved in rapid political change? The types of learning involved are no different, but their institutional form—the socializing agencies—may be quite different. Lane, referring to the intergenerational replication of political beliefs and loyalties within the family as the "Mendelian law" of politics, states, "While imitation and common social stakes tend to enforce this law, the socialization process may work to repeal it."[42] Although individual cases of repeal may have their motivational roots in disturbed family relationships, it is ordinarily extrafamilial institutions that provide the new values and behavior patterns involved in political change. Especially in new nations, where family, local community, and ethnic group are likely to be working for the enforcement of this Mendelian law, political leaders striving for change will attempt to create national institutions for the countersocialization of individuals whose orientations have already been formed to some extent along traditional lines. The kinds of institutions that have been used in this way are youth movements, schools and universities, military forces, and special training villages. Any of these can become an assimilating institution, attempting to reorient young adults, adolescents, or even children, and resocialize them to a new national ideology and a new way of life. In their more coercive forms, associated with totalitarian governments, such institutions explicitly attempt to destroy family and other traditional groups as well as inculcating new values. There is evidence to indicate that these institutions for adult socialization are most effective in achieving this aim when they manage to exclude counteracting social stimuli through isolation of the trainees, to maintain consistent goals within the institution, to manipulate rewards and punishments in the service of official training goals,

42. Robert E. Lane, *op. cit.*, p. 502.

and to use both formal instruction and opportunities for imitation and practice of new roles.[43] In other words, a complete social environment in which the individual becomes temporarily involved may be necessary to effect drastic alterations in his motives, habits, and values after childhood.

One of the few systematic studies of political socialization of American college youth is the famous one by Newcomb, who showed that girls from conservative families who came to Bennington College with conservative political and economic attitudes changed over their years as students and acquired more liberal attitudes.[44] Although Bennington College may seem a far cry from any situation one is likely to find in Africa or Asia, its institutional setting for attitude change in young adulthood would seem to be generalizable: isolation of students in an atmosphere of homogeneous political values, with conformity pressures and rewards for acquisition of the new values, and a great deal of exposure to and practice with the novel political orientations.

In every new nation, including those that are making no strenuous efforts to modernize their populations, there are assimilating institutions operating to introduce at least part of the population to new ways of life and to new political ideologies and images. These include schools, universities, industrial and bureaucratic organizations, and religious groups. Very little research has been done to assess empirically the effects on individual political attitudes and values of these institutions, and this would seem to be a task of high priority for students of the political modernization process in the new states.

Summary

RATHER than dealing with a variety of political orientations, this chapter has been concentrated on authority patterns. The following kinds of hypotheses for comparative research on political socialization in new nations have been mentioned:

43. For a more thorough discussion of the effectiveness of these factors in adult socialization, cf. Robert A. LeVine, "American College Experience as a Socialization Process," in R. B. Clark, et al., The Study of College Peer Groups: Problems and Prospects for Research, New York, Social Science Research Council MSS., 1961.

44. Theodore M. Newcomb, Personality and Social Change, New York, Dryden, 1943.

1. Propositions linking the age at which a given political behavior pattern is acquired by the child, and (*a*) its resistance to change in a situation in which it is no longer adaptive, (*b*) its functional importance for the maintenance of the political system (or some unit within the political system), (*c*) its greater strength under conditions of political crisis.

2. Propositions linking certain traditional political syndromes such as "authoritarianism" to cultural patterns of child training in the family and other primary groups.

3. Propositions linking the individual's degree of deviation from the traditional political behavior patterns into which he was socialized with (*a*) the degree of his involvement in extrafamilial institutions of a modernizing nature, and (*b*) the nature of the socialization patterns of the modernizing extrafamilial institutions in which he is or has been involved.

Index

Aborigines Rights Protection Society, 66
Afghanistan, education and income, 254, 258, 272, 274
Africa, 48–54
    archaeology, 52
    cultural modernization, 202–204
    education and income, 275
    equality and politics, 216–218
    ethnic fragmentation, 118
    folk art, 53
    kingdoms, 50, 51, 71, 117, 179–180, 203, 290–293
    land tenure, 238–240
    law, 220–246
    property succession, 240
    social stratification, 179–180
    women and marriage, 236–238
Akbar, 34
Algeria, education and income, 255, 260, 262, 275
Alliance, The (Malaya), 134–136
Andhra (Indian state), 106
Anti-Fascist People's Freedom League, 136–138
Arab League, 45, 107
Ashanti Tribe, 50, 117, 124
Asia, education and income, 271–274
Asoka, Emperor, 35, 39
Atatürk, Kemal, 224, 225
Authoritarianism, 59, 98, 289–299, 302–303
Azerin Turks, 107

Babylonia, 72
Baganda, 50, 51, 117, 203, 290–293
Baghdad Pact, 45

Balewa, Sir Abubakar Tafawa, 49, 152
Bandaranaike, S. W. R. D., 122–123
Bandung Asian-African Conference, 39, 48
Berbers, 124, 126, 146–149
Bhagavad-Gita, 32, 33, 198
Bhutan, 39
Brahmanism, 33–34, 40, 176, 177
British Colonial Policies, 187, 197
British North Borneo, 136, 276
    education and income, 252, 253, 256, 262, 272–274
Brunei, 136
Buddhism
    Burma, 116
    Ceylon, 41–43, 122
    India, 28, 38, 40
    Indonesia, 46, 48
Buganda. See Baganda
Bureaucracy, 185–187
Burma, 130
    dress, 127, 138
    education and income, 255, 260, 272–274
    national integration, 136–139
    religious orientation, 28, 116, 238

Capitalism, 99
Carnegie Corporation, v
Censuses, 126
Center for Advanced Studies in the Behavioral Sciences, viii
Ceylon, 41–43, 106, 121–123
    education and income, 255, 259, 260, 262, 263, 272–274

Ceylon (*cont.*)
language, 43
religious orientation, 28, 42–43
technology, 42
Children
in Baganda, 293–294
in *kibbutz*, 294–296
political orientation of, 281, 285–288, 299–301
Chile, education and income, 254, 258, 262, 263, 269–271
China, 59, 66, 71, 86–87, 93, 205
education and income, 253, 256, 262, 272–274
emperor-subject relation, 284
Christianity
in Lebanon, 142–145
and the state, 74–77
in Uganda, 51
in Western Europe, 66, 68
Church and State. *See* Religion and the State
Colombia, education and income, 252, 253, 256, 262, 269–271
Colonialism and Neocolonialism, vi, 66, 99
Commercial Minorities, 112, 119
Committee for the Comparative Study of New Nations, The, v–viii
Communalism, 106–107
Communism, 78, 87, 92
India, 36, 140–141
Indonesia, 132–133
Comparative Method of Study, vi–vii, 15–20
Conflict of Laws, Law of, 233–234
Congo (Léopoldville), 86, 106, 112, 187
education and income, 253, 256, 259, 262, 275
ethnic fragmentation, 118
Cultural Policies, 29, 54–56
Africa, sub-Saharan, 48–54
Burma, 28
Ceylon, 28, 41–43
Ghana, 28
India, 28, 31–41
Indonesia, 46–48
Ivory Coast, 28
Nigeria, 28
Pakistan, 28, 43–45
Custom, 113, 241–243

Cyprus, 117
education and income, 252, 255, 257, 260, 262, 272–274

Democracy, 24–25, 64, 77, 102, 207–212
Development, Material, 57, 81–82. *See also* Industrialization
Dravidians, 33–35, 125
Druzes, 142–144

Education, 2–3
and income, 248–277(*tables*), 252–256, 258, 260, 262, 268–275
India, 36–37
literacy, 250–255, 269, 272, 275
and opportunity, 190–193
political and cultural conflict, 125
role in economic development, 277–279
survey, 252–275
Egypt, ancient, 52
Egypt, modern, 78, 224
education and income, 255, 257, 260, 262, 275
personal adjustment in, 298
Eire, education and income, 254, 258, 261–263, 268
Elite classes, 2–7, 169–170, 217. *See also* various countries
England, 210–211, 230
Entrepreneurs, 183, 185–187
Equality and Politics, 204–206, 212–219
Ethiopia, 4, 113
education and income, 255, 260, 275

Families and Politics, 281–289
Feudalism, 171–175, 207–212
France, 80–81
French Equatorial Africa, education and income, 253, 256, 262, 275
French West Africa, education and income, 255, 260, 262, 275
Fulani, 150

Gandhi, 32, 198, 199
Garuda (Indonesian emblem), 47
Ghana, 54, 59, 67, 78, 83–85, 93, 204
cultural policies, 28, 50, 51

education and income, 254, 258, 262, 275
Gita, 32, 33, 198
Greece, classic, 70
Guinea, 54, 59, 67, 78, 82–83, 85–86, 93
  French orientation, 49
  Islam, 51
Gusii (Kenya tribe), 296–298

Hasan II (Moulay Hasan), 148–149
Hatta, Mohammed, 131–133
Hausa, 150, 152
Hinduism, 176–177
  Ceylon, 41–43
  India, 28, 36, 38–40, 176–177, 198
  Indonesia, 46, 48
Historicism, 14–15, 20
History and Social Studies, 10–16
Hong Kong, education and income, 254, 258, 262
Houphouet-Boigny, Félix, 49

Ibo, 150
Ideology, 61
India, 59, 80, 93, 131, 151, 187
  archaeology, 39
  caste system, 39, 165, 177–178, 215
  cultural policy, 28–41, 197–199
  education and income, 254, 257, 258, 262, 272–274
  equality and politics, 214–216
  family group living, 283
  holidays, 36
  languages, 32–33, 105–106, 112, 126
  law, 224, 244
  national integration, 139–142
  religion, 36–40, 176, 197–199
  technology and industry, 37, 98
  urban living, 285
Indian National Congress, 66, 106, 139–142
Indonesia, 59, 78, 80, 93, 187
  archaeology, 47
  Chinese residents, 116
  cultural policies, 45–48, 125
  education and income, 255, 260, 262, 272–274
  holiday, 47
  languages, 47, 112
  national integration, 130–133

regionalism, 106, 113, 123–124, 126
  religion, 38, 45–48
  urban living, 285
Industrialization, 57, 60–62, 97
  Japan, 57
  Soviet Union, 58
  Western nations, 58
Indus Valley Civilization, 44
Integration, National, 119–130. *See also* Cultural Policies
  Burma, 136–139
  India, 139–142
  Indonesia, 130–133
  Lebanon, 142–145
  Malaya, 133–136
  Morocco, 145–149
  Nigeria, 150–153
Iran, 4
  education and income, 254, 258, 262, 272, 274
Iraq, 107, 114, 224
  education and income, 253, 256, 262, 272–274
Ireland. *See* Eire
Islam
  Africa, 51, 53
  Ceylon, 42
  cultural modernization, 199–202
  India, 36–40
  Indonesia, 45–48
  Iraq, 107
  law, 223–225, 231
  Lebanon, 142–145
  military tradition, 16
  Pakistan, 28, 38, 43–45
Israel, Ancient, 71
Israel, Modern, 52, 117, 255
  education and income, 255, 260, 262, 268, 272–274
  kibbutz system, 290–296
Ius Civile, 231
Ius Gentium, 231
Ivory Coast
  French orientation, 28, 49
  Islam, 53

Janaganamana, 35
Japan, 57, 60, 61, 71
  education and income, 254, 258, 261–263, 272–274
Java, 46, 47, 124, 130–133

Jordan, 124
  education and income, 254, 257, 258, 262, 272–274

Karens, 137–138
Kashmir, 116
Kenya, 232
Kibbutz, 290–296
Kurdistan, 107, 115

Ladakh, 39
Land Tenure, Africa, 238–240
Languages, 3, 110–112
  Ceylon, 43
  India, 32–33, 105–106, 112, 125
  Indonesia, 47, 112
  Malaya, 112, 125
  Pakistan, 125
Laos, 107, 114
Latin America, 4–5
  education and income, 269–271
Law, 73–74, 76
  Africa, 220–246
  England, 230, 232, 235, 244
  India, 244
  personal, 222–229
  Roman, 230
  territorial, 223
  United States, 220–230
Lebanon, 126, 131, 214, 224
  education and income, 255, 257, 260, 272, 274
  national integration, 142–145
Leninism, 58, 61, 65, 78
Lex Fori, 229
Liberia, 4
  education and income, 253, 256, 275
Libya, 118
  education and income, 255, 260, 275

Machiavelli, Niccolo, 171, 174
Macrosociology, 20–24
Maghrib, 116, 149
Mahabharata Epic, 32, 34, 36
Malaya, 59, 106, 112, 113, 115, 130
  education and income, 255, 260, 262, 272–274
  national integration, 133–136
Malaysian Federation, 136
Mali, 59, 68, 78, 84–85, 93
  cultural policies, 51, 54

Maronites, 142–144
Marriage, Africa, 84–85, 236–238
Marxism, 78, 181
Mass Communication, 22, 29
  India, 31
  law, 227
Messianism, Political, 63, 78, 79, 84
Middle East, 38, 112. *See also* Near East
Military in National Life, 16, 60
Mobilization Systems, 63, 65, 67, 69, 77–82, 91–101
Modernization, 57, 58, 60–62, 67, 69
  cultural, 193–195
  structural, 181–193
Moguls, 28, 34, 44, 198
Mohammed V, 147–149
Morocco, 106, 116, 124, 126, 131, 224
  education and income, 255, 260, 262, 275
  national integration, 145–149
Moslem League, 66

Nasser, Abdul, 117
National Integration. *See* Integration, National
Nationalism and National Identity, vi, 2–4, 22, 66, 107, 108
Near East, 189. *See also* Middle East
  education and income, 272–274
Negritude, 49, 53–54, 112, 204
Nehru, Pandit, 34, 39–40, 105–106, 140–142, 151
Nepal, education and income, 254, 258, 272, 274
Netherlands, Indonesia policy, 46
Newspaper Circulation, 261
  tables, 253, 256, 258, 260, 268–275
Ngoni (African tribe), 293
Nigeria, 59, 80, 107, 112, 131
  cultural pluralism, 28, 49–52, 113, 127
  education and income, 254, 258, 262, 275
  national integration, 150–153
  urban living, 285
Nkrumah, Kwame, 49, 83–85, 87, 101, 204
Noblesse Oblige, 164, 210
North Borneo. *See* British North Borneo

North East Frontier Agency, 39
Nu, U, 136–138
Nuer (tribe in Sudan), 296–298

Occupational Structures, 181–190
Ottoman Empire, 171–175, 190, 212–214

Pakistan, 43–45, 91
  constitution, 44
  education and income, 255, 260, 272–274
  Islam, 28, 38, 43–45
  law, 224
  regionalism, 113
  technology, 45
Panama, education and income, 252, 254, 258, 262, 269–271
Paraguay, education and income, 253, 256, 261–263, 269–271
Philippines, 93, 112, 114, 125, 187
  education and income, 255, 257, 260, 262, 272–274
Plato, 73, 90
Plural Cultures, 2–3, 21–22, 28, 109–119. *See also* Cultural Policies
Political Behavior and Orientation, 281, 285–288, 299–302
Political Religion, 82–101
Political Systems, 62–104
  democracy, 64, 77, 102, 207–212
  mobilization systems, 63, 65, 67, 69, 77–82, 91–101
  reconciliation systems, 64–65, 67–69, 73–77, 93–95
  theocracy, 59, 66, 68, 69, 70–73, 88
  totalitarian democracy, 63–65, 79, 103
Politics and Social Stratification, 204–219
Population Problems, 190, 276, 284
Primordial Conflict, 109–119, 153–157
  blood ties, 112
  custom, 113
  language, 112
  race, 112
  region, 113
  religion, 113
Protestantism, 76, 196
Puerto Rico, education and income, 254, 255, 257, 260, 262, 269–271

Ramayana Epic, 34, 35, 125
Rationalism, 66
Reconciliation Systems, 64–65, 67–69, 73–77, 93–95
Regionalism, 113
Religion, 64, 87–92. *See also* various religions
  and science, 196–197
Religion and the State
  Burma, 28, 116, 138
  Ceylon, 28, 42–43
  India, 28, 33–36, 125
  Indonesia, 47
  Lebanon, 142–145
  Pakistan, 28, 43–45
  Philippines, 125
  Western nations, 66–68, 74–77
Rhodesia and Nyasaland, 80

Sarawak, 136
Sarekat Islam, 66
Saudi Arabia, education and income, 253, 256, 272, 274
Science and Religion, 196–197
Senegal, 51, 59
Senghor, Léopold, 49
Sham'un, Camille, 145
Shan States, 107, 137–138
Shiites, 107
Singapore, 136
Sinhalese, 41–43, 107, 115–116, 122
Socialization, Political, 280–303
Social Stratification, 158–219
  Africa, sub-Saharan, 179–180
  cultural aspects, 164–166
  India, 175–178
  medieval West, 171–175
  Ottoman Empire, 171–175
  peasant societies, 168–171
  relation to politics, 204–219
  roots, 162–163
  structural aspects, 166–168
  tribal societies, 168–170
Social Studies Techniques, 9–20
Somalia, 116
South Africa, 65
  education and income, 252–253, 256, 262, 275, 276
Southeast Asia Treaty Organization, 45
Soviet Union. *See* Union of Soviet Socialist Republics
Stability, Political, 281–301

Sudan, 107
 education and income, 255, 260,
  262, 275
Sukarno, 130–132
Syria, education and income, 255,
  260, 262, 272–274

Tagore, Rabindranath, 35, 199
Taiwan, education and income, 255,
  257, 260, 262, 272, 274
Tamils
 Ceylon, 41–42, 106, 115–116, 122
 India, 34
Tanganyika, 112
Technology
 Ceylon, 42
 India, 37
 Pakistan, 45
Thailand, 4, 107
 education and income, 255, 260,
  262, 272–274
Theocracy, 59, 66, 68, 69, 70–73, 88
Tilak, 32
Tocqueville, Alexis de, 69, 102–103,
  212
Totalitarian Democracy, 63–65, 79,
  103
Touré, Sekou, 49, 82, 83, 86
Traditionalism, 2–3, 9, 168–171,
  175–180, 281–289
Tribal Societies, 168–170, 218, 226–
  228
Tunisia, 224
 education and income, 255, 260,
  262, 275

Turkey, 4
 education and income, 254, 258,
  262, 272–274
 employer-employee relations, 284
 living by family groups, 284

Uganda, 50, 51, 203
Ulamâ, 200–201, 213, 214
Union of Soviet Socialist Republics,
  58, 60, 61, 82, 91, 95, 97
United Arab Republic. See Egypt
Untouchables, 39, 40
Urbanization, 284–285
Uruguay, education and income, 254,
  255, 260, 262, 269–271

Vande Mataram, 36
Venezuela, education and income,
  252–254, 256, 262, 269–271
Vietnam, 113
 education and income, 254, 258,
  272, 274

Weber, Max, 14, 18, 20–21, 26, 162,
  177, 185, 196
West African National Congress, 66
Women
 in Africa, 236–238, 294, 297
 in a kibbutz, 296
Workers and peasants, 187–190

Yoruba, 150, 228
Yugoslavia, education and income,
  253, 256, 257, 262